IN GRIOT TIME

IN GRIOT TIME

AN AMERICAN GUITARIST IN MALI

Banning Eyre

 Temple University Press
PHILADELPHIA

Temple University Press, Philadelphia 19122
Copyright © 2000 by Banning Eyre
All rights reserved
Published 2000
Printed in the United States of America

Maps on pages xii and xiii from *Mande Potters and Leatherworkers: Art and Heritage in West Africa* by Barbara E. Frank published by the Smithsonian Institution Press, Washington, D.C.; copyright © 1998. Used by permission of the publisher. Editorial changes by Blue Heron, Inc.

♾ The paper used in this publication meets the requirements of the American National Standard for Information Sciences—Permanence of Paper for Printed Library Materials, ANSI Z39.48-1984

Library of Congress Cataloging-in-Publication Data

Eyre, Banning.
    In griot time : an American guitarist in Mali / Banning Eyre.
        p. cm.
    Includes bibliographical references and index.
    ISBN 1-56639-758-8 (cl. : alk. paper) — 1-56639-759-6 (pbk. : alk. paper)
    1. Music—Mali—History and criticism. 2. Griots—Mali. 3. Musicians—Mali.

ML3760.E9 2000
780'.96623 21—dc21   99-045338

Frontispiece: Djelimady Tounkara. *Photo by the author.*

To my father and mother,
Jack and Cornelia,
who always inspired me
to look beyond myself

Contents

Photos follow pages 64 and 150

List of Terms

West African music has its own terminology, as loaded with unexpected twists as the music itself. I've avoided unfamiliar language where possible, but the terms below are pretty much part of the terrain.

balafon [BA-la-fone] Wooden slatted xylophone found in a variety of tunings throughout West Africa. Principal griot instrument of Guinea.

Bambara [BAM-ba-ra] The predominant language of Mali. The Bambara people, who emerged from the Manding roughly 400 years ago, were known for their resistance to Islam.

boubou [BOO-boo] Traditional gown worn by both men and women in West Africa.

denkonli [den-KOHN-lee] Literally "baby head shave." Bambara name for the naming or baptism ceremony that almost always involves griots.

doso ngoni [DOH-soh nGO-nee] Six-string hunter's harp.

griot [GREE-oh] Umbrella term for an inherited status found in numerous West African societies south of the Sahara, north of the coastal jungles, and west of Lake Chad. The word's origins are disputed, and some reject it as tainted by colonial attitudes, but ever since Alex Haley published *Roots* in the late 1970s, the word has been part of the lexicon. Griots can fill many different social roles including musical bard, family councilor and advisor, historian, praise singer, instrumentalist, and diplomat.

horon [OH-rohn] A member of the Manding noble class. *Jelis* sing the praises of *horon*. *Horon* are also referred to as *jatigui*.

jeli [JEL-ee] A Manding griot, usually a musical entertainer, either an instrumentalist or a praise singer. One translation of the word is "blood," and birth to a *jeli* family is the only widely accepted way to achieve this status. The correct

ix

plural is *jeliw*, but for the sake of readability in English, I use the adaptation *jeli*s in this text.

jelimuso [JEL-ee-moo-so] A female jeli, almost always a praise singer. The plural is *jelimusow*.

jeliya [JEL-ee-yah] The art of the *jeli*s.

kamalé ngoni [KAH-mel-en-GO-nee] Literally "young man's harp," a smaller version of the *doso ngoni*.

kora [KOR-ah] Twenty-one-string bridge-harp played by the *jeli*s. Principal griot instrument in Gambia.

Manding (also ***Mande*** or ***Mandingo***) Ethnic group spread through Mali, Gambia, Guinea, Senegal, Guinea Bissau, Cote D'Ivoire, Niger, and Burkina Faso. In Mali, most Manding now speak Bambara, an offshoot of the older Mandinka.

ngoni [nGO-nee] Spike-lute played by the *jeli*s. The principal *jeli* instrument in Mali and a likely ancestor of the American banjo.

nyamakala [NYA-mah-KAH-lah] Bambara term for a set of professionals that includes *jeli*s, *numuw* (blacksmiths), *garankéw* (tanners), and *funéw* (Islamic orators).

toubab [TOO-bob] General West African term for a white person.

Acknowledgments

I would like to thank all those who have inspired and supported me through the years of writing this book, above all Djelimady Tounkara and the Tounkara family and all the musicians who shared their art with me in Bamako; also my friends, Sean Barlow, Dirck Westervelt, Anne Peters, Joyce Miller, David Gilden, and Leigh Rhett; my agent, Ben Camardi; for sharing their expertise, Lucy Durán and Kassim Kone; for their love, my family; for their guidance, my editors, Jeff Hush, Phyllis Rose, Pam Friedman, Doris Braendel, and Suzanne Wolk; for his advice, V. S. Naipaul; and for his financial support, Babani Sissoko.

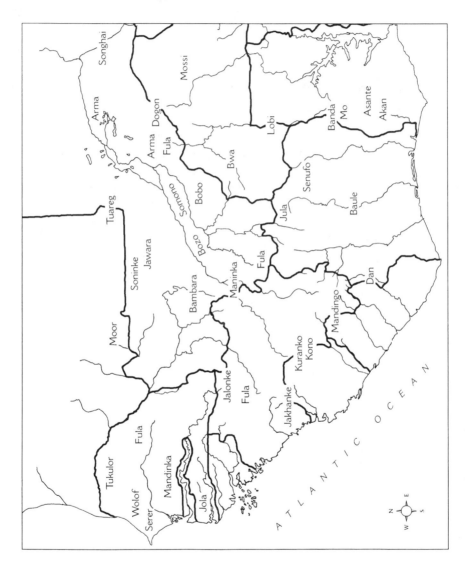

Map 1. West Africa: Peoples

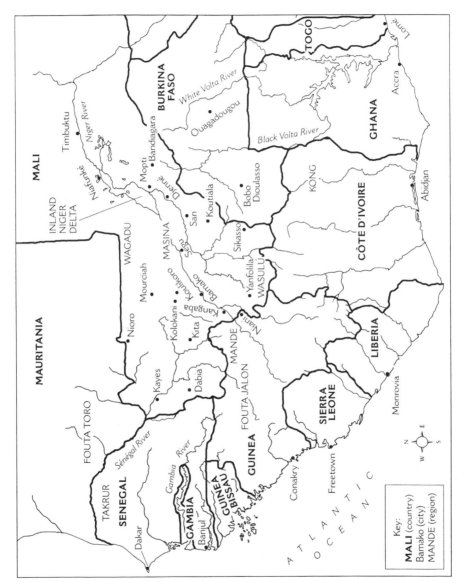

Map 2. West Africa: Places

IN GRIOT TIME

1

Apprentices and Kings

Ce do fe baro be do son hakili la: **Talking to one man sharpens the wits of another.**

(Bambara proverb)

jelimady Tounkara has powerful hands. His muscled fingers and palms seem almost brutish to the eye, but when he grasps the neck of a guitar and brushes the nail of his right index finger across the strings, the sound lifts effortlessly, like dust in a wind. In Bamako, Mali, where musicians struggle, Djelimady is a big man, and all of his family's good fortunes flow from those hands.

Since the early 1970s, Djelimady (pronounced JEH-lee-MA-dee) has played lead guitar in the Super Rail Band of Bamako, the only "Manding swing" orchestra to survive into the 1990s in Mali. When I first visited Bamako, in January 1993, the Rail Band still performed on weekend nights at the Buffet Hotel de la Gare, right next to Bamako's red stone, colonial-era train station. I found Djelimady there, rehearsing with the band in a cave-like concrete store room by the tracks. In return for government paychecks, the eight or ten core members of the Rail Band met there to rehearse on weekday mornings. I went as a journalist, hoping to record the band and their story for American radio, not imagining the musical apprenticeship that would unfold.

I had spent a decade exploring African music and had visited five African countries. I had heard countless recordings of traditional and contemporary music from around the continent. I knew the beauty of Manding music, but not its power. For Manding griots, more properly called *jelis*, do not simply amuse their listeners. *Jelis* can persuade the mighty, dignify ordinary lives, and sometimes their music can make them as wealthy as any musician in Africa.

I showed up unannounced at the Buffet Hotel practice room, but Djelimady greeted me warmly. Standing more than six feet tall, with broad shoulders and an open face, he clasped my hand and smiled as I introduced myself in rudimentary French. Djelimady's jet-black hair and mustache were trimmed short, and he wore a colorful shirt and pressed white trousers. Furrows traversed his brow as he studied me. When he smiled, his face opened into a mask of joy, but when the smile passed, the furrows returned and the mask became inscrutable—vaguely bemused, a little stern and wary.

Djelimady spied my guitar and asked to play it. It was a modest instrument by professional American standards, a chestnut brown Yamaha acoustic, slim and light. But it played easily and produced a bright tone. Djelimady inspected the instrument and began to play. I had known he was an extraordinary guitarist, skilled at transferring the rapid, flowing lines of Manding traditional instruments onto the guitar. But his reputation and the recordings of the Rail Band I had heard did not prepare me for the direct experience of his musicianship. He cradled the instrument with the confidence of an old Delta bluesman, and he tickled the strings with his forefinger, producing impossibly fast and fluid melodies, music of startling clarity, boldness, and innocence.

Djelimady noted my gaze and offered to show me something. He played the accompaniment to the central epic of the *jeli* repertoire, "Sunjata," the story from which all the others flow. The full-blown song recounts the miraculous life of Sunjata Keita, first king of the thirteenth-century Malian Empire. All I heard that day was a brief, stately cycle of notes, simple but bristling with tough certainty. Djelimady laughed as I labored to imitate his articulations on the guitar. I could reproduce the sequence of notes, but not the emphasis and timing that made them Manding guitar music.

When I returned to the Buffet a few days later, Djelimady was surprised to see I had made progress, and he showed me more. During the month I spent in Mali, I returned to the Buffet whenever possible, and before I left I had learned the accompaniment to "Sunjata" passably well. Pleased, Djelimady invited me to his family compound west of town one night and let me record a musical session with him and some of his relatives. The result was the most satisfying recording I had made in Africa.

When I met him, Djelimady already embodied an epoch of modern West African history. Raised in a *jeli* family near the western city of Kita, Djelimady came to live in Bamako in 1965. He arrived during the turbulent years that followed the country's independence from France. Modibo Keita, a socialist and an Africanist, was Mali's president at the time, and he had established a system of state-sponsored musical ensembles that epitomized the idealism of that era. Modibo Keita believed that by melding the cultural expressions of the territory's many peoples, he could build an African nation. As a talented young guitarist in the capital, Djelimady rose quickly through this system to earn a seat in the Ensemble National du Mali.

The state-funded dance bands of that era were forging a new music for a new society. They transformed the ancestral airs of the griots (pronounced GREE-ohs) to create a sound that professional urban couples could dance to in Western-style clubs. Sassy horns. The swing of dance band jazz. The lilt of Cuban *son*, *mambo*, *cha cha cha* and *rumba*. All the musical strands of that time were interwoven with the melodies and flourishes of Manding music, a core that reached back to the glory days of the Malian Empire.

In learning "Sunjata," I had come face to face with a legacy far older than the Rail Band's venerable swing. Everywhere I went in the country, when I took out my guitar and played "Sunjata," I made friends. That brief sequence of notes could short circuit a hustle in seconds, and its effect had nothing to do with Djelimady's prestige or the caliber of my playing. It had to do with Sunjata himself. Sunjata Keita was Mali's George Washington and Thomas Jefferson rolled into one, a founder and a philosopher, a figure whose story and song are known to every Malian child. John Johnson, the Manding scholar, has called the Sunjata epic "a virtual social, political, and cultural charter of society."

The Sunjata epic is a story of magic, transformation, and delayed justice. It has many variants, but most begin with a hunter's prophecy to Sunjata's father, then the ruler of a small kingdom. The king is instructed to marry a hideously ugly woman brought to him from the land of Do. The woman, Sogolon, is actually a buffalo in human form, and the king must struggle to consummate their marriage. Driven by the prophecy that they will beget the future king of Mali, he persists, and at last they produce a boy. But Sunjata begins life as an invalid child, unable to walk or speak, an unlikely candidate for such an august destiny.

After the old king dies, another of his sons takes the throne, and Sunjata's mother gradually loses patience with her indolent seven-year-old. Her final humiliation comes when she is forced to ask another woman for leaves from a *baobob* tree, a cooking ingredient, and then must endure the other woman's taunts.

"Oh son of misfortune," Sunjata's mother wails in one telling of the epic, "will you never walk? Through your fault, I have just suffered the greatest affront of my life! What have I done, God, for you to punish me this way?" Sunjata replies, "Very well, then, I am going to walk today. Go and tell my father's smiths to make me the heaviest possible iron rod. Mother, do you want just the leaves of the *baobob* or would you rather I brought you the whole tree?" The boy then bends the iron rod into a bow while lifting himself to his feet. As his griot composes the "Hymn to the Bow," Sunjata dislodges a young *baobob* tree from the dry earth and lays it down before his mother's hut.

Suddenly mighty and dangerous, Sunjata is driven into exile by fearful rivals, and during his travels he befriends the leaders of neighboring kingdoms, all of whom will later become his vassals. The story climaxes with Sunjata's victory over the sorcerer king, Soumaoro Kanté, at the battle of Kirina. Sunjata wins the battle by exploiting Soumaoro's occult vulnerability—a spur from his totemic animal, the cock.

It is a victory found in myth. It would have been dismissed by historians as African superstition were it not for two brief passages in the writings of Arab political historians. Ibn Battuta and Ibn Khaldun both visited Mali during the century that followed Sunjata's death. These writers confirm the existence of a king named Sunjata Keita who established a vast, peaceful sovereignty supported principally by the mining and trans-Saharan gold trade. Those two passages have forced historians to consider the tales of the *jeli*s in a serious light. Malians, of course, require no such substantiation. The pride stirred by Sunjata's story, while especially potent for the Manding people, touches the modern descendants of many Malian ethnic groups: the Bambara, the Fulani cattle herders, the Bozo fishermen, the Tamasheck and Songhai of the north, the Bobo of the south and east, even the remote, cliff-dwelling Dogon, famous for their preservation of animist religion.

As I left Bamako, Djelimady said to me, "You've learned well. I think if you came here for six months, I could teach you to play the way I do." Those words would stay with me. Back in the United States, the more I read and listened, the more I understood that Djelimady's offer to teach me was an opportunity. I wrote to him from Boston and sent him $100 as a contribution to the new house I had heard he was building for his family. I told him that I had saved some money and was prepared to move to Bamako and study with him, leaving my job, my apartment, and my band.

We spoke just once on the telephone before I left. I told Djelimady that I expected to pay him for putting me up and teaching me, but I wondered if he might like part of that payment in the form of something I could bring from the States. "Yes," he said. "An amplifier. Bring me a Roland Jazz Chorus guitar amplifier."

I found a used Roland for around $500 and a 1,000-watt power transformer that would let the amplifier run off 220v current. I built a wooden box to protect the amplifier during the flight. I assumed that this would be only a down payment on my eventual debt to Djelimady, but it seemed a start. The physical difficulty of bringing such a thing to Mali would provide evidence of my seriousness. In October of 1995, nearly three years after I first watched Djelimady's hands move across the frets of my Yamaha guitar, I flew from New York to Bamako, loaded to capacity with a heavy metal trunk, two guitars, and the Roland amplifier.

Flying into Bamako on a Monday night, I looked out the airplane window to see dim patches of light separated by miles of darkness. I felt a wave of apprehension and scrawled in my notebook, "What have I done?" Even in all that darkness, I could see the reddish dust of the city, coloring the occasional lights with a smoky mist. As we landed, only the strip lights marking the runway and the blue neon glow of the terminal building emerged from the shadows.

Inside the dust-coated terminal, I spotted Djelimady as I waited in the passport line. He towered above everyone, emanating confidence. I knew instantly that his celebrity was working its charm on the officials, as he had made his way far beyond the barriers that restrained people meeting flights. Djelimady sent a security officer to speed my arrival, a matter of spiriting my passport to the head of the line, assigning porters to my seven pieces of luggage, and cajoling the customs man, who instinctively pulled aside my trunk, amplifier, black handbag full of computer gear, tape recorders, and camera accessories.

When the critical discussion over the release of my luggage began, I said nothing. I stood by smiling benignly while Djelimady shook hands and spoke in grandiloquent Bambara and his official directed the customs inspector in a sterner tone. The strategy worked. Before I knew it, we were on the curb outside loading things into Djelimady's old white Nissan. The porters liked my U.S. $1 bills, but Djelimady's official seemed to disdain the ten I offered him. In fairness, I did underpay him; he had spared me the travel ordeal I feared most, a close customs examination.

Djelimady had come to the airport with his brother Madou Djan Tounkara and also a young man named Oumar Diallo, whom everyone called Barou. Even before I made it through the customs hurdle, I saw Barou waving from the crowd. A thin, animated fellow with light brown skin and curly hair, Barou grinned my way like a long lost friend. Apparently we had met during my first visit, though I did not remember him, much to his disappointment.

Knowing that my luggage would overburden any single car, I had arranged for two to meet me. I rode into Bamako with my second benefactor, a French expatriate named Philippe Berthier who operated Mali K7, a recording studio and cassette reproduction facility in Bamako. Philippe and Djelimady greeted each other guardedly as we loaded the car. Philippe, it turned out, was not a fan of the Rail Band; he considered them old-fashioned. For all his achievements in Bamako, Philippe had a mixed reputation among the city's musicians. I don't know whether these chilly tidings reflected any real malfeasance on Philippe's part or simply the normal animosities that exist between music producers and recording artists. Either way, in a city of many musicians and few producers, this was a deep divide, and though I was riding with the producer, I had cast my lot with the musicians.

As we drove along the increasingly busy road that leads from Bamako-Senou Airport toward the Niger River and the city, the sensations of Bamako returned to me. I peered into the night and glimpsed silhouettes and shiny faces etched by the light of bare, solitary light bulbs. The pungent sting of wood smoke blended with the dust and exhaust fumes and the tangy odors of ripe and rotting fruit. I saw brightly lit rooms opened to the street, with vendors selling cigarettes and drinks in neon parlors—cobalt blue, fire-engine red, white, and battleship gray. Women squatted around small, coal-fired stoves grilling beef brochettes, whole fish, and bananas, which they served on torn sheets of brown paper or skewered on wooden kebab sticks. Men in loose robes called *boubou*s straddled bicycles and mobilettes (motor bikes) and wove among cars, pedestrians, and hucksters. I began to see *bashée*s, pickup trucks, painted green and packed with commuters jammed onto wooden benches under a makeshift roof.

We crossed a modern stanchion bridge, newly opened since my first visit, and reached Avenue Sheikh Zayed, the main road leading out of Bamako toward Djelimady's neighborhood, Lafiabougou. Just past the Lafiabougou market, Djelimady—leading the way in his slow-moving Nissan—took a right onto a ravaged, packed-dirt road. Philippe slowed to a gingerly crawl, shifting across the road at odd angles to avoid deep holes. After about a quarter-mile, both cars turned sharply to the left, passing between newly painted white pillars into a tiny car park that was also the central courtyard of a concrete house, still less than half built. One day, this would be home to Djelimady's extended family. For the moment, the few completed rooms along the right side of the court-yard housed renters and family guests, now including me.

We got out of our cars in the neon-lit courtyard. People came for-ward and Djelimady began to make introductions. First he presented me to my immediate neighbor, a serious gentleman of fifty named Mamadou Keita. "This is the Colonel," said Djelimady, and Mr. Keita nodded dutifully. "He's a friend. You can trust him. I've told him to look after things here." I got the impression that Djelimady had hired the Colonel as a security guard. They both warned me that I must lock my room at all times because there were many "bandits" around. Turning to me in an aside, Djelimady advised me to give the Colonel a little money from time to time to ensure his good will. "How much?" I asked. "Whatever you like," he said, shrugging, "just something."

Djelimady introduced me to his eldest son, Samakou, a handsome fel-low in his early twenties who shook my hand vigorously. Samakou lifted my 150-pound trunk from the back of Djelimady's car and carried it into my bedroom. He smiled with satisfaction as he put it down, barely seeming to strain. A gray, latticed metal door led into my two-room suite. Each room had a two-foot neon light mounted above the door-way and a single metal-slatted window, bolted shut. Aside from that, the outer room was absolutely empty and the inner room, the bedroom, contained only a woven reed mat spread over most of the floor, a wooden bench, and a foam mattress covered with fabric depicting car-toon images from the comic strip Dick Tracy. Speech balloons ema-nating from the comic strip characters' mouths read, "Stick 'em up" and "Eat lead."

Philippe, the producer, stepped inside to inspect. He had told me in the car that he might be able to arrange a room for me in his own compound in a few weeks, in case things didn't work out with Djelimady. Now he drew on his cigarette and blandly pronounced, "This is good." But the room Djelimady had prepared for me was better than good. It was everything I had hoped for—private, safe, wired for electricity, and large enough for me to set up a small office and write.

After loading my things into the main room of my new home, I dug around in my baggage for gifts—a digital sound processing unit that Philippe had requested by fax, the power transformer for Djelimady, and copies of my first book for each of them. *Afropop! an Illustrated Guide to Contemporary African Music* is a colorful reference book. Unable to read its English text, Djelimady admired the photograph of Senegalese singing star Baaba Maal on the cover, then turned right to the Mali section and noted that there was no photograph of him. "Next time," I told him.

At the Tounkara family compound, some two miles further into Lafiabougou, I met an overwhelming number of Djelimady's family members that night, beginning with his wife Adama Kouyaté, his tall, aged mother Ina and aunt Nene, at least three of his daughters, his brother's wife, and various half-brothers, nieces, nephews, and neighbors. In my jet-lagged haze, I despaired of ever learning all their names.

I then ate my first Malian meal, rice and sauce served in a metal bowl. Recalling what I had learned in earlier travels, I ate using the fingers of my right hand. With that simple gesture, everyone seemed to relax. It suggested that I might survive in their world. I declined water, explaining that I would prefer at first to buy a case of bottled water, just to be safe. I had feared this moment, not wanting to give offense but well aware that water presented the greatest danger to my health and that a precedent had to be established from the start. Djelimady, having already warned me that mosquito bites cause malaria, was sympathetic. He sent a boy to buy me a Coke.

By the time we had eaten, returned to my place, and sipped a couple of bracing shots of Malian green gunpowder tea prepared by the Colonel, it was nearly two in the morning. My new friends left me alone, but though I had scarcely slept in a week, I was too excited to do so now. During the next few days I would fall asleep constantly—in the car, at the Buffet Hotel de la Gare, at the Tounkara compound, even during rehearsals and concerts. People would laugh at me and I would wake abruptly, scarcely able to believe where I was.

Early each morning, Djelimady would either come for me or else send Barou in the Nissan. Within the peach-colored concrete walls that sealed off the Tounkara compound's large, square courtyard, the women's cooking and washing were generally well underway when I arrived at 7:30 or 8:00. I would sit with Djelimady, and his wife would bring us each a tall glass of warm, weak coffee, sweetened with sugar and thickened with powdered milk. She would hand me a section of day-old French bread. Never a fan of the continental breakfast, I found this African variation unsatisfying, but I ate every crumb, as there was no opportunity to eat during the Rail Band rehearsal, and we rarely made it back to the compound for lunch before 2:00.

The shock absorbers on both sides of the Nissan were shot, and it clanked horribly even on relatively good roads. Djelimady always stopped for gas at the Elf station at the corner where we turned onto Sheikh Zayed. He never put much gas in the car, just enough for the trip at hand. For 1,000 CFA (French African Community) francs, around $2, he would get two liters, just enough to make it into town and back. That way, if someone borrowed the car, they would not use Djelimady's gasoline. Running out of gas now and then when calculations failed was a risk worth taking in the interest of frugality.

On the way back from Bamako for lunch, we always stopped at a roadside fruit stand so Djelimady could buy a melon or papaya. The prices fluctuated, and Djelimady often fell into heated bargaining, sometimes driving off angrily to find a better price at the next stand. "Ever since democracy," he would complain, "prices are no longer fixed. People think they can charge whatever they like." Djelimady also suspected that the fruit-selling women jacked up the price when they saw a white person in the car. "It's racist!" he would growl. Tensions vanished, though, when we returned to the family to linger over lunch in the shade of the inner verandah.

Afternoons provided the closest thing I knew to free time during those early months. More often than not, by the time I had rested a little, fielded the stream of uninvited guests who frequented my house, and taken a moment to wash myself while it was still light, it was time to return to the compound for dinner.

The Tounkaras' courtyard was large for a single family, about five hundred square feet. Two smaller families might easily have shared the same space. But given the large number of relatives who had come to live there, the place felt crowded. Within the courtyard, Djelimady always took the central seat just to the left of the doorway that led back to the main verandah and the largest bedrooms. Out in the courtyard, the men congregated on the left side, which included the compound's one concrete-walled lavatory and washing area and also the courtyard entranceway with its ramp leading down to the dirt street. The women occupied the right side of the courtyard with its cook fires, well, and food storage area.

Children were everywhere. One evening at dinner, I counted twenty sitting around the TV set or nestled in various mothers' arms. One little girl, not yet two, was terrified of me and cried whenever she saw me, to everyone's amusement. A girl of four usually cared for her, often keeping the baby swaddled and tied to her back or slung across a jutting hip. The older girl would flash me a coy smile as she moved off to quiet her bawling burden.

Two twin boys of ten—Lasine and Fuseini Tounkara—were especially extroverted and friendly to me. They were beautiful children. They had the trademark Tounkara poise about them, walking with shoulders back and chests thrust forward, smiling often. Lasine was almost always the first to greet me when I arrived at the compound. He would take whatever I had in my hands or else smack his firm little hand into mine for a quick slap handshake. "Benneeg!" he would bark. Lasine and Fuseini were identical down to their slightly hoarse voices. Adults liked to say that they couldn't tell them apart and called either one of them using the word *fulani*, Bambara for twin. The twins' mother, Ami, had been widowed three years earlier by another of Djelimady's brothers, Issa, who had once been the bassist in the Rail Band.

Untimely deaths explained the presence of many women and children in the compound. The size and scope of Djelimady's household testified to his success but also to the substantial burden that all successful Malians must bear. Djelimady attributed his brother Issa's sudden death to alcohol, but, as with so many deaths I would learn about during my stay, nobody really seemed to know why Issa had died. In those early days, Issa's twin sons spoke to me constantly in Bambara, somehow expecting that I would magically understand them.

Every evening, two Tounkara children carried the television out from one of the bedrooms and placed it at the focal point of the courtyard for the night's broadcast. Since Mali's 1992 democratic constitution had legalized private radio, Bamako had produced around twenty radio stations. But there was still just one state-owned television station, Office de Diffusion

Radio et Television de Mali (ORTM). Private television was illegal, as in almost all African countries. ORTM broadcasted from 7:00 until about 11:00 P.M. every weeknight and all day on weekends. Bamako's radio stations could broadcast what they liked, and the more political stations, like the print media, could be very critical of the government. Television news on ORTM mimicked the appearance of Western-style media, but it ignored controversial events and aired only measured doses of debate between the government and its opposition. Still, Djelimady rarely missed ORTM's hour-long evening news program, *Le Journal.*

I found the broadcast dull, but I loved the conversation and cuisine that accompanied it. We ate rice and savory meat sauce or smoked fish, sometimes salad, beef brochettes, or fried potatoes. Sometimes the Tounkara women served a doughy millet porridge called *tow*, which came with a somewhat slimy but flavorful sauce made from the dried flower of the *datu* plant. Though *Le Journal* rarely reported on the United States or on anything familiar to me, I loved the way Djelimady and his brother Madou discussed the stories. They felt obliged to approve or disapprove of everything reported.

The Chinese foreign minister visited Mali. "That's good," said Djelimady. "The Chinese have been our friends since the time of Modibo Keita." Jacques Chirac announced that he would not abandon Africa. "He's a bastard," said Djelimady. "He was with de Gaulle in World War II when they wouldn't pay the African soldiers. You can't trust him." The Nigerian government executed nine dissidents, including activist author Ken Saro-Wiwa. "Very sad. That country is lost," said Djelimady. The Malian president's wife announced the opening of her annual two-day music festival, Tabalé, and told the nation that the proceeds this year would go to aid the handicapped. "She's a great woman," Djelimady boomed at the mention of the president's wife, "Mali's Hillary Clinton." The citizens of Quebec voted, by a hair, not to separate from Canada. "Excellent," he said as we watched the faces of stunned Quebecois learning of the razor-thin referendum defeat. "Canada is good. Why would anyone want to leave it?"

For Djelimady, the word socialist had positive associations—it was synonymous with democratic. During *Le Journal,* he would use these two words regularly to heap praise on figures as diverse as Bill Clinton, Mali's President Alpha Oumar Konaré, Yasir Arafat, and Francois Mitterand. Djelimady's list of global demons began with Jacques Chirac but also included Muammar Khadafy, Saddam Hussein, and American Republicans, whom he said were racists.

After dinner came music. Djelimady would call for his acoustic guitar and he and I would go out to the street. The twins would bring out a couple of lawn chairs for us, and we would generally work until around midnight. These were not exactly lessons. Djelimady would play things. I would record him, and when there was something I thought I could tackle, I would interrupt him and force him to repeat it. As I tried to imitate him, he would correct me, and it all went down on tape. There was no particular system. He didn't give me exercises to practice, and in the beginning he never asked me to play anything he had taught me before. When he talked, it was usually to dramatize the history of a song or to reminisce about the glory days of the Rail Band. "We did this version with Mory Kanté in '72. Oh, the people used to die for it!" That sort of thing. In this way, I found myself progressing little by little, and during those evening sessions on the stoop, I felt I was getting what I had come for; the frustrations and distractions I experienced at other times seemed unimportant.

On my second morning with the Tounkaras, I woke late from a deep sleep and was not ready when Barou arrived at my house to take me to the compound for breakfast. Djelimady scolded Barou for our delay, and I soon learned the reason. "Our brother in town has lost a daughter, nine years old," he told me. Impatiently gesturing as he described how children are always recklessly running around, he explained that the girl had fallen into a hole and died. We ate breakfast and headed out in the Nissan.

We maneuvered the busy roundabout near the train station, where the traffic circles a tall, French-style monument to the Republic of Mali. We bypassed the chaos of downtown and made our way to the Banconi neighborhood, a little way up one of the dry, rocky hills that skirt Bamako on both sides of the Niger. We parked on the street and walked into a compound about three times the size of Djelimady's. Some two hundred people were gathered, sitting silently on benches, chairs, and a large central mat, women on one side, men on the other. A few shade trees offered scant protection from the sun, even as they shed crisp, sickle-shaped leaves, a sure sign that the dry season had begun.

Among the Manding, the sons of your father's brothers are your brothers, and the daughters of your mother's sisters are your sisters. This causes confusion for the foreigner, especially when combined with the fact that polygamy allows for brothers and sisters with the same father but different mothers. When someone wants you to know that a sibling is a full sibling, he clarifies with the phrase "same mother, same father."

More often, the relationship is left ambiguous. At the time, sorting out such complexities was beyond me. When Djelimady introduced me to his grieving "brother," I simply shook his hand and retreated.

The brother sat surrounded by elders. He wore a dark blue *boubou* and a white skull cap. Djelimady and Madou took their places with their brother and spoke softly in Bambara before moving off to make room for new arrivals. From the street behind us came the tinny drone of a mosque where an Imam was intoning through a megaphone speaker. Soon the old, bearded Imam entered the compound, chanting. He made his way into the central courtyard, where he paused to speak a few words with the family members at the center. On his cue, the wake ended abruptly, and people began a quiet but rapid departure.

The death observed, Djelimady returned to himself. We drove on to the Buffet Hotel de la Gare, where the Rail Band was gathered for rehearsal. The musicians had news. One of Mali's popular young *jeli* singers, Fodé Kouyaté, had just been by to ask if the Rail Band would back him for his performance in the upcoming Tabalé '95 spectacle. This would mean performing in front of thousands of people alongside a lineup of African musical luminaries. It would also mean participating in the pet project of Mme. Konaré, that lovely and generous socialist. "And you will play with us," Djelimady told me with smile. It seemed a difficult undertaking for my first week in town, but Djelimady's confidence buoyed me.

That evening after dinner, I sat out on the street playing guitar with Sambry Kouyaté, Djelimady's seventeen-year-old nephew. Sambry was teaching me the one song he knew on guitar, "Kemé Burama." Two teenage girls lay across the hood of Djelimady's Nissan, one this way, one the other, chatting where their faces met at the center. Five or six children were gathered around on stools, the twins claiming the best seats. A half moon hung bowl-like in the sky. Djelimady came out to inspect our progress, and after a few minutes he asked whether I knew what the song was about.

"It's a very important story," he said, shooing away one of the twins to take his seat. Djelimady explained that the last great Manding fighter, Almami Samory Touré—who happened to be the grandfather of Guinea's first president, Sékou Touré—had made bitter war on the French at the end of the last century. Touré's younger brother Ibrahima had been his general and a great fighter, and the song "Kemé Burama" celebrates him. "Kemé," Djelimady explained, is Bambara for "one hundred," and it refers to Ibrahima Touré's strength in battle, equivalent to that of a hundred men.

"Their war camp was just nearby," said Djelimady, gesturing to the end of the street where a flat, empty plain separated Lafiabougou from the riverside neighborhood of Djikoroni. "The Tourés made war on the Wasulu kingdom from here. It was brutal. They killed and killed. But Kemé Burama spared the musicians. He spared the griots. He killed or enslaved all the others. But there have never been slaves among the griots. Tounkara, Diabaté, Kouyaté," he said, listing names of griot families. "These were never slaves. Even the whites did not make the griots work. Ibrahima saw the griots as a weapon and treated them well. That's why they sing about him."

After the Wasulu wars, though, the Tourés faced the more imposing forces of the French. Djelimady explained that the brothers later fled to Guinea, where Ibrahima was killed. Years later, Samory was captured in what is today the northern Ivory Coast. "My father remembered seeing Samory paraded down the street in Kita," said Djelimady, in a way that deepened the silence of the children. "He was just a boy at the time."

A few days later, I was riding in the car with Barou, and I told him how impressed I had been by Djelimady's story. "Be careful, my friend," said Barou unexpectedly. "Apart from music, Djelimady knows nothing. Manding guitar, Bambara music—that he knows. Other than that, nothing."

"He knows history," I said.

"*Griot* history," replied Barou. "Griot history and actual history. Not the same thing."

By this time, I had spent hours listening to Djelimady hold forth on many subjects as we rode along Avenue Sheikh Zayed between Bamako and the Tounkara compound and lingered over long meals in the courtyard. Once when we were driving, I remarked on the large Khadafy logos painted on many of the green Sotrama minivans that carted commuters all over the city. Djelimady responded by pointing to the towering mosque that marked the halfway point of our route into town. "Khadafy built that for us," he said blandly. "They call it the Islamic Center."

"Really?" I asked. "Why did he do that?"

"Don't know," shrugged Djelimady. "He likes Mali, I suppose."

Djelimady informed me that many Bamako landmarks had been built by foreign benefactors. The new bridge across the Niger bore the name of the Saudi Arabian king who had financed it. The road we took into town every day got its name from the man who had paid to pave it in 1993, HH Sheikh Zayed bin Sultan Al-Nahyan, president of the United Arab Emirates since 1971. Zayed, I later learned, was so proud of his gifts to Islamic countries that he took out a full-page ad in the *New York Times* to trumpet his virtues as an educator, an environmentalist, and "a statesman of vision and generosity." His gift to Bamako had reduced Djelimady's hour-long commute to a tolerable twenty minutes. Djelimady was forever feeding me such information, and it troubled me to have his veracity impugned by his own good friend.

Using the books at my disposal, I checked into Djelimady's history of "Kemé Burama." In fact, the warlord Samory had kept a war camp south of Bamako. He had captured plenty of land during his rampages, including a good deal of the Wasulu kingdom to the south and east. Wasulu was mostly the land of the Fulani, who had come from the north and been displaced there as the result of an earlier war. Samory's purges seemed to have strengthened the survivors. The Wasulunké, I was often told, were known for their powerful fetishistic magic, and also for their music.

At the far extreme of Lafiabougou, beyond the Tounkara compound, a narrow valley cuts between two thousand-foot mesas, creating a perfect set for a guns-blazing, Hollywood western skirmish. The actual battle fought here at the village of Wayanko in 1883 pitted Samory Touré's army, led by his brother, against an exhausted and ill-prepared French regiment commanded by Lieutenant-Colonel Gustave Borgnis-Desbordes. The Tourés had triumphed initially but had ultimately been routed by the better-armed French, who then claimed Bamako and made it their base of operations on the upper Niger. As Djelimady had reported, Samory's men then fled south into Guinea.

In essence, Djelimady's account was accurate. I couldn't verify some of the more colorful details, such as the claim that Ibrahima Touré spared the griots of Wasulu or that his men liked to kill French soldiers by dragging them behind horses over the rocky terrain surrounding the Wayanko mesa. But I had no reason to doubt them.

So why this skepticism from Barou? Barou, for all his closeness to the Tounkaras, remained an outsider among them. To begin with, he was not a *jeli*. Although he might play his portable keyboard, a hand-operated drum machine, or bass at the wedding and baptism parties where Djelimady and his young relatives earned much of their money, Barou did not merit respect as a musician among them, and he was never well paid. Barou was also not Manding. His mother, a Fulani woman from Burkina Faso, had married a French military man, long since departed from the scene. This unusual background helped to account for the way Barou could blend smoothly in such a variety of situations. From the moment he waved to me from the crowd at the airport, Barou seemed be telling me that he was the man to mediate my experiences in Bamako. His caution concerning Djelimady's authority on nonmusical subjects was the first of many.

Barou lived with his mother, his two brothers, his wife, and their shy two-year-old daughter in a small compound at the Lafiabougou terminus, the final stop for the Sotrama minivans and green *bashées* that serve as public transportation into Bamako. This proximity to the Tounkara compound made it easy for Djelimady to send for Barou at a moment's notice. *"Fulani,"* Djelimady would snap at the nearest of the twins, "get Barou. I need someone to take the car to the mechanic. Quick! Quick!" Barou would always oblige. If I ribbed him, suggesting that he did a lot for his friend, Barou would simply say, "I consider Djelimady the greatest guitarist in Africa. I am honored to be his friend."

Just as I used Barou to help me understand my experiences with the Tounkaras, Djelimady used Barou to communicate with me on sensitive matters. It was Barou who requested that I make a weekly payment for the food I ate at the compound. I volunteered 10,000 CFA, about $20.

"Thank you," said Djelimady, as though it had all been my idea. "Normally, I wouldn't accept, since you are a friend. But with my brother and his wife away in America, I have to earn for everybody. Money is a problem now."

With this matter settled, the pattern of my apprenticeship to Djelimady became clear. Life began to feel normal, and I took comfort in the illusion that I knew what lay ahead.

2

The Naming Ceremony

Bee togo ye i ko: **Everybody leaves their name behind.**

(Bambara proverb)

The first time I attended a Rail Band rehearsal, it became clear that Djelimady considered the band part of my training. He told me to bring my electric guitar to the rehearsal and instructed the rhythm guitarist, a quiet fellow named Ali Dembélé, to begin showing me parts for the songs. Djelimady directed the rehearsals, sometimes with passion and vigor. But that dungeon-like back room, with its ceiling fans and wide double doors opening onto a sunny garden, also served as Djelimady's office. The rehearsal itself often became a backdrop for Djelimady's other activities, which included conferences with relatives, wealthy patrons of the arts, the Buffet Hotel management, fellow musicians, politicians, and fans.

The day after the wake for Djelimady's niece, the renowned *jeli* singer Fodé Kouyaté came to rehearse the band for his spot in the upcoming Tabalé extravaganza. "Hey, man. What up?" said Fodé, breaking into flawed English when he saw me. Fodé's manic demeanor and tired eyes suggested a man on the move, and indeed Fodé traveled most of the time—to Paris, Brussels, Abidjan, Conakry, London, Washington. In rehearsal, Fodé coached the band meticulously, pointing and gesticulating and singing in the ear of one musician after another. When at last he was pleased with the music, he would freeze, close his eyes, and croon long, beautiful notes in his angelic tenor voice.

"Fodé is crazy," Djelimady said after our first rehearsal. "He is my wife Adama's brother. Completely insane." I wondered whether this family tie had had anything to do with Fodé's decision to have the Rail Band back him in this prestigious gig. Whatever his reason, it was a shrewd choice. The Tabalé show featured fourteen acts. It would take place on Friday night at the indoor Palais de la Culture, just across the Niger River from downtown, and then on Saturday night at the larger, outdoor Modibo Keita Stadium. That left time for just two rehearsals, and the Rail Band's experience would be a big asset.

On the opening night of Tabalé, the elite of Bamako filled the cavernous, 1960s-era Palais de la Culture. Backstage, glamorous female singers, or *jelimusow*, dressed like parading queens and mingled with harp- and guitar-toting sidemen wearing grand *boubou*s or else the heavy, brown-patterned fabric known as *bogolon*, or mudcloth. The different styles of dress helped to distinguish the griot musicians from those playing in the Bambara and Wassoulou styles. Djelimady used his pull with the security guards at the gate to win entrance to the back parking lot. He had hoped to get away early, but his finagling actually landed the Nissan deep in the parking jumble and guaranteed that we would be there to the bitter end.

Fodé Kouyaté's brief three-song set was one of the first and went well. He gathered the musicians in a huddle just before we took the stage and told us he wanted us to be *"tres posé,"* in effect, cool. He eyed me nervously, as if doubting his decision to include me. I managed not to embarrass him. Djelimady wowed the crowd, prancing forward in his black and white suit, as if possessed by the stream of electric notes that poured from his guitar. Fodé's set was over in a flash, but by the time the remaining eleven acts had played, it was 3:00 in the morning. By then Djelimady had introduced me to many of Bamako's professional musicians.

Senegalese singer Baaba Maal played the final set. Though not a *jeli*, Baaba carries himself with the same exalted demeanor. His performance was visceral. It brought the enthusiastic crowd to their feet in roaring acclamation. Djelimady beamed. "Baaba Maal has shattered the Zaireans," he said, referring to the penultimate act by Congolese superstar Kofi Olomide, with his saucy dance music and his four ample female dancers, who had swiveled their spandex-clad posteriors in slow unison before the dazzled fans. It amused me that Djelimady viewed the two headliners as engaged in some sort of showdown. Malians, like virtually all Africans, love Congolese music, but Djelimady was right: The crowd had picked a winner in Baaba Maal.

The next night, Djelimady's young cousin, Adama Tounkara, accompanied us to the stadium for the outdoor show. We sat together in metal chairs on the grassy playing field before the stage. As we waited through the chilly November night, Adama pointed out musicians on and off-stage and told me stories about them, and he made an expert critique of each performance. Adama played the small traditional spike lute known in Mali as the *ngoni*, and he played it well. Though he was just twenty years old, I could tell that Adama commanded respect among the musicians of Bamako. Many came over to greet him deferentially. There was a familiar rhythm to their exchanges, as short rote phrases shot back and forth: "My brother." "How is it?" "No problem." "And the wife?" "She is well." "And the family?" It was a rhythm I would hear again and again.

The stadium program lacked the discipline of the Palais performance the night before. A low ticket price had attracted a big, rowdy crowd. Caught up in the enthusiasm of the moment, performers ignored the MC, playing additional songs after they had been instructed to stop. Some twenty thousand people in the stands shouted disapproval when each set ended, only to scream with excitement when they learned who the next act would be.

This time, Fodé's set came third to last, at 5:00 in the morning. By then it was cold enough to see breath in the bright stadium lights. Once again our time on the stage proved exhilarating. Fodé wore black and white and a funny helmet-like hat with a feather plume. He played to the audience in grand gestures, taking a long introductory solo on his transverse flute before firing up the band, then running down the wooden stairs at the front of the stage. With his cordless microphone, he stepped out onto the field, then turned back toward the stage and called Djelimady forward to solo. The crowd, which had not dwindled despite the cold and the late hour, was scarcely visible to us behind the lights. But their roaring told us that Fodé had triumphed.

The sun had begun to peek over the dry mountains of Bamako as we left the Stade Modibo Keita. Kofi Olomide and his spandex-clad girls were still on the stage, closing the show after Baaba Maal had played an eerily subdued set in the predawn mist. We arrived at Djelimady's compound at about 8:00 A.M. to find Madou standing in the doorway. Barou appeared, tucked tightly into a leather jacket. He'd been awakened by one of the children in the lingering cool of night and summoned to appear. While everyone spoke rapidly in Bambara, Barou told me, "The wife of Djelimady has left the house. She became afraid when you did not return. We must go and find her."

We got into the Nissan and drove to my house, where the Colonel informed us that Djelimady's wife had come by twice that morning looking for her husband and me. Barou saw me to my room. "The wife of Djelimady thought that you and Djelimady had come here with women," he said with a chuckle. "She was not afraid as I told you. She was jealous."

Gradually I adjusted my expectations of life. Eating strange foods in the dark with a bare hand, never speaking English, and bathing with a bucket of cold water and a scoop did not bother me. The hard part was never being alone. The Tounkaras and the people around them saw to it that I had something to do at every waking moment. The women and girls smiled a lot and occasionally engaged me in conversation, but they tended to keep their distance. The men and boys all wanted to befriend me and accompany me everywhere. The young *jelis*, particularly Djelimady's precocious nephew Sambry Kouyaté and *ngoni*-playing cousin Adama Tounkara, rehearsed me tirelessly. Adama lived just around the corner from my house, and any time I was not occupied with Djelimady, he would turn up at my door and insist that we work. I always welcomed him.

Adama had unusually large eyes that seemed to bulge from his serious face, giving him an extraterrestrial countenance. He was slight and lanky and spoke in quick, decisive tones. On one of my first days with the Tounkaras, Adama took me to the far end of Djelimady's compound, where the younger women gathered in the evening. He introduced me to a pretty, very pregnant woman sitting on the floor with her legs stretched out before her. "My fiancée," said Adama simply, "Diallo."

The statement seemed so incongruous that I wondered if he was joking. Adama seemed too young and unformed to have a fiancée. The impression that he was joking was reinforced when Djelimady's wife—who, confusingly, was also named Adama—chimed in, "It's not true. *I'm* his fiancée."

I didn't give this much thought until a week or so later, when Adama and I were sitting in my room working on a piece of music and three of his friends came rushing in babbling excitedly in Bambara. Suddenly everyone was on their feet shouting. Adama widened his eyes to the greatest extreme possible and raised his arms in exultation. I assumed that he or someone must have won the grand prize in the government-run horse race betting fever that grips Bamako twice weekly. Later, when I told this to Barou, he laughed and said, "No. Adama didn't win with the horses. He won with a woman." Adama's fiancée, Miriam Diallo, had delivered twin boys that morning. "He's going to have to play a lot of *ngoni*," said Djelimady. "It's good. But it's a problem."

I first saw the twins at the Diallo household the next morning. Moussa Kouyaté, the Tounkaras' family griot, drove Adama and me over to inspect them. Moussa was not a musician, nor did I ever hear him reciting the old histories of Mali. Moussa's relationship to the Tounkara family reflected a different aspect of griotism. His job was to mediate disputes within the family and to negotiate sensitive matters, such as weddings and births, with other families. Among the Manding, the concerned parties in an important matter rarely discuss it directly. Rather, they ensure clarity and preserve decorum by speaking through an intermediary, generally a griot. In ancient times a griot worked for only one family during his life. If the patriarch of that family died, he might even take his own life, unless his master had specifically given him to a surviving relative.

Few families can afford their own griot today, and the entire tradition has either changed with the times or else died, depending on whom you ask. Moussa Kouyaté took great pride in pointing out that he worked only for the Tounkaras and that he still performed the tasks of a family griot exactly as in antiquity. In the matter of Adama, his twins, and the Diallo family, Moussa had work to do. Adama Tounkara and Miriam Diallo were not married. Adama was an impoverished *jeli*, and the widowed matriarch of the Diallo family did not approve of her granddaughter's marriage. Now this unsanctioned union had produced not one but two new mouths to feed. To heighten anxieties further, the babies were already sick. One of them had yet to drink from his mother's breast nearly twenty-four hours after his birth, and the other had done so only once.

When we arrived, the twins, their mother, and two or three attendant women were gathered in a small room with a single bed, a mattress on the floor, two chairs, and a screenless window. With no fan and too many people, the room was hot. There these tiny fellows wrapped in cloth had spent their first day. Unlike Lasine and Fuseini, the ten-year-old twins at the compound, these babies could not be mistaken for one another. One had a long face and virtually no hair; the other was round and pudgy and his head sprouted large black curls.

As we left after the short visit, Moussa Kouyaté told me that there had been trouble between the two families when Diallo became pregnant. He explained that through a number of diplomatic negotiations between the two families, he had brought about a peaceful settlement. "Now everyone is happy," he beamed. I looked over at Adama, somber and distracted, and I knew this was not true.

That night after dinner, Djelimady and I were sitting outside the main door, playing guitar on the street, when Adama and a friend arrived on foot. Adama looked haunted but said little and didn't linger. Pivoting indecisively at the doorway, he said goodnight and the two walked off. But they returned quickly and, after a few words in Bambara, Djelimady turned to me and said, "The children are sick. You should take them to get medicine. You can bring back the car in the morning."

Adama and I headed into the night in Djelimady's Nissan, picking up a doctor friend at the terminus and then collecting the babies, carried by Diallo and one of her sisters. We made the obligatory stop for gas and drove to Gabriel Touré Hospital, a ranging complex of dimly lit two-story buildings.

The hospital inspired no hope or confidence. Outside the open doorway leading into the building marked *Pediatrie*, male nurses and orderlies sat on benches, smoking cigarettes and making tea on a coal stove. One of them was asleep on a mat on the ground. Inside, fluorescent lights revealed the main lobby, from which a staircase and two hallways led off into darkness. Drawn to that light, mosquitoes swarmed in, ants streamed across the lobby floor, and an enormous spider hung in the hallway, constructing its web at head level.

Chipped green paint on the walls and cracks in the dirty floor gave the hospital a chilling decrepitude. Hand-painted signs above doorways read ominously, *Reanimation, Surveillance*. Adama and I sat down on a wooden bench next to a trash can lid half filled with discarded peanut shells while the three women and the babies went into a reception room. As they entered, I caught a glimpse of a man at a desk with nothing before him but a pad of paper and a scale big enough to weigh a baby. Another fellow seemed primarily concerned with keeping the door closed. Two lean cats pranced in the front doorway and then made their way down one of the deserted hallways. A baby cried from somewhere beyond them.

Adama looked desolate. He smoked cigarettes and often took my hand to say things like, "Banning, you are my best friend. I am grate-

ful to have you in my corner." I was touched but also puzzled that there
weren't other friends in his corner. Adama seemed out of his depth and
nobody was coming to the rescue. He told me that he himself was quite
sick and he wondered whether the twins had not made him so. He was
talking not about infection but deviltry.

The women and babies soon emerged to sit on the benches in the
lobby. "This is our hospital," said Diallo's sister quietly, as if apologiz-
ing. The babies cried. Adama looked over at their pale, quivering lips
and had to turn away. The doctor produced a handwritten prescription
and Adama and I set out to fill it. The fellows drinking tea outside gave
us wrong directions to the pharmacy, which was barely a hundred yards
away. "That's dangerous," observed Adama grimly. The guy at the pharmacy pulled himself away from the TV to fill our order, which came to
a mere 805 CFA. When we returned, the doctor told us we had been
overcharged.

The women and babies went back into the treatment room but soon
returned with another prescription that we had to fill at an outside
pharmacy. By then it was nearly midnight and we had trouble finding
an open pharmacy. As we sat in the car waiting for the doctor to return
with the medicine, dark flute and vocal melodies and the insistent triplet
rhythms of a Bambara pop song drifted from a radio. This time the bill
came to nearly 5,000 CFA. I paid.

Back at the Diallo house, the sicker baby made a feeble attempt to
breast-feed. He had turned a corner. Adama and I dropped the doctor
off and went to find some food at the edge of the Lafiabougou market,
a short walk from our homes. Knowing Adama had not eaten all day, I
offered to buy him a meal. While he devoured a plate of noodles with
meat sauce, I drank a beer purchased from a bar across the street, Le
Segovien. Adama let me know that, like most good Muslims in Bamako,
he did not drink alcohol. He seemed to disapprove of my doing so. I
didn't care. If I was his best friend, he would have to take me as I was.

That cold Castel lager, the only beer commonly served in Bamako,
tasted exquisite. I had scarcely tasted alcohol in two weeks. The
Tounkaras, all nominal Muslims, never drank, so for more than a week,
neither had I. Feeling the effect of that beer and loving it, I kidded
Adama, saying he really ought to try it, but the humor seemed to escape
him. We sat on wooden stools at an open-air kiosk just next to a foul-
smelling roadside drainage ditch. The kiosk's radio was playing Bob
Marley, and Adama paused to do a brief mime of the dead reggae singer.

Closing his large eyes and pressing his chin forward, he struck a distinctly Marley-like pose. Such was Adama's sense of humor.

As the babies recovered, Adama turned his attention to the problem of arranging a baptism for the following Monday. Malians use the French word *baptême*, but in fact the term "naming ceremony" describes this event better, since the principal action involves the public announcement of the new child's name. The Bambara name for the ceremony, *denkonli*, literally means "baby head shave," a reference to the fact that women shave each baby's head before the ceremony. The *denkonli* must occur one week after the baby's birth. Its central action involves a griot speaking the baby's name into his or her ear, three times for a boy, four times for a girl. The griot also utters a few phrases into the child's ear, phrases that hint at the connections between the child's name and the history of Mali. This experience forms the basis of *jeliya*— the griot's art. Throughout his or her life, that child will hear those phrases cross the lips of countless praising *jelis*.

For Adama, preparations for the twins' *denkonli* involved notifying people in person all over Bamako, rounding up musicians to play at the party following the ceremony, and making a variety of purchases. "I have to buy a mattress for the babies, a new *boubou* for Diallo, food for the guests. And my money is finished," Adama complained. I offered to help with the mattress, which cost 15,000 CFA, but explained that my generosity would have to end there.

The next day Adama and I dropped Djelimady at the Buffet de la Gare to rehearse with the Rail Band, and we went off to buy the mattress and track down musicians and invitees. These errands took us to the far end of Bamako, along the busy Route de Koulikoro, named for the city where Sunjata pursued the sorcerer king Soumaoro into a cave from which he never emerged. On our way back into Bamako, I heard a sharp whistle. Sensing no concern from Adama in the passenger seat, I ignored it, but when we turned right onto a dirt road past a huge cardboard cutout of Michael Jackson and ambled along the rutted surface toward our next stop, a motor scooter with two military men on it pulled up alongside the car and commanded us to stop.

The problem was that the Nissan had been purchased in Togo and still had foreign plates two years later. We had been stopped as part of an ongoing customs crackdown. Customs charges pay for the largest portion of the government's annual budget, and efforts to collect these revenues were being stepped up as part of the anticorruption, pro-people approach of the new government. Djelimady had voiced enthusiastic support for the policy, but rather than pay the fees he owed on his car, he preferred to talk his way out of it if ever he got stopped. Lacking Djelimady's status and authority, we had to return to the Buffet and fetch him.

"You didn't explain enough," he said enigmatically when we found him. We returned to the checkpoint in a taxi and Djelimady began his routine, smiling and shaking hands. One of the officers turned out to be his "little brother," and he succeeded in liberating the car with no money changing hands. But the incident put an end to Adama's automotive recruitment activities.

Gatherings at the Tounkara household grew tense as the naming ceremony neared. Heated discussions in Bambara tantalized my imagination. One afternoon, a shouting match erupted at the doorway where people congregated in the shade of the house at that time of day. Djelimady, his wife, and his mother all held forth in angry tones. Moussa Kouyaté, the family griot, listened with concerned, priestly calm. Adama Tounkara paced at the perimeter looking haggard, saying nothing. Adama had shed his western-style street clothes in favor of a brown and white *boubou* ensemble with blue umbrellas on it. He looked festive despite the gloom that hung over him.

I learned from Djelimady that the argument concerned the Diallo family's wish that two naming ceremonies be held, one at each household. "That's not the tradition," my mentor complained. Normally there is single ceremony at the father's home involving a men's session in the morning and a women's session in the afternoon. The Tounkaras were not about to depart from this norm. They considered the Diallos' request a vengeful effort to make them spend more money.

The griot Moussa Kouyaté set out for the Diallo home, and Adama and I went to invite another musician to the naming ceremony. We went on foot across the long, open space where Samory Touré had kept his war camp, into the neighborhood of Djikoroni. I plied Adama for information along the way. He explained that his fiancée's mother had gone to live with her husband's family and that Diallo had opted to stay behind in her grandmother's household. That gave the grandmother full authority over the girl.

"Diallo's grandmother doesn't want us to marry," Adama told me. "And it's all because I am a griot." I was intrigued that the *jeli*s of Bamako seemed to merit a special reverence for their cultural contributions but were not exempted from the stigma that musicians bear in other societies.

The message seemed to be: God bless the *jeli*s, but don't let your daughter marry one.

To complicate matters, Adama told me that nobody, not even his own family, quite believed that he was penniless. Djelimady's wife openly claimed that Adama kept a secret cache of money.

"Well, do you?" I asked.

"No!" he protested. "It's gone. All gone. And these days, there aren't many weddings. Really, I don't know what I'm going to do."

Moussa Kouyaté succeeded in making peace between the two families, but the settlement involved a price for Adama's marriage to Diallo of 150,000 CFA, about $300, more than the average Malian earns in a year. This meant that before he could marry Diallo and legitimate the twins, Adama would have to come up with that sum. As Djelimady had said, Adama would have to play a lot of *ngoni*.

Fortunately, playing *ngoni* seemed about the only thing Adama wanted to do. During this stressful week, he continued to rehearse me, more determined, driving, and impatient than ever. "I'm going to work you hard," he snapped at one point when I couldn't put the beat where he wanted it. "You're going to learn all the accompaniments to all the songs and play them for Djelimady. Then he will see that you are serious."

On the Sunday before the naming ceremony, Adama stopped by my house complaining of nightmares. He showed me fresh wounds on his forehead, hand, and leg, apparently inflicted when he had awoken in the night convulsing and screaming and flinging himself against the concrete wall by his bed. I asked him why he thought this had happened. "Perhaps it's a devil," he speculated. I had read that an attack of malaria begins with a night of violent dreaming, and I suspected that this might be the true explanation.

That night the Tounkara courtyard filled with relatives, many elderly and all well turned out. Some of them had come from the family's ancestral village near Kita for the naming ceremony. The names for the two boys had been chosen, Lasina and Fuseini, family names.

"But those are practically the same names as the older twins," I said to Barou. "Won't that be confusing?"

"It's tradition," he replied. "Twin boys often take those names."

Gray metal chairs were stacked by the door in anticipation of guests. The chairs, which had been carried from a nearby rental site by the children, all bore painted numbers, ensuring that they would be accounted for later. Over in the cooking area, two goats were tied to a tree where they would remain until slaughtered for the baptismal feast.

As darkness fell, Moussa Kouyaté arrived and more discussion began. The entire family circled around, women on the right, men on the left, children nesting around the oldest Tounkaras, Djelimady at the center and Moussa before him. Only Djelimady's wife continued working in the cooking area as the debate escalated. Djelimady's half-brother Yéyé seemed especially incensed, his ravings becoming so intense that I feared he might turn violent. In response to that aggression, Djelimady's mother flew into a fury, as did his wife, and ultimately even Djelimady lost his composure and began rasping out a tense stream of Bambara. Adama Tounkara broke his silence at last, stopping his pacing to speak in an angry but utterly defeated tone of voice. Everybody was talking at once in a cacophony I found horrifying on the night before a ritual family celebration.

Then Moussa spoke quietly to Djelimady. In the midst of disgruntled muttering, the griot gently made his case for civility and reason. Djelimady and others took issue with him, but in a more subdued tone. By the time he got up to make yet another trip to the Diallo household, he had soothed the waters.

Miriam Diallo arrived with her twins and provoked a round of applause. The babies vanished into the house, absorbed into its endlessly accommodating rooms. A young man I would come to know as a most excellent guitarist arrived. Boubacar Diabaté, or Badian, was Djelimady's protégé and Adama's good friend. On seeing him, Djelimady called for the guitars, but there was to be no playing then. The children had carried the family boom box out to the street and wired it into Djelimady's old, spent Roland Jazz Chorus—the one I had replaced—to create a raucous blast of distorted party music. Barou explained to me that on the night before a naming ceremony, the children celebrate, dancing and playing card games on the street until just before dawn, when the Imam comes to perform the men's ceremony.

Young guests arrived in casual dress. Adama made the rounds restlessly in his wide-lapel turquoise jacket and his black and gold Malcolm X T-shirt, which bore the words "By any means necessary."

The next morning at about 6:30, the men's ceremony began, with the male Tounkara elders positioned on a mat to the left of the doorway. They dispensed *kola* nuts to guests as they entered the courtyard. These red nuts, with their bitter white meat, have a mildly narcotic effect similar to that of coffee. *Kola* nuts figure in every rite of passage in Malian society.

I had been asked to videotape the event. I would not have dared request this privilege, but it turned out that all such events get taped. Asking me to do it was simply a way to save money. I began with a pan of the courtyard and almost immediately heard a clamor arising from the elders' mat. Though I couldn't see what was causing it, I soon understood, when through the lens of my camera I watched four people carrying Adama, eyes closed and limbs flapping, into one of the back rooms. Adama had succumbed to whatever demons were besieging him. He lay unconscious while his sons received their names.

I was appointed to drive Adama to a friend's place to rest. We stopped at a pharmacy, where a Tounkara relative dressed in a tuxedo produced a lengthy prescription—treatment for malaria. The total came to nearly 8,000 CFA, paid mostly by me with a little help from Badian, the guitarist. When we got Adama into bed, the tuxedo-clad relative prepared an IV bag, injecting the contents of glass quinine vials into the IV fluid with a hypodermic needle. He nailed the bag to the wall using a rock as a hammer and inserted the IV into Adama's vein. As the fluid began to flow, Adama asked me to return with guitars for him and Badian. I ignored him and went home to sleep.

That afternoon at the lively women's ceremony, Adama appeared— rejuvenated—in an elegant brown *boubou* with yellow embroidery. He made his rounds, played *ngoni*, danced, and seemed to fulfill his paternal responsibilities, right down to making sure that I got plenty of footage of the Diallo family in my video. "Make sure you film the grandmother," he kept insisting, as though pleasing his foe might make up for everything else.

Fifty or so guests arrived, more than filling the rented chairs. Most were women dressed in gowns and head scarves and adorned with makeup and jewelry. Though they rarely smiled, their faces glowed. With the two amplifiers out on the street, Adama and a friend plugged in their *ngoni*s and Badian plugged in my electric guitar, leaving one input jack for a singer. Young Sambry stood to the side in a deep blue *boubou* and thumped out rhythms on a large, shoulder-slung drum called a *doundounba*. Djelimady and all the men of his generation remained sequestered in the courtyard throughout.

As the long afternoon unfolded, a succession of *jelimusow* took their turns at the microphone, complaining that the instruments were too loud but getting no response from the celebrant string players. The *jeli*'s singing style relies on projection. Singers belt out long notes from deep within their chests, producing a sound that Western writers have compared with blues shouters and R&B belters. At street parties, this elegant form of expression takes on the intensity of rock 'n' roll, with everything amplified to the greatest possible extent. Hearing *jeli* street music for the first time that day, I was startled by its rawness and by the musicians' disorderly approach. They seemed distracted. Songs went on and on with no apparent arrangements. During breaks, Badian would fiddle with the amplifier settings, producing whistling feedback, while the singer held the microphone close to her mouth crowing, "Allo! Allo!"

Nevertheless, when the music proceeded, the gathered women got up from their chairs in groups and paraded slowly past the *jelimuso*, often handing her a 500 or 1,000 CFA note as they passed. I continued videotaping until the party broke up at sundown.

A mood of relief prevailed at dinner. The family ordeal was over, though Adama's larger ordeal of parenthood had just begun. He lit up a cigarette. "This will be my last cigarette," he told me with confidence. "After this, it's over."

The next day he was smoking as usual, begging cigarettes and money with which to purchase them. I wondered how this young man who could not support his own smoking habit was going to raise 150,000 CFA to marry the mother of his children. But I had been in Bamako just two weeks then; I had much to learn about the resourcefulness of *jeli*s.

3

Praise for Hire

The art of eloquence has no secrets for us; without us the names of kings would vanish into oblivion; we are the memory of mankind.

Mamadou Kouyaté, from his telling of the Sunjata epic

One of the many accounts of griot origins dates back to the life of the prophet Mohammed. It describes a bold infidel named Surakata who attempts to kill the prophet and demonstrate the impotence of Islam. After Mohammed commands the desert sands to rise up in waves and mire Surakata's horse, and then to recede and release it, the pagan ceases his assault and is converted. Surakata begins shouting the glories of Allah and his messenger Mohammed, and the flattered prophet engages Surakata as a kind of missionary advance man who revs up crowds with inspirational speeches—prototypes of today's *jeliya*.

This story, read often on Radio Mali during the early days of the independent Republic, suggests that the task of *praising* preceded the musical and diplomatic responsibilities of griots. It also reveals a distinct ambivalence toward them, as Surakata becomes the object of potent jealousies. Scholars still puzzle over the fact that griots used to be buried in the husks of dead *baobob* trees rather than in the ground. Europeans saw this as an act of contempt, and though its real meaning remains obscure, there is general agreement that it was no honor.

As an apprentice *jelimuso* in Mali, anthropologist Barbara Hoffman observed the subtle vulnerabilities that draw today's *horon* (nobles) to the *jeli*s who praise them. Nobles love to denigrate griots, but griots' words contain undeniable power for them, the force called *nyama*, a drug that nobles fear but cannot resist. Hoffman writes, "I have seen many a *horon*'s hand quake as it thrust forth a bill, sometimes accompanied by a verbal plea, 'ka nyama bò' (please take away the *nyama*)."

Years before I visited Bamako, I interviewed Mali's most famous guitarist, Ali Farka Touré, in Boston. Farka took pains to point out that he is Songhoi, *not* Manding, and certainly not a griot. "Griotism is an art of exploitation and flattery," he growled. "The words may be pretty, but they are not true." I had never heard the honesty of griots called into question, but then I held a romanticized view of griotism. As long ago as 1834, a European traveler in West Africa wrote that griots proclaimed the virtues of their subjects "as impartially as European tombstones do those of the dead." Such skepticism is as common as the griots themselves, and I would run into it often in Bamako, beginning with Barou's caution about "griot history."

For the Manding, official griotism begins in the time of Sunjata. The griots in the Sunjata epic play instruments and serve as advisors, negotiators, and public praisers of noble patrons. Through the words of the griots, family names have become the glue that binds the present to the past. Today, anyone who bears the name Kouyaté traces his ancestry to Sunjata's heroic griot, Balla Faséké Kouyaté. The name means literally "there is a secret between you and me," suggesting both a unique intimacy and an implied threat.

Roderic Knight says that some griot names seem to have been given to "people of famous warrior families who were inept or fearful in battle." For instance, Suso, which means literally "stabbing the dead," was earned by a timid fighter who lagged behind the lines, driving his spear into the corpses of slain enemies. Each Manding spear left a signature mark, so that after the battle, every soldier's kill could be tallied.

During the six centuries that separate Mohammed's convert crier from the *jeli*s of the Sunjata epic, some of the griot's traditional roles survived within a select African class: hunters. Hunters traveled. They saw and heard things unknown to those in their sedentary villages. In their journeys away from home, hunters had a daily need for entertainment, so there came to be among them musicians who did what the *jeli*s do today. They played long musical epics full of praise for brave hunters and their exploits. The hunter-griot's instrument of choice was the seven-stringed *simbi*, a combination of a harp and a lute and a clear ancestor of the twenty-one-string *kora*.

Knight argues that most *jelis* today are too proud to acknowledge the ancient connection to hunting, but Djelimady was pleased to report it. "This is the true origin of the griot," he told me excitedly when he invited a hunter musician to the compound for a soirée. "As the desert moved south, there were not many animals left to hunt. It was now the time of the farmers. The hunter-musicians passed on their art to the griots. *Et voila!*" Djelimady smiled with satisfaction, as though he had answered any remaining questions I might have about griots.

After Barou, Madou Djan Tounkara was my best guide through the mysteries of life with the Tounkaras. As tall as Djelimady, but thinner, Madou had a subdued presence. He walked with stiff resolve, slowly, as if in pain. When he spoke, his deep voice was rarely inflected with emotion; he won my attention with his words. "You have been lucky," he told me after the twins' naming ceremony. "You have seen the family at an important moment. Now, Banning has become a Tounkara."

Madou adored the youngest children and never seemed happier than when coddling a baby and speaking gently into its ear. Older children feared him. With a single Bambara phrase, a quick, forced whisper like the sound of an air brake releasing, Madou could bring an end to any activity. If a boy failed to heed him, Madou would wade in and deal him a smack behind the ear. He needed only stand up from his chair and raise a hand and children around him would scatter like minnows. Once Moise, a disheveled twelve-year-old who seemed forever in trouble, came to Madou crying because he had gotten his finger stuck in the grill of a fan. Madou carefully helped the boy remove his finger and then gave him a whack that sent him off bawling.

Madou was gracious to a fault with me, always entreating me to eat more than I really wanted and indicating when social situations required a particular behavior from me. I must always sit in the front seat of the car. When eating a meal, I must always take the seat next to Djelimady. When the wash water comes, the oldest person washes his hands first and then passes the bowl to the left. No one should eat until everyone has washed his hands. Madou also taught me Bambara with the patience of Job, translating phrases and explaining nuances of meaning for as long as I could bear to listen and scratch definitions my notebook. "You see, he is intelligent," Madou would say as I scribbled. "Intelligent people write things down."

When we watched *Le Journal* in the evening, Madou let his gregarious brother do most of the talking, but he followed world events more closely than Djelimady did and held at least as many opinions. More than once I found myself seated in front of the television between Djelimady and Madou, watching a public service announcement on the subject of AIDS.

Compared with many African countries, Mali's AIDS infection rate was low, but rising. Where other governments had been squeamish about openly discussing sex, Mali had embarked on a frank program of warning citizens about the disease, often through humorous television sketches. In one, a man chats with the mechanic working on his motorbike. The customer complains about having to wear a condom during sex, to which the mechanic replies that, unlike the motor bike, you cannot be repaired if you get AIDS. The customer scoffs. They argue, and in the end the mechanic triumphs with the line, "The only cure for AIDS is a condom," a truth that the customer repeats with comic despair.

The Tounkara brothers always laughed when they heard that line: The only cure for AIDS is a condom. Then Madou would pose an odd question to me: "Do you believe in AIDS?" The first time I heard this question, I stalled, wondering what might lie behind it. "Yes," I finally said. Madou thought for a moment before allowing that he supposed he did too, but I had the feeling that he was just being polite. This exchange, which was repeated a few nights later, left the impression that Madou had asked the paramount question concerning the AIDS phenomenon. The mystery was not how you avoid getting the disease, or how you treat or cure it, but whether you believe that it is real.

The second time he asked this question, I replied immediately that, yes, I knew a number of people who had died from the disease in the United States, Zaire, and Zimbabwe. "AIDS is definitely real," I asserted.

Madou repeated his hollow affirmation, "Yes, I believe it." This time Djelimady spoke up, announcing that he did not believe in AIDS at all.

"What do you think people are dying from?" I asked him.

"Chronic malaria," he replied, explaining that doctors, scientists, and African governments had invented AIDS as a way to get funding. He said that African health officials counted malaria and other deaths as AIDS cases because they knew the high numbers would attract foreign money. He implied that this worldwide scam had the added advantage of allowing governments to meddle with people's sexual behavior. He'd be damned if he was going to fall for that.

Barou had warned me not to disagree with Djelimady on factual matters. "You will never convince him," he had said. "You will only make him angry." Just the same, I told Djelimady that while I believed governments might inflate numbers to get more money, that didn't mean AIDS was a fiction. He listened patiently, too polite to bicker. Madou said nothing.

During my first week in Bamako, Madou came into my room and told me that he had a problem with money. He asked to borrow 10,000 CFA, which he said he would pay back later in the week. Years of experience had taught me not to expect repayment of money "lent" to my African friends. "Do you mean lend or give?" I generally asked when faced with a request for money. This usually brought ardent promises, but rarely reimbursement. I wondered, though, with Madou, so upright and proper. Perhaps he would surprise me. I gave him the money. He asked that I not mention the loan to anyone.

The next day, as Djelimady, Madou, and I were driving through town, we stopped beside a government building and Madou got out. He returned looking frustrated and gave a vague explanation. He said he was owed money by the government for services rendered in the past. He told me that the payment had been approved and that now it was just a matter of getting the funds from the treasury. Madou had worked for years in the hotel business in Abidjan, the wealthy, cosmopolitan capital of Cote D'Ivoire. He had returned from there quite recently, so I wondered how the Malian government could owe him money, but Madou's gloomy air discouraged prying.

Barou laughed when I told him this story. "There is no way that the government is paying Madou Djan any money," he assured me. "He is the one who stole money from them."

"Stole?" I asked.

"A long time ago," Barou explained, "during the presidency of Modibo Keita, Madou was a constable in a government agency. I don't know the details, but later, after Moussa Traoré came to power, Madou was accused of stealing money, and he had to leave the country. That's why he lived so long in Cote D'Ivoire. If he had come back here, he would have gone to prison. After 1991, the old government was gone. He felt safe coming home."

A few days later, during one of our Bambara lessons, Madou told me that he had learned to speak five African languages while living in Abidjan. Newly aware that Madou's years in Abidjan might have been more a period of exile than of exploration, I asked him, "How long did you live there?"

"Seventeen years," he replied.

His answer seemed to confirm Barou's story. Madou had a strong sense of family, and nothing about him suggested that he would willingly leave the fold for so long. That very morning, he had had to take his mother to the hospital for an evaluation of her failing eyesight, and he had told me with pride, "Our mother is 84 years old. Our father lived to be 103. I couldn't even tell you how many children he had."

If in fact Madou had been driven from home by scandal, it might explain his melancholy aura. It did not lessen my affection for him. Strangely, Madou was one of the most reassuring people I knew in Bamako. I felt as though, having lived so long as a stranger himself, he sensed my thoughts.

On that particular day, I was preoccupied with the imminent arrival of an American colleague. Dirck Westervelt was a fellow musician and a friend since our school years in the 1970s. Dirck had planned to come and stay with me in Bamako for a couple of months. I had encouraged him to come but was also worried about how it might affect my interactions with Djelimady and his family. Long-term guests had never been part of our arrangement, and as the day approached, I became apprehensive. I confided to Madou my nervousness about bringing another person into the overcrowded compound.

Madou understood and knew what to say. "Even if you have ten strangers come and visit you, it is no problem," he told me. "Even if you are not here and someone comes and says they are your friend, they can stay here. Our grandfather used to say, 'Any day that at least one stranger does not enter my home is a day that I say God has forgotten me.'" Madou then explained that among the Manding, aiding strangers amounts to a kind of insurance. When Tounkaras began to land in Boston, he suggested, they too would find hospitality with me.

I understood this. A young journalist who had once shown me two weeks of hospitality in Conakry, Guinea, had later come to live with me for over a year in my Boston apartment. In coming to live with the Tounkaras, I had entered into an exchange the ultimate terms of which could not be predicted. This family of *jeli*s was only too happy to serve me, knowing that, as with all their services, payment would come. *Insha 'Allah*: if God wills it. But the complications I might someday face back home seemed remote in the face of those before me. I felt calmed by Madou's words.

One evening at the compound, Adama Tounkara and his guitar-playing friend Badian showed up after dinner and told me that they wanted to make a recording. I was tired, and I knew the project would preempt my evening lesson with Djelimady, but I agreed to participate. Adama explained that he did not actually want me to play guitar, just to operate my tape recorder while he performed with a few friends.

"Adama," I complained, "I came here to learn guitar, not to be a sound engineer."

"My friend, please," he implored me. "This is important."

Adama, Badian, and a young girl gathered in the sitting room in the back section of the compound. Dim, incandescent light barely revealed the overstuffed couch and armchair. Adama had moved the central table out of the way, blocking most of the couch. He and Badian had strewn wires and equipment on the carpet. The room felt close and chaotic. The two players struggled with connecting wires, effects boxes, and a microphone to one big guitar amplifier—the Roland I had brought for Djelimady. At first there were buzzes and crackles. Adama fussed with the connections until the racket settled into an oscillating hum.

The girl sat to the side, silent and bored. Though she had her thinly braided hair tied in a knob atop her head and wore a dark blue robe and elegant gold earrings, she did not seem glamorous. She sat inside an open-top hamper, her rear end jammed down into a wash bucket that had been placed inside and her legs dangling indelicately outside, not quite reaching the floor. In one hand she held the microphone, an old wedding-party warhorse that had its cable doubled back and taped to its shaft, presumably a protection against a sudden yank on the cord. In the other hand, she fidgeted with a crumpled sheet of notebook paper with some fifteen lines of scribblings in Bambara on it.

The girl was Ina Tounkara, one of Djelimady's nieces from the family's ancestral village. Barely twenty and just recently fatherless, Ina had come to Bamako for the naming ceremony and was now staying on to try her luck singing *jeliya* in the capital.

Just before the recording began, Moussa Diabaté, a guitarist I had met at the Tabalé shows, arrived. A little older than Adama or Badian, Moussa carried an aura of professionalism. He took up my acoustic guitar, tuned it, placed the capo on the seventh fret, fired off a couple of quick, clean riffs, and was ready to go. The session started with "Lamban," a *jeli* standard.

As soon as the musicians began to play, Adama's listlessness gave way to absorption. His deadpan face came to life and mirrored the creaky, darting lines his fingers etched on the *ngoni*. The *ngoni* has no frets, so the fingernails on the fretting hand must scramble to find precise locations at which to press its wound nylon strings against the doweling neck, and they need to work fast as the picking finger and thumb spin out volleys of notes. Adama's eyes bulged when he stepped out with a flash of improvisation, and he smiled as if flirting with a girl when he fell back into his accompaniment. For him, the musical conversation was everything. In every other situation in which I'd known him, Adama seemed a ghost by comparison.

Adama and Badian worked to impress each other, rewarding each other's efforts with smiles, nods, grunts, and murmurs of "Oooooooh," uttered with ever so slightly rising intonation and volume. The three instruments made a rich sound together. Through the guitar amplifier, Adama's *ngoni* took on a biting tonality. Moussa balanced this by producing a muted, rhythmic sound on the acoustic guitar, the combined effect of the sweat-bathed strings on my guitar and the fact that he played mostly low notes high on the fretboard. Between these two, Badian—the most gifted improviser of the three—played Djelimady's imitation Gibson electric guitar. He used a watery sound that let him burrow deep into the weave of melodies to provide texture and then rage to the surface with stabbing solos, full of angular rhythms and screaming melodies. At his best, Badian played with the freshness and fire of Jimi Hendrix.

Like Adama, Badian liked to play with a lit cigarette drooping from his mouth. The sight always reminded me of that famous photograph of Mississippi Delta bluesman Robert Johnson, staring dead into the camera with a fresh cigarette similarly positioned. As he played, Badian would puff occasionally, letting the ash get as long as possible until it finally fell, splashing gray dust over a stretch of the guitar fingerboard. Ignoring the trail of ashes, Badian's fingers would plow through on the next pass.

As much as these young players impressed me, Ina Tounkara proved the revelation. Though stuffed into a clothes hamper and reading from a crib sheet, Ina sang like a nightclub angel. Her powerful alto conveyed warmth the average griot wailer couldn't dream of, just as a French horn makes a cool contrast with the brashness of a trumpet. She never hesitated or faltered, never gave the slightest hint of regret. Ina remained aloof from the congratulatory gestures and sounds exchanged among the players. The only audience that counted was the *jatigui*, the noble who would receive the cassette, the person whose particulars she transformed from scrawls on a page into incandescent *jeliya*.

The cassette they were making, I eventually learned, was for a patron of young *jelis*. Ina's bit of paper contained the family names she had to work into the text as she sang standard songs—"Diaoura," "Lamban," "Tara." Like the players, she had a base of memorized material to work with, but her art, and hence the value of the tape, would depend on her ability to improvise, to tell the patron's story in a way that both entertained and surprised him, unleashing the coveted power, *nyama*. In the two hours of recording, there were no second takes. The performance was recorded with a single stereo microphone, electronic humming and all, and when the two tapes were full, the work was done and the musicians began to pack up.

Djelimady had poked his head in a few times during the evening, smiling and nodding for the most part. Afterwards, he criticized Adama for straying too far from the original *ngoni* parts. "These young players want to change everything," he complained to me. "Put in a little reggae, a little this, a little that. But you lose the sound of the *ngoni*." Adama had now returned to his taciturn self and paid no attention.

"How much do people pay for these cassettes?" I asked Adama the next day as we drove through Lafiabougou.

"That depends," he hedged.

"But what is the range?"

"If it's someone who has money, it can be a lot." Adama did not like to explain anything to me unless forced to.

"Adama," I pressed, "I'm not going to ask for a share. I don't mind helping you make recordings, but you need to help me by giving me real information. Tell me some numbers."

He told me that a cassette could bring in from 10,000 to 50,000 CFA, or $20 to $100. I asked him what they would get for the tape we had made the night before and he said that the four of them would share about $50. In a country where the average person makes around $300 a year, this didn't seem bad. I would realize later that this patron was getting a bargain for two hours of personalized *jeliya*.

While Americans celebrated Thanksgiving, I attended a lavish baptism in Lafiabougou. I walked there from the Tounkara compound with

Harouna Kouyaté, Sambry's younger brother and one of Djelimady's many nephews. With the same generous features—wide noses, full lips, animated eyes, and forward manner—these two boys were easily spotted as brothers, Harouna fifteen and Sambry seventeen. As with so many of the young people at the Tounkara compound, their father was dead. Their mother, Djelimady's sister, lived as the second wife of a merchant in the village of Tokoto, near Kita. Harouna had told me that his mother was chronically sick and that the new husband did not treat her well. Sweet, though openly manipulative, Harouna held my hand as we walked, and he expressed hushed, tender concern for his mother, while not forgetting to request 2,500 CFA for the train so that he could go and visit her, as well as for a pair of shoes—size 42—that I could send to him when I got back to Boston.

The Thanksgiving baptism took place on the street next to one of the largest and most elaborate houses in Lafiabougou. Towering three stories above the street, this boxy, peach-colored edifice had stucco walls with pebble inlay, large windows sealed off with bars, and small balconies, terraces, and archways. On the roof sat a mammoth satellite dish and a verandah big enough for twenty, shielded from the sun by a round thatched roof. Lafiabougou contained a number of impressive houses, though none more grandiose than this. That day, the owner's first child was to be named at a grand *denkonli*.

The band was still setting up as we arrived. It included Adama Tounkara on *ngoni*, the Bobo pop musician Dounanke Koita on guitar, and his three brothers on bass, drums, and percussion. One of the great singers of the Wassoulou tradition, Daouda "Flany" Sangaré, stood by smoking cigarettes. Soon these musicians would be joined by four *jelimusow*. The ensemble interested me because I hadn't realized that musicians from all these traditions would collaborate this way.

As the music started, children occupied most of the rented steel chairs that formed a wide circle on the street. Gradually the children were displaced as women arrived. While we waited, Harouna took my hand again and pulled me aside, anxious to tell me the story of how such wealth had found its way to Lafiabougou.

According to Harouna, the man of the household, then thirty-six years old, had gotten a job working for a wealthy Arab sheik in Saudi Arabia about two years earlier. One day, the Malian had seen an opportunity to advance himself. He had stolen two large sacks of cash from the sheik and promptly left the country. He had been apprehended at the Bamako-Senou airport and promptly jailed, but the government had released him after he'd agreed to split the money with them. The man had then used what remained of his booty to build this house and, with an eye to the future, to launch a transport company with a fleet of thirty-two trucks. Harouna pointed out one of these hulking vehicles parked alongside the house. He told me that while many people knew the secret of the patron's staggering wealth, nobody would talk about it.

Harouna seemed to admire the rich Malian, not only for his money but because he had struck a blow against the much-resented Arabs. At the same time, Harouna knew that what the man had done was wrong, hence the secrecy. I made a point over the next few weeks of remarking to various companions as we passed by the home of Harouna's thieving entrepreneur, "That's an awfully big house. I wonder how that guy got all his money?" No one ever seemed to know.

As the baptism unfolded, there was a good deal of fussing over who would be allowed inside the lavish compound. Most of the guests remained crowded into the circle of chairs out on the street, as they would at any other Bamako street celebration, waiting as fruit, popcorn, peanuts, water, soft drinks, and, in a departure, beer, were carried out from the house. Though the compound was bigger, the refreshments and the music better, and the guests more numerous and well heeled, this party seemed in essence little different from the one I had filmed at the Tounkaras' after the birth of Adama's twins. All that changed, however, when the *jelimusow* began to sing.

The would-be divas at the Tounkara party had spent most of their time quarreling with the musicians and complaining about the sound. Guests had handed them the odd 500 CFA note, but the total take had been negligible. This kind of singing had hardly seemed to me a profession at all. I now realized that Adama Tounkara and Miriam Diallo's unmarried status and poverty had reduced the viability of the event from the musician's point of view. What I would now see was an occasion worth a *jeli*'s while.

The first woman to sing wore an ivory-colored gown that glittered as though covered in diamonds. Her face shone translucent brown—the result of skin-lightening treatments—and a rosy patch at the crest of her cheeks gave way to impassive eyes that flashed from within a wreath of black brows and plucked lashes. No hair showed from beneath the furled wrap that swaddled her head like a crown. As she rose from her chair and seized a microphone, her matching high-heeled shoes bore into the dust but remained pristine, as though some magical force protected her from the ground up. With a single glance she won the musicians' attention, and they continued to watch her closely through the performance as she commanded them to play softer, louder, faster, to solo, or to change songs without stopping.

The *jelimuso*'s first note scored the air like a steamship horn announcing entry to port. I had begun to doze in one of the metal seats but sat bolt upright at the sound. Her voice shivered weirdly through the air, apparently because the guitar amplifier she sang through had the "chorus" effect turned on. No accident there. A sound that no American jazz singer would tolerate had become *de rigeur* at Bamako street parties.

By this time, an extraordinary collection of women had taken their places in the dense circle of chairs. Like the *jelimusow* themselves, these women had dressed aggressively, in some cases radically—yellow, green, and red flowers embroidered onto black, see-through cloth; glittering hearts on blue cloth with pleats and embroidery; the waxy sheen of new fabric, striped shoes, and vinyl-quilted purses big enough to contain bricks. Many had spectacular hairdos made from store-bought hair extensions painstakingly constructed into coiled, ropy hills that fanned out or gathered into knobs, bouffants, or braids that wiggled, looped, flowed, clung to the skull, or stuck out like long, spindly carrots. As if these trappings said all that need be said, the women rarely smiled or showed any outward expression. Their conversations were close and private, their laughter conspiratorial.

Most of them scarcely seemed to notice the griot singer's opening blasts—until, that is, she sang one of their names. At the mention of a family name—Diallo, Touré, Traoré, Keita—the women of that family would rise unhurriedly and move out into the circle of musicians and guests. The women would form a close line and parade slowly past the singer. As each woman passed, she would hand money to the *jelimuso*, sometimes reaching into her purse in the showiest manner possible. The singer's performance intensified at these moments, her voice loud and declamatory. She seemed to pay no heed to the parading women, but collected their offerings in her free hand until the wad became unmanageable. Then she would pause and turn to deposit the cash in a guitar case that gradually filled with a salad of bills, some as big as 5,000 CFA.

I noticed that there was one woman who carried a page torn from a notebook. She studied it and rose frequently to whisper in the singer's ear. The page listed the names of guests observed at the party. It was the *jelimuso*'s key.

With events in full swing, the new mother and baby at last made their way from within the compound to take seats at the inner edge of the circle. A large stack of gifts—metal pans and bowls, colorful plastic buckets, bed sheets, and fabric—had been assembled in front of the mother's seat, but these offerings paled next to the *jelis*' growing cache. Sometimes, after a long stretch of praising, the *jelimuso* would shout to the musicians, *"Chauffez, chauffez!"* "Make it hot!" The drummers would soar into overdrive and Adama and Dounanke would exchange fiery, electronically distorted licks on *ngoni* and guitar. Only then would the women in the circle at last drop their reserve and dance. They lifted their shoulders, let their elbows go loose, and flung their forearms around like disembodied props, all the while crouching and stomping their shoes into the dust. For the first time, they let themselves smile.

A cameraman with a large, shoulder-held video camera followed the action. As night fell, he mounted a spotlight on his camera. Now the singer's subject received not only the words and storming voice of *jeliya* but also a shower of white light that made the colors on her dress go electric. Under the circumstances, not even reluctant subjects could refuse to dance and to give.

When at last the man of the house came out to dance, it was nearly 8:00 at night, and the musicians stopped to eat. This would have been the end, but as Harouna and I left, I heard the man telling the musicians they should continue playing until everyone was satisfied. "I will pay," I heard him say, and the musicians, exhausted but knowing the patron's means, played on.

I was back at the Tounkara compound having dinner with Djelimady and Madou when Adama returned. "Good gig, wasn't it?" I asked him. He shrugged. The man had not paid much in the end, he explained, and the singers had taken most of the money. He told me that his pay for over five hours of music had been 3,000 CFA, about six dollars.

Such low pay betrayed Adama's lack of political finesse. "There were too many musicians," he complained. Perhaps, but such a thing could not have happened to Djelimady. When he played a street party, nobody took him for granted. He would stand up when he played a solo and confidently circulate among the women, pressing his guitar forward as if showering them with notes of praise. They would put 5,000 CFA bills directly into his mouth and he would clench them in his teeth. The *jelimuso* would stand back until he sat down. When it came time to divide the day's earnings, Djelimady's share would be nearly as large as theirs. That, he once explained to me, was understood from the outset. If a singer slighted him, he would never play with her again. Adama had the kind of musical talent that such power is built upon, but there it ended. When his *ngoni* went into its sack, he behaved more like a beggar than a councilor of kings. The results spoke for themselves.

One night in early December, I got a lesson in Djelimady's more formidable political skills. Organizers within the griot community of Bamako had arranged a concert at the Palais de la Culture to honor a living legend among their ranks, aging *ngoni* player and media personality Djeli Baba Sissoko, a luminary of *jeliya* for nearly four decades. After dinner at the compound, without prior warning, Djelimady glanced at his watch and said he was going to make an appearance at this event. "Do you want to go?" he asked.

"Of course."

"All right," he said. "But I warn you. We won't stay long. I don't plan to be up half the night." Before I knew it, we were in the Nissan at the Elf station, buying the customary two liters of gas.

Along the right side of Avenue Sheikh Zayed stood a single line of street lights. These lights represented for Djelimady one of the proud achievements of the Konaré administration, tangible proof that with democracy came progress. The lights arched over the long, straight road, casting an orange hue that, by comparison with Bamako's dim, shadowy side streets, felt like real illumination. Low on oil and squeaking ominously, Djelimady's Nissan moved through the dense, smoky evening air, crossing the Niger River on the new bridge and taking us to the back gates of the Palais de la Culture, where a hundred or so musicians and eager fans crowded in restlessly, competing for the attention of the guards.

The situation looked hopeless, but when Djelimady stepped out of the car—dressed "American" in black trousers, a white T-shirt, dark vest, and black leather baseball cap—things changed. Djelimady improvised in these situations with the same sureness and mastery with which he improvised on guitar. He stood tall, flashed a smile, and greeted everyone like his brother. There was simply no denying him. We entered the fenced-off parking area beside the dust-red hall, this time carefully positioning the car near the entrance for an easy getaway.

The crowd lingering on the concrete verandah proved a who's who of Bamako *jeliya*. Djelimady introduced me to Tata Bambo Kouyaté, one of Mali's top recording artists, and her husband Modibo Kouyaté, another legend of griot guitar. The diminutive Tata Bambo wore a midnight-blue gown flecked with gold. Her head wrap seemed enormous around her small head, but within it I recognized the high cheekbones and finely molded face I knew from cassette jackets. We met Diallou Damba, the griot singer who had most impressed me at the Tabalé concerts, and her husband Balla Kone, who Djelimady informed me was *"un grand"* of *ngoni* and guitar.

Inside, Djelimady introduced me to Guimba, Mali's most popular comedian and the star of many television sketches. Guimba was a phenomenon. Even as he played out didactic TV vignettes on the great issues of the day—democracy, AIDS, and the Konaré administration's new vision for Malian government, a policy dubbed "decentralization"—Guimba could make the evening television viewers at the Tounkara compound laugh like fools. In one public service spot, Guimba plays a gardener who lectures his apathetic employer about the importance of decentralization. "It doesn't concern me," says the employer, reclining in his easy chair. Just over the hedge, wielding a garden hose, Guimba lets out the oft-heard African expression of amazement, a quick, high-pitched "Eeh!" and then, brandishing the hose like a weapon, he explains that the patron might think the change in Mali's governmental structure doesn't concern him, but he'll soon find out he's up to his *neck* in it. The randomly spraying water and Guimba's musical delivery conveyed comedy even without the language. Djelimady and Madou found this sketch funnier with each repetition, even though it played two or three times a night.

Having penetrated the outer walls of the Palais and entered the side lobby, we soon slipped in and took seats in the front row of the mostly full orchestra section. It was the first time I had seen the old hall from the audience's perspective. It felt run down and the sound system was inadequate, but the room had a grand sweep to it that helped to ennoble anyone performing there. To the right side of the stage, just above where Djelimady and I were sitting, I noticed that one huge panel of the wall was painted with a portrait of an old man dressed in white robes and holding an oversized *ngoni*. This was the greatest griot of the late colonial era, Banzumana Sissoko, who died in 1987, bringing Mali to a virtual standstill, just as his radio performances had done for decades.

Banzumana's tough, uncompromising musical oratory is credited with making the nation of Mali possible in the first place. He refused to sing the praises of anyone living and so was immune to charges of using *jeliya* to exploit the vanity of rich and powerful figures. "In the rivalries between African parties," said the blind griot near the end of his life, "I refuse to take a firm stand on one side or the other. I like the winner; therefore, I like nobody before the end of the battle." Banzumana is one of the most complex and intriguing figures in modern Malian history, and his looming specter in that hall dwarfed the performers on the stage.

On this particular night, Bamako's *jelis* fawned extravagantly over old Djeli Baba Sissoko, all under Banzumana's watchful gaze. The evening's entertainment began with members of Djeli Baba's family dancing onstage while two *jelimusow* sang their praises. Five talking drummers crouched on their knees and pumped out solid rhythm that boomed through the hall. The Sissoko family danced in the style reserved for griots. Men unfolded their *boubous* along the full length of their arms so that the flaps hung like wings to the floor. The dancers then turned jerkily from side to side, twisting their bodies from the shoulder and lifting elbows and fists to fold and unfold their draping robes as they circled slowly. The movement seemed awkward, like that of groggy storks drying their wings. It conveyed an almost arrogant sense of self-assurance. The Sissokos carried on this way for nearly half an hour and had to be cajoled from the stage by a nervous MC.

Guimba came next, telling the crowd that Mali's culture was its greatest asset. Again the wiry comic's barrage of voices, and the delighted reactions he won from the crowd, suggested humor lost to me in Djelimady's whispered translations. Guimba commented on the evening's news report that the French had recently mined a fortune in diamonds near the city of Kayes and had not paid Mali the appropriate fee for the privilege. I took the message to be that the country had to be smarter with its riches, including its cultural riches. Guimba sketched out little dialogues, using voices I knew from the television— an excited squeak followed by a burly grumble—and body language to get billowing laughs from the crowd, which by now filled three-quarters of the hall.

At the back of the stage, a small collection of amplifiers and drums sat huddled together, dwarfed by the thirty-foot ceiling and broad stretches of empty floor that surrounded it. Two groups came on to use these instruments, each playing just a single song, while Djelimady eyed his watch and fidgeted. Then, barely an hour into the show, came the moment he was waiting for, the grand entrance of the honoree. Attended by a coterie of splendidly dressed men, the old griot in gold and black made his way down the long central aisle while the crowd rose in acclamation. Djelimady made his move. He stood up and walked slowly along the front of the stage, timing his steps to arrive at the stairway just in time to grab Djeli Baba's hand and raise it high for all the world to see. As the old man made his first step onto the stage, three television cameras trained squarely upon the two of them: Djeli Baba and Djelimady.

Djelimady returned to his seat wearing a hero's grin. He leaned over to me and said, "Let's go."

"That was quick," I chided, as Djelimady slid the Nissan out of its strategic parking space and headed back toward Lafiabougou.

He laughed quietly and said, "You understood."

"Of course."

"Well," he said without apology, "that's how it is with us."

The more I learned about *jeliya*, the more aware I became of the gap between its cultural meaning—however debased in modern times—and my own project of learning its guitar music. Playing griot guitar did not tie me to the ancestors; rather, it posed a purely technical challenge. It demanded daily concentration, and the satisfaction it brought me was abstract and uncomplicated, an anchor of sanity in a world that grew more ambiguous each day.

In our lessons, Djelimady identified the single technique I most needed to develop: the way the first finger on the right hand actually picks the strings. I soon took to waking up each morning, switching on the BBC news on my short wave radio, and, without even getting out of bed, reaching for my small electric guitar to play a mindless exercise that involved extending that forefinger and playing the same note over and over again, upstroke followed by downstroke, as fast and as long as possible. Djelimady had explained that this, more than anything else, defined the unique character of fingerstyle Manding guitar. When executed correctly with just the right finger position, pressure, and speed, it becomes a voice, Manding guitar music's indelible soundprint.

Djelimady knew exactly how this robust, trilling voice should sound, and when he listened to my attempts—*diddle-diddle-diddle-diddle-diddle-diddle*—he would note when I did and did not achieve it. "No. No. No.

Yes! No." Children watching our sessions laughed at my frustration. But frustration gave way to understanding. My fingers were learning to speak with this new voice.

"You want to know my secret?" Djelimady asked one evening during our lesson.

"Sure," I said.

He stood up and walked over to the Nissan with his guitar in his hand. He proceeded to lean against the parked car, cradling his guitar in his arms so he could play standing up. He then raised his left foot and placed his left calf across his right shin and held it there. Balancing on one foot and tickling a single note repeatedly, he looked up at me and said, *"Voila."*

"That's your secret?" I asked.

"That's it," he said. "I spent a good part of the 1970s doing this." I gave it a try, but it didn't seem to help; I stuck to lying in bed and the BBC.

"Why do they call the music *bajourou?*" I once asked Djelimady. He told me that the name meant literally "big string." I liked this name, for it said a lot about the elusive guitar voice I was working to control. The essence of the griot guitar technique seemed to be a matter of coaxing the largest imaginable sound from the strings of a guitar or *ngoni.* It struck me as a metaphor for much of what I had seen in Mali, a country where people's attitudes and presentation suggested wealth, even though theirs was one of the poorest countries in the world. From something small came something very big.

As I ventured out to street parties, concerts, and impromptu recording sessions, another paradox became apparent. As beautiful as *bajourou* music could sound at its best, I found that the music suffered in almost every setting in which musicians performed it. The dismal amplification at most of the street parties made delicately purring lines into angry snarls, and the singer's praising obligations called for dragging songs out far beyond their inherent musical interest. Then, in concerts and especially on cassettes, griot singers all seemed to share a distressing affection for drum machine rhythm tracks. In addition to sounding cheap and awful, these mechanical grooves strangled the natural flow of the music, leveling out the elliptical give-and-take that engages its internal lines. Even when a singer used a live drummer in a concert, the drummer tended to play the same sort of stiff accompaniment, nothing like the fluid and inventive rhythms I had heard from trap drummers in Central and Southern Africa.

The one consistent exception to this rule was the Rail Band, whose music was wonderful and genuinely swinging. There, the fleet melodies of griot guitar became an element in a larger tableau that also included Latin and Congolese rhythms, reggae and rock. Something as subtle as griot guitar, it seemed to me, could be masked or stifled as easily as the telltale flavor of thyme gets lost in a spicy stew. Nothing ever sounded better to me than when Djelimady pulled out his acoustic guitar at night and played *bajourou* songs in the moonlit street, all alone, for nobody.

This concerned me. Having come all this way to learn the music in context, I found I preferred the music *stripped* of its context. I thought about John Miller Chernoff's book, *African Rhythm and African Sensibility*, a bible for Westerners who delve into African performance arts. Chernoff says that to learn African music, you must immerse yourself in the social world that produced it, a world that encompasses ideas, beliefs, rituals, and values. Chernoff concludes his chapter "Style in Africa" this way:

> At an African musical event, whether listening to the comments of the spectators, or observing good and bad dancing, or understanding the improvisational principles and decisions of a great drummer, we should be conscious of the fact that music-making in Africa is above all an occasion for the demonstration of character.

Quite so. Djelimady could win special treatment from Malian officials because, through his proud solos with the Rail Band, they had learned to admire him as a person. A *jelimuso* could gather more cash in her waiting hand if she succeeded in evoking a deceased ancestor's mantle of respectability and placing it on the person being praised. These things fascinated me, but there was no getting around the fact that my core interest as a musician was the *sound* of the music, and, more often than not, the context, rather than enhancing and deepening my appreciation, obscured it with sideshows. It occurred to me that there might be something corrupt in my approach to *bajourou* music, that in a way I might be like those French diamond miners whom Guimba had ridiculed. I was digging up treasures to take away and turn to my own ends. And what kind of character did *that* demonstrate?

Had I been learning African music in a more structured environment, my attitude might have posed a problem. If I, like Chernoff, had gone to study in a village known for its drumming, but then found I preferred to play my drum all alone in the forest rather than with the village troupe, my interest would have seemed perverse to everyone. But the *jeli*s had no system of apprenticeship. The act of learning was another improvisation, and I was free to fashion my own approach. I spoke with many griot guitarists in Bamako, and virtually every one claimed to be self-taught. Some would talk about borrowing a guitar from an older player, or learning by watching someone else play. But the notion of a "guitar teacher" who gave "lessons" seemed to have no place or precedent.

Djelimady boasted about the guitarists he had taught, but I never saw him teaching anyone other than me, except in rehearsals. His playing itself set a standard that good players struggled to emulate and top, but he had no organized approach to instruction. He never said, "Work on this exercise twenty minutes a day and come back next week." Learning from Djelimady was like reaching into a rushing stream of water hoping to pull out a fish before it slithered away forever. If I had not tape-recorded our sessions so that I could go back and dwell on a short passage for hours at a time, I would have found it difficult to learn anything from him.

Now and then, Djelimady would indulge a certain vanity in having a live-in student and would show me off. "Play 'Sunjata,'" he would tell me, when one of his friends visited the compound. Then he would chuckle as the visitor puzzled or gasped over a white American reproducing Djelimady's articulation and phrasing on guitar.

A British record producer named Ben Mandelson—the man who years earlier had first encouraged me to look up Djelimady if I passed through Bamako—once made a recording of an acoustic super-trio involving Djelimady, a rival *jeli* guitarist named Bouba Sacko, and Lafia Diabaté, a male vocalist who sang years ago with the Rail Band. Like me, Ben recognized that *bajourou* music contained a beauty that was hard to appreciate in Malian recordings. Ben had simply imagined his own way to present the music. Ben called this group Bajourou and the debut CD he produced for them "Big String Theory," a clever name no doubt lost on the Malians. No matter; this was Malian music for outsiders.

After we returned from the Palais de la Culture following our brief appearance at the tribute to Djeli Baba Sissoko, Djelimady and I sat out on the street and played for an hour or so. Near the end, we left aside the disciplines of *bajourou* music and settled into a free-form jam. Djelimady played one of his own songs and I improvised, tossing in fragments of blues and jazz and managing the odd *bajourou*-flavored riff.

"Yes!" said Djelimady, offering rare praise. "You know," he said, "Manding music and jazz. It's the same thing. The same thing exactly. If you can fit this style into jazz songs—*ba ba ba ba ba!*—that will be something. The person who succeeds in doing that will be famous all over the world."

While we played, high above us in the dry, rocky hills west of Lafi-abougou, farmers were burning off the parched vegetation left behind by the rainy season. The fires spread in fast-moving circles away from their points of ignition. Driving home that night, buoyed by Djelimady's words, I looked out through the warm, smoky air toward hills wearing crowns of fire.

4

Slaves of Music, Music of Slaves

No more shall they in bondage toil.
O let my people go!
Let them come out with Egypt's spoil.
O let my people go!

From an early published version of the spiritual "Go Down Moses"

My friend Dirck Westervelt arrived in Bamako about five weeks into my stay. Dirck plays piano, bass, guitar, banjo, and a few more exotic instruments. But the only instrument he brought to Mali was a five-string banjo. It was small and light and, more importantly, it was an instrument with African ancestors. For Dirck and me, traveling to Africa could only be an encounter with otherness, however much we identified with the music. For the banjo, this was a homecoming.

"Donne moi banjo," Adama Tounkara demanded upon meeting Dirck. The ngoni player took the American banjo into his hands and began scratching at the strings with his forefinger. After puzzling around to find his bearings, Adama began to play a traditional Manding song on the banjo. He smiled with surprise as the quick melodic sputters he normally played on *ngoni* or guitar sprang forth in the banjo's percussive voice. Within minutes, Adama seemed at home with the instrument, though he had never played one before.

Most *ngoni* players in Mali also play some guitar, and most Manding guitar players have studied the sound and music of the *ngoni* and can approximate it on guitar. Adama was the first of many *jeli* guitarists and *ngoni* players to acquaint themselves with Dirck's banjo. Each time, it amazed me to see how rapidly they adapted to the instrument.

There are places in Africa—Ghana and South Africa, to name two— where the banjo once had a role in the indigenous pop music. Decades ago, in the heyday of Dixieland music and early swing jazz, the banjo was an American cultural export, and some English-speaking African countries came by the banjo this way, as they did trumpets, trombones, saxophones, upright basses, and pianos. But people in Mali, Guinea, Senegal, and the Gambia have a different connection with this American instrument. For the musicians who first created the banjo were in all likelihood slaves taken from what are now these four African countries, and perhaps also Angola. In fashioning the first banjos in the West Indies, Louisiana, and the Appalachian states, Africans were attempting to recreate an instrument they knew from home, the instrument Malians call *ngoni*.

The Wolof people of Senegal know this same instrument as *halam* or *hoddu*. It may well be the oldest lute in Africa and goes by many local names. People near the West African coast, where many of the earliest slaves brought to the New World came from, sometimes called it *bania*. Most musicologists believe that this name, *bania*, along with the idea for the instrument itself, survived the rigors of slavery and that that is why seventeenth- and eighteenth-century texts from the Americas contain so many references to black musicians playing a stringed instrument called *banjer, banjah, banjar, banjil, banshaw, banza,* or *bandore*.

The name varies, but the fundamentals remain constant. The slave instrument's body was a drum with a skin head, rather than a wooden box like the lute or guitar has. Its strings were generally made from gut or some other organic substance, not wire. Often it had a short string at the bottom, where the lowest-sounding string on a guitar would be, except that this string, usually played with the thumb, produced a high drone note, not a bass tone. Finally, the instrument had no frets, so that the player had to position the fingers on his fretting hand precisely in order to achieve the desired pitch. Modern banjos have wire strings and metal frets, but the frets are a relatively recent development. When they first made fretted banjos, players would cover the frets with a copper plate that let them play non-standard notes, as they had on the older instrument.

Americans eager to find connections between African and American music have made big claims about the African origins of the blues and jazz and about the strands of griot music in American folk. From the African side, it is popular to claim that everything the Americans came up with already existed in Africa. In truth, the story is so complex and poorly documented as to rule out such sweeping generalizations. More than two centuries passed between the arrival of the first Africans on American shores in 1619 and the first documented emergence of "Negro spirituals" in the 1860s. What was forgotten and what was preserved and passed on during those centuries can never really be known. That said, I have little doubt that the banjo came from Africa. Aside from my experience with Malian *ngoni* players, who greeted Dirck's banjo like a familiar object, I find the scholarship of music librarian Dena J. Epstein especially persuasive.

In her book *Sinful Tunes and Spirituals, Black Folk Music to the Civil War*, Epstein presents a weight of evidence sifted from mountains of letters, memoirs, newspapers, and other texts from the slavery years on both sides of the Atlantic. Epstein avoids overarching conclusions, but she turns up some remarkable findings. For instance, a number of her texts give accurate descriptions of *balafon*s, West African xylophones constructed by American slaves in the eighteenth century. A 1776 *Virginia Gazette* refers to the music of the "sprightly and enlivening *barrafoo.*" That the writer does not explain the term suggests that it would have been commonly understood by his readers. Later, after musical activity by blacks in America had been more effectively curtailed, Epstein finds no further mention of this instrument. It has vanished along with other lost Africanisms.

Epstein's work says a lot about the banjo. I offer just one example, one I like because it argues the worthlessness of slave culture but in fact documents a solid African contribution to Western music. Epstein's translation of a 1810 French tract aimed at defending the practice of slavery reads:

> As to guitars, which the Negroes call *banza*, see what they consist of: they cut lengthwise through the middle of a calabash. . . . This fruit is sometimes eight inches or more in diameter. They stretch upon it the skin of a goat which they adjust around the edges with little nails; they make two holes in its surface; then a piece of lath or flat wood makes the handle of the guitar; they then stretch three cords of *pitre* (a kind of hemp taken from the agave plant, vulgarly called *pitre*), and the instrument is finished. They play on this

instrument tunes composed of three or four notes, which they repeat endlessly; this is what Bishop Grégoire calls sentimental and melancholy music, and which we call the music of savages.

The savage origins of the banjo did not concern my Malian friends. All that mattered to them was its sound and its potential usefulness in one project or another. Oddly enough, though the Manding *jeli*s could play the banjo easily, musicians from non-*jeli* traditions seemed more interested in collaborating with Dirck and his banjo. This is partly because the long-dominant *jeli*s tend to be set in their ways. After an initial burst of interest in the banjo, they usually dismissed it as a novelty.

Mali's most progressive young *ngoni* player, Basekou Kouyaté, could hardly contain his excitement when I told him a banjo player was coming to visit. Basekou had attended a banjo conference in New Lebanon, Tennessee, in 1991 and had played for a roomful of mostly white American banjo masters. American bluesman Taj Mahal met and befriended Basekou there, and he once told me that when Basekou played, "You could hear mosquitoes walking like T-Rex in that room, because this was the first time they had ever seen where the instrument came from."

Almost as soon as Dirck settled down in Bamako, we went to visit Basekou. But the *ngoni* master's excitement about the banjo cooled once he heard Dirck playing Barou's electronic keyboard. After that, the message to Dirck was: Next time you come to play, forget the banjo; bring the keyboard. Partly this reflected the fact that Dirck was an excellent pianist and only a competent banjo player. Partly it was another example of the *jeli*s' love affair with electronics. Keyboards, it seemed, had passed the test and earned a lasting place in griot music. The banjo, despite its venerable origins, had not.

Djelimady was the first to voice outright skepticism about the banjo. "I like your friend Dirck," he said to me one morning. "He's a good musician and a nice guy. But why did he bring that banjo here? Does he really think he will ever be able to play *bajourou* music on it?" Djelimady had once played a mandolin and seemed much more convinced that it could find a place in his music. Dirck, to his credit, stuck to his plan and sat out on the street with Djelimady and me night after night, trying to fit his banjo-playing fingers around Djelimady's racing *bajourou* melodies. As hard as it was for me to learn from Djelimady in these free-form sessions, it was harder for Dirck. The wide spacing of the frets and the instrument's tuning system complicated matters, as *bajourou*'s rapid phrasing depends on maintaining particular intervals between adjacent strings.

Dirck experimented with a variety of tunings, but clearly the instrument had evolved away from its African ancestor, and as optimistic as Dirck was, Djelimady remained dubious.

Around that time, I went through a period of trying to teach Djelimady some American guitar tricks. He was taken with my ability to play swing blues on the guitar, keeping up a walking bass line and throwing in syncopated chords to create the feeling of a rhythm section. "Yaaaaah!" Djelimady would growl when I played a twelve-bar blues in this style. "Show me that."

This was easier said than done. For starters, one element of the blues that did *not* come from Africa is the twelve-bar form that gives shape to so many classic blues and rock 'n' roll lyrics. Compared with the underlying structures in Malian music, this form is long, and I knew from experience that Malian musicians tend to get lost in it, just as young American players do when they first attempt it. It's one thing to feel that sense of coming around when the blues singer delivers a so-called "turn-around" line, the phrase that ties the end of the form back to its beginning. *"Believe me when I tell you, you can love me like a man."* Or, *"Well, I shouldn't be here trying to sing these railroad blues."* Every listener hears the sense of the form when guided by the singer. It is quite another thing, however, to live and breathe that form so that every note you play fits into it and you can improvise freely without thinking about it. This aspect of American blues grew from European song forms. The old Mississippi Delta players rarely used it. As blues became popular club music in cities like St. Louis and Chicago, the twelve-bar form gradually became religion, but even as accomplished a musician as Djelimady needed to spend some time wrestling with that form before he could play it.

The first time I visited Bamako, I discovered this fact in a bar one night, when the band asked me to play a song with them. "Let's do a blues," they said. Their concept of "doing a blues" was simply to hang out on a single dominant seventh chord and play bluesy riffs for twenty minutes. Not understanding this, I broke into a twelve-bar form. By the end of one repetition, the band was lost.

As I tried to teach Djelimady my swing accompaniment, Dirck kept the form on Barou's keyboard so we wouldn't have to worry about it. But there were other problems. The hand positions, chord forms, and rhythmic inflections I used were all alien to Djelimady. It amazed me to see this man who could wail through *bajourou* music, Manding swing, Zairean *soukou*s, Cuban songs, French pop hits, and could even do a lively if idio-syncratic version of flamenco guitar, suddenly stalled. His hands moved stiffly and haltingly, as though he had been in a car accident and suddenly forgotten everything he knew about the guitar. It felt awkward to put such a magnificent guitarist in so compromised a position.

Of course, when he stopped trying to play my rather stylized accom-paniment and simply let himself go with a solo, Djelimady was brilliant. This points to an aspect of the blues that is plainly African, the man-ner of melodic expression and the emotional coloring that comes from using particular collections of notes or scales. Leaving aside the note bending and in-between tones that account for a lot of the expression in the blues and also many forms of African music, most blues music relies on a single scale, a *minor pentatonic* scale. Instead of using all seven notes of a major or minor scale, blues songs limit themselves to a set of just five notes. Five-note scales exist all over the world. Chinese music commonly uses a pentatonic scale, but you would never mistake it for the blues. On the other hand, the particular arrangement of notes that makes up the minor pentatonic scale is common in Mali, and the char-acter with which Malian players and singers express themselves using this scale has led many observers to characterize Malian music as "bluesy," hence making a significant African origin of the blues seem all but a foregone conclusion.

However, these bluesy Malian sounds do not come from the reper-toire of the *jeli*s. *Bajourou* and other forms of Manding music use seven-note scales and have, for the most part, a more consonant, European, or in some cases Arabic sound. The *jeli*s do introduce dissonance into their music. Manding musicians bend notes and alter tones within the scale, and they use unusual scales that some hear as "jazzy." But they do not use the minor pentatonic scale, and even though a *jelimuso* can belt out a song with the power of Big Mama Thornton or Tina Turner, the music itself does not sound inherently "bluesy."

To get an idea of how clear this distinction is to Malians, consider the fact that musicians there commonly divide the music of their country into two large categories: Manding music (in all its seven-note or *heptatonic* vari-eties) on the one hand, and *pentatonic* music (sometimes *pentaphonic* or just *penta*) on the other. This second category is enormous and includes Was-soulou music from the Malian south, the Arab-tinged, northern Niger River styles played by Ali Farka Touré, and musical repertoires associated with regional ethnic groups like the Bobo, Senufo, Dogon, Bambara, Bozo, and Mossi. As a well-rounded guitarist, Djelimady is proficient in many of these pentatonic styles. He has also listened to a lot of blues, so when it comes time to blow a blues solo, he's there, and he has lots to bring to the table. But if you ask him to cover the chord changes on "Nobody Knows You When You're Down and Out," expect trouble.

After a few weeks of struggling with the swing blues accompaniment I gave him, Djelimady seemed to lose interest, and we never played much blues after that. But whenever I watched a young *jeli* traverse centuries with Dirck's banjo in his hands, and whenever I heard a blues inflection or a New Orleans shuffle rhythm in a traditional Malian song, I returned to my musings on the deeper mysteries of African and American music. It all led back to the slave trade, of course, and as I soon learned, slavery, like music, also looks different from the African and American perspectives.

One Friday night before Dirck arrived in Bamako, a concert was held near the Lafiabougou market. I mentioned it at dinner to Djelimady and Adama Tounkara, but they had no interest in going. "Well, I'm going to go," I said. "I like to see the venues, who comes, what music they play. It's all interesting to me." Djelimady just looked at Adama and said, "He's not like us."

Djelimady gave a cynical preview of the show. Griot singer Djessira Kone and her group, led by guitarist Bouba Sacko, would do the usual wedding numbers, "Lamban," "Bajourou," "Diaoura." It would be good, but overdone. "We have so much more folklore yet to exploit," Djelimady complained. "Why do they always have to play the same songs?" Pentatonic *balafon* player Seydou Balani would play next but, according to Djelimady, he was "not a serious artist." He would offer showbiz, not music. Moussa Kouyaté, the Tounkara family griot, concurred, but said he would join me anyway.

The concert hall turned out to be an old movie theater, long since defunct, as few people go to the movies in Bamako. More than a thousand decrepit metal seats crammed the floor. The ceiling towered thirty feet overhead. The stage was enormous and bathed in plain, incandescent light, a wall of chipping paint looming behind the musicians.

Djelimady had been right about the predictability of the *jeli*'s set, but Seydou Balani's pentatonic *balafon* music was terrific. Far from showbiz glitz, this was just the sort of music that got me thinking about the Louisiana connection. The rhythms were romping, driven by the washtub-sized *doundoun* drum that hung around the player's neck. Two ladies played calabashes while *balafon* players cranked out a weave of bluesy melodies. Two dancers invited people from the audience, including me, onstage to join in their revelry. Even Moussa seemed pleased despite himself.

Things went downhill from there. A man wearing a wool cap, a pink windbreaker, and a rook sack came on stage to lip-sync and dance to music from a boom box placed on a chair. During his performance, the microphone he had placed near the boom box rolled off the chair and hit the stage with a thud. The artist casually danced over to the chair and replaced it. He got a laugh, but only tepid applause for his performance. Then a singer named Tata Diarra used this same "playback" rig to dance to a Congolese number. Moussa studied her closely, then leaned over to inform me that Tata's belly-wiggling dance was "a dance of slaves."

"Slaves?" I asked.

"Yes," he replied.

"But are there *still* slaves in Mali?" I asked. Moussa did not answer me directly, but as we left the concert that night, he explained that there had long existed a kind of social hierarchy in this part of Africa. At the top were the *jatigui* or nobles, like the Keitas who had descended from Sunjata Keita and before that from Bilali, the prophet Mohammed's *muezzin.*

"Historians have written that Bilali was Mohammed's slave," said Moussa. "But that is not true. Bilali was a free African, the first black man to pray to Allah."

After the nobles, Moussa explained, came the *numuw* or blacksmiths, followed by the *garankéw* or tanners, and below them the *jeli*s, whose job it was to sing the praises of the nobles. Each group could be identified by its family name. For example, Tounkara, Diabaté, Sissoko, and Danté were all names that generally signified *jeli* families. Next came the Kouyatés, griots whose job was exclusively to praise and serve the *jeli*s and their nobles. After them came the *funéw*, Islamic orators who speak rather than sing praises, and then the *gawlo*, Fulani entertainers charged with praising *funé*, *jeli*, and noble alike. With each step down this rather confusing social ladder came an associated right of solicitation. For example, a *gawlo* could demand money from all those above him on the ladder, but a *jeli* could not demand money from a *gawlo*. Finally, at the very bottom of the hierarchy, Moussa explained, came the slaves, or *jon*.

I would later learn that there were gradations of slaves as well. Slaves captured in war were prized and sometimes became the confidantes of kings; everyone knew that if the king was overthrown, his captured

slaves would be buried in the same grave. The children of these captured slaves were less dangerous and more expensive. The lowest order
of slaves were those sold in the market. Often deprived of their language
and knowledge of their ancestry, their condition came closest to that of
the Africans sent to the Americas as chattel, with no hope of recover-
ing their pasts.

When Moussa talked to me about slaves, I hesitated to press him for
details, fearing the subject might be sensitive. Strangely, though, slavery was not a sensitive topic. In fact, many times in Bamako, I was
stunned to hear one person taunt another with the statement, "Your
family were the slaves of my family." Imagine what would happen if a
white American ever said that to a black. Here, it all seemed like so
much good fun.

I first encountered this taunting phenomenon the day I turned up at
the Tounkara compound with my friend Djiby Camara, a bass player in
kora virtuoso Toumani Diabaté's group. "Ah, Camara," said Djelimady
upon seeing Djiby. "My slave!"

"Tounkara!" Djiby replied, "You and all the Tounkaras were the slaves
of the Camaras."

I cringed, vaguely recalling that there had been some sort of rancor
between Djiby and Djelimady during my first visit to Bamako. I imagined I had made a terrible mistake in bringing Djiby to the compound.
The two men were smiling to keep up appearances, but their words
betrayed animus. After I heard this same exchange repeated almost ver-
batim two or three times between various people, I at last demanded an
explanation. As usual, it was Barou who clarified things.

"That's *sanakouya*," he said. "Joking cousins. Don't you remember
from the Sunjata story?"

That night I went back to my tattered edition of the epic as translated
by British savanna scholar G. D. Pickett, and there it was. Pickett spells
it *sanakhou* and translates the term as "bantering brothers." It refers to a
historic and universally recognized agreement that the members of two
specific families have the right to insult each other with impunity. The
original *sanakouya* relationship comes from the point in the Sunjata story
when a hunter named Traoré receives advice from an old woman on how
he can kill the buffalo that has been terrorizing the people of Do.

In the story, many have died trying to kill this evil creature, and the
king of Do has promised the pick of all the eligible maidens in the land
to the man who can fell the beast. The old woman gives Traoré the

secret of success, but on one awful condition. When the moment comes for his reward, he must choose the ugliest woman in the crowd. The story turns on this event because once killed, the buffalo's spirit passes into the ugly woman and she goes on to become Sunjata's mother. But for the moment, Traoré finds himself in a spot. In plain view of the good people of Do, he must pass over scores of nubile beauties and select the most hideous among them as his prize. This exposes him to derision, none so fierce as from the Kondé family. From this almost comic moment of heroism and mockery, the first *sanakouya* relationship is established between the families Traoré and Kondé. To this day, members of these two clans know that they can insult one another without repercussion. And how do these insults manifest themselves? With the charge of slavery.

"Ah, Kondé, you are my slave."

"Traoré! No, it is you who are my slave." And so the routine goes, right down to the present.

I never learned the origin of the Tounkara/Camara *sanakouya* arrangement. But it is just one of many handed down in the epics of Manding *jeliya*. When I eventually discussed this with Djelimady, he told me that *sanakouya* was another example of Sunjata's genius as a ruler and one of the keys to the king's peaceful reign. In times of genuine tension between families, Djelimady claimed, such banter provides a safe outlet for hostilities. Words that might lead to violence or permanent rifts can be aired with no long-term damage to the families involved.

It had been a long time since people were kidnapped or captured in battle and forced into slavery in Mali. Even when that did happen, African slavery was a different matter from the wholesale human trade practiced by Europeans in the New World colonies between 1550 and 1850. Moussa Kouyaté's social ladder suggested that slavery was simply the lowest possible social status a person could have. It was not necessarily permanent. A slave could sometimes work for or buy his or her freedom, and children of slaves did not automatically become slaves themselves. The more I understood what Malians meant by the term slavery, the more I realized that it was not some remote practice lost in the mists of history, and that it was not viewed with horror as in America. The memory of African slavery lingered as a historical fact, like European serfdom. And how different was serfdom from the condition of the two girls who did most of the work in the Tounkara compound every day?

One of these girls was Djeneba, about twenty years old and originally from Segu. Djeneba lived among the Tounkaras as a kind of benign
shadow figure, pulling one of the other girls' foam mats into the store
room to sleep at odd hours of the day, crowding in at night on a thin,
woven mat with the other chore girl, with whom she rose before everyone else in the morning to start fires and set water to heat. Djeneba
stood barely five feet, but she was built like a wrestler, biceps flexing
within her well-worn shirts. Her saucer-shaped face featured a receded
nose, firm lips often ready with a smile, and muddy eyes full of deter-
mination and a strange bemusement.

Djeneba worked tirelessly even in the heat. Countless times each
day, she bent double to haul washing water from the deep well at the
back of the courtyard. She cut mountains of vegetables into sauce-sized
bits. She hefted the cauldron used to heat water for cooking and washing. She scrubbed clothes and hung them out to dry on the fly-covered
clothesline that ran across the courtyard. She lugged buckets of filthy
water and foul garbage out to the street. She swept the concrete floor
after every meal.

Often Djeneba and the other servant girl worked right alongside the
Tounkara women, and then only their attire and hairstyles distinguished
them from the Tounkaras. On holidays, Djeneba never dressed up or wove
costly extensions into her shortish, frizzy hair. But she helped the other
girls with theirs and seemed to enjoy a friendly rapport with them. Whenever I brought my camera to the compound, Djeneba, like everyone else,
demanded that I take her picture. Sometimes I would see Djeneba leaving from the Lafiabougou terminus in a *bashée*. She never failed to flash
me a smile and say my name. I never knew where she was going.

These girls were paid little. Someday, I was told, they would have
enough money to return to their villages and marry. So, though their
condition was not permanent, it was thoroughly subservient.

When at last we spoke openly about the subject of slavery, Djelimady
made it clear that he knew the difference between the servitude of girls
like Djeneba and the appalling degradation suffered by Africans taken to
foreign lands. He once told me that Sunjata's own brother sold many
Manding to Arab traders. "He had his reasons," said Djelimady, not seeming to blame the man. "He didn't know what would happen to them." By
the 1890s, when warlord Samory Touré had his day at the Wayanko mesa,
people had a clearer idea of what might await an African sold to or captured by the white man. "Samory taught his people that any blacks who

were given to whites became slaves," Djelimady once told me. "He told his followers, 'We must kill them. If you see a white man, kill him.'" This helps to explain the legendary ferocity of Samory's fighters.

Djelimady also told Dirck and me a poignant story about meeting Louis Armstrong in Bamako during his last African tour, shortly before his death in 1971. "He had a name," said Djelimady, "a name passed down through his family. And we walked through Bamako neighborhoods until we found the family with that name. Oh, my God. Louis Armstrong! He cried when he met this family. It was unbelievable."

Literally so. To begin with, the name Djelimady recalled was Kunta Kinte, the slave name from Alex Haley's novel, *Roots*. In addition, Armstrong's last African tour took place in the early 1960s, and its itinerary did not include Bamako. Griot history.

If slaves fell at the bottom of the Malian social ladder and nobles at the top, griots of all varieties settled in between. And the compromised position of the musician class in Malian society never struck me more clearly than the time Dirck and I accompanied a group of *jeli*s to the Tounkaras' ancestral home, Kita, for a *"grand concert."* Kita is a place no tourist would go; my West Africa guide book doesn't even mention it. But its cultural riches, especially its local *jeli*s, have made it an important destination for music researchers. The so-called "city of holy water" had been Sunjata's second capital, after his birthplace, Niani. A roster of the town's best known *jelimuso* includes some of the best: Fanta Sacko, Backo Dagnon, Kandia Kouyaté, Yayi Kanouté, Awa Juguna Diabaté, Hadja Soumano, Dogomani Dagnon, Souadou Somano, Mamou Diama Diabaté, Sali Diabaté, and Ina Tounkara.

When Dirck and I heard that Djelimady and Barou would both be going to Kita to do a concert with a *jelimuso* named Manian Damba, we decided to go. It would be a long haul for a short visit, but if we had any doubts about making the journey, the rehearsals we heard at the Tounkara compound clinched the decision. Manian sang like an angel, and under Djelimady's direction the two guitarists, two *ngoni* players, bassist, and Barou on keyboard drums came together in superb arrangements.

Kita sits in the craggy highlands 160 kilometers west of Bamako, near the headwaters of the Senegal River. Our entourage of ten arrived at the train station at 7:00 on a Saturday morning, laden with instruments and amplifiers. West African trains are narrow and noisy and generally full of people, often with babies, plenty of luggage, and even small livestock, mostly chickens. The air-conditioned cars seem desirable at first, but beware. The air conditioners tend to be feeble or broken, and in these cars you can't open the windows. Aside from denying you a breeze, this puts you at a disadvantage when the train pulls into a town and women and children on the platform rush to the open windows selling fresh fruit, beef brochettes, peanuts, cold drinks, and shot glasses of gunpowder tea.

At Kita, a relative of Djelimady's met us with a Land Rover and ferried us from the station to the Diabaté compound, the family home of Djelimady's mother. There, people were eating and watching a television broadcast from Niger pulled in with the aid of a huge parabolic antenna that loomed over the courtyard. These people, in this remote location, were in better touch with the world than we were at the Tounkara compound in Bamako!

We walked to the Centre D'Education Populaire in the Segu Bougouni neighborhood of Kita, near the base of a steep, rocky hill. The hall, such as it was, consisted of a school-yard-like enclosure surrounded by a sky-blue and beige seven-foot concrete wall. The three hundred or so seats that had been moved in filled only a small portion of the floor, an area roughly the size of two basketball courts. Even with all the equipment set up on the concrete riser where the musicians would play, it was clear that the sound system would be pressed beyond its limits to fill the space. Barou had the job of organizing the musicians and equipment.

When the sound seemed as good as it was likely to get, we returned to the Diabaté compound for a meal. Inside, where the musicians were dressing for the show after dinner, I picked up a guitar and began to play a *bajourou* song Djelimady had recently showed me. A *funé*, or talking griot, in a blue robe looked me over and remarked sourly, "That's wrong."

"Oh?" I said. "What's the right way?"

"I could show you," he said, "but I don't feel like it." This was my introduction to the eminent *funé* Ishaka Kouyaté, and already I didn't like him.

On our way back to the hall, a few of us, including Barou, Dirck, and myself, ducked into a sleepy bar for a couple of beers. As we approached the concert, we heard music already underway. Barou looked nervous. "Uh oh," he said. Djelimady was furious that Barou was turning up late. Manian couldn't hear herself. Some of the instruments were making distortion in the amplifiers. The overall sound seemed a parody of what we had heard in the Bamako rehearsals, and Barou couldn't do much to improve it.

None of this seemed to bother the audience, who soon filled the three hundred seats. The show heated up as best it could, and, eventually, well-dressed patrons began approaching the stage to give Manian money, just as they would at the street parties I had seen in Bamako. During a break, while Ishaka Kouyaté regaled the audience with griotism, Djelimady took me around and introduced me to more of his relatives than I could possibly keep straight. As things worked out, I never returned to Kita during my stay in Mali, but until the end, I would hear Djelimady saying, "You remember so-and-so, don't you? You met him at Kita." He always seemed disappointed at my failure to recollect this *"grand frère"* or that *"grand cousin."*

During the second half of the show, the temperature dropped precipitously. Even I, raised on Canadian winters, found it chilly, but the musicians forged on bravely. Manian wore a pink gown and struggled to project resplendence even as the public address system sabotaged her. Now and then I would see her casting an icy glance at her microphone. The crowd never swelled beyond the seating capacity, though open spaces yawned on every side. To their credit, those present did fulfil their role, crowding the stage to dance, hand out money, and hold up the hands of those honored by the singer, just as Djelimady had done at the benefit for the old griot in Bamako.

When the gig ended, long after midnight, the crowd vanished into the night, leaving the musicians waiting onstage while the organizers counted the money, clearly less than they had anticipated. The long wait did not bode well. Cold, exhausted, and with nothing to look forward to but the train ride home, now just hours away, we sat dejectedly. *"Ah, la vie d'un musicien,"* went the refrain. *"C'est dur!"*

When at last one of the organizers called from across the empty yard, Djelimady skulked over. Soon we heard loud arguing that echoed bleakly within the concrete walls. The organizers could not honor the contract. They said they would pay the rest of the money later. "But will they?" I asked Barou.

"If they do," he replied, pausing to draw on his cigarette, "I won't see any of it."

At the train station, we found most of the musicians sitting on the equipment alongside the tracks, shivering in the chill before dawn, silent and glum. Dirck took out his banjo and began plucking out a melancholy Appalachian mountain tune. For once, nobody asked to play the banjo.

PHOTO 1
Djelimady Tounkara at a street party. *Photo courtesy of Dirck Westervelt.*

PHOTO 2
Adama Kouyaté, wife of
Djelimady Tounkara.
Photo by the author.

PHOTO 3
Moussa Kouyaté, the Tounkara
family griot. *Photo by the author.*

PHOTO 4
The new father. Adama Tounkara and one of his twin sons. *Photo by the author.*

PHOTO 5
Solo Tounkara and Djelimady
Tounkara counting money.
Photo by the author.

PHOTO 6
Madou Djan Tounkara, Solo Tounkara, and Djelimady Tounkara heading out for a round
of Tabaski visits. *Photo by the author.*

PHOTO 7
Barou Diallo with his daughter
Photo by the author.

PHOTO 8
Adama Kouyaté *(center)* and other family members in the Tounkara compound. *Photo by the author.*

PHOTO 9
Women dancing in the Tounkara compound. Adama Kouyaté is in white. *Photo by the author.*

PHOTO 10
Adama Tounkara (banjo) and Fode Sacko (ngoni). *Photo by the author.*

PHOTO 11
Dounanke Koita (guitar).
Photo by the author.

PHOTO 12
Lobi Traoré playing his guitar
at Ma Kele Kele.
Photo by the author.

PHOTO 13
Habib Koité at home.
Photo by the author.

PHOTO 14
Salif Keita performing at the
French Cultural Center in
Bamako.
Photo by the author.

PHOTO 15
Yayi Kanouté.
Photo by the author.

PHOTO 16
From right to left: Toumani Diabaté, his son Sidiki, his father Sidiki, and another Kora student in Toumani's compound. *Photo courtesy of David Gilden.*

5

Bamako After Hours

I believe music is legitimate work. Not everyone can be a bureaucrat or businessman. Music is all I know in life.

Lobi Traoré

The first time I accompanied Djelimady on his weekly Saturday night Rail Band gig, I expected to watch the show, as during my first trip to Mali. Back then, I had spent Christmas Eve at the Buffet Hotel de la Gare under the colored lights that routinely stretch across the open-air dance floor during the month leading up to the band's big New Year's extravaganza. The Buffet is a modest venue. In the performance area, low, round tables nestle among trimmed shrubs, and potted flowers extend to the edges of the garden nightclub. On two sides, palm trees shoot up and fan into dark, feathery orbs, and on a third, the train station itself stands in almost eerie silence against the blue-black sky.

I remembered the Buffet's African patrons who had come to that Christmas show, most of them older and apparently wealthy. The women had been dressed up as at an afternoon street party, only they came with their husbands, men in business suits who seemed to be government functionaries or perhaps even ministers out for a weekend dance. Interspersed among these couples, a handful of American Peace Corps volunteers had sat drinking beer. Occasionally they'd been lured to the dance floor by the grand, old swing of the Rail Band.

Like all the white people who patronized the Buffet on a Saturday night, I had found myself on that first visit at the mercy of a fellow I later came to know as Old Baldy, an aged hustler who worked the crowd there. Baldy had called himself a griot, but he was just a has-been percussionist. Though he still liked to sit in with the band and scrape out Cuban rhythms on a serrated gourd or take a spin on the dance floor with a woman half his age, he lived, above all, to drink. "I've got 250 CFA," he would say. "Make up the rest and we'll have a big beer together. You and me!"

Three years later, the Buffet's atmospherics hadn't changed. The brownstone train station and the palm trees still loomed. The functionaries and their wives still trickled in. And Old Baldy was there, working the Peace Corps contingent. Only now I found myself watching all this from a back row seat on the bandstand. During the week, the Rail Band rehearsed systematically, concentrating on just one or two new songs at a time. In the show, they played everything—well-worn arrangements of Manding folklore, pentatonic songs, Cuban and Zairean classics, and the odd reggae tune. Having learned just two songs before my first Saturday night at the Buffet, I had not expected to be onstage for the entire three-hour gig. But in the afterglow of our appearances with Fodé Kouyaté in the Tabalé performances, the Rail Band seemed to adopt me, and they insisted I remain with them from start to finish.

The rhythm guitarist, Ali Dembelé, would tell me the key of each song before it began, and when the song started he would show me a part to play. I had to struggle to hear him, pressing my ear up to the old Italian-made Ranger guitar amplifier while staring at his squirrelly fingers as I tried to mirror repetitive but tricky accompaniments. Ali would wait for me to join in and then he would switch to a different part. Frequently, unable to imitate him precisely, I had to invent and improvise as best I could. These solo flights through the tight formations and orchestrated shifts of Rail Band songs proved stressful. Listening intently and watching everybody's faces—especially Djelimady's—for signs of approval or disapproval, I struggled to keep my balance.

Between songs, I would jot down little notes so that I could quiz Ali during lulls in the next week's rehearsals. "Ali, what's that accompaniment on 'Silanidé' again?" I would ask, switching on my tape recorder for thirty seconds of precious tape. If I was going to be onstage with one of the legendary dance bands of West Africa, I wanted to know what

I was doing. Happily, after a few weeks of scrambling, I was able to relax during the gig at the Buffet. And then, when at last I raised my eyes from the fretboard and looked out at the colonial-era hotel and its smattering of genteel patrons, I saw them from yet a new vantage point, from within the music itself.

The Rail Band's music spoke of a new Africa, a summing up of past glories in a brave embrace of the best the outside world had to offer. In the 1960s and '70s, Mali's government had effectively commanded the bands it supported to develop the nation's folklore. Bands did not have to abandon the Western sounds they had been busily commandeering before independence, but they had to play them in a new way, informed by local traditions. Active support for a pro-African social policy became a precondition for commercial viability as a musician, and Mali's music would never be the same. Now, decades later, the Rail Band's two saxophone players—old Kabine Keita and wiry, graceful Mamadou Ouedraogo—shifted between mambo blares and old Manding folk melodies. Singers Damory Kouyaté and Samba Sissoko wielded their microphones and danced together like Las Vegas nightclub stars, but they sang with the passion of *jeli*s. And when Djelimady stepped off the stage and strode among the dancers, soloing with rock idol bravado, his lofty musical lines fell upon them like the cascading praise melodies of antiquity's *kora*-wielding troubadours.

To play with the Rail Band at the Buffet Hotel de la Gare on a Saturday night was to travel through time. The crowds I saw were sparse. But among the swaying middle-aged couples and beer-happy Peace Corps troops, I sensed ghosts from the past: political schemers flushed with power and mingling with their boosters; railroad moguls buoyed by profits from a bustling overland trade, firmly in their hands at last; Russian and Chinese operatives out to steer Mali toward the communist ideal; noble Malians and their family griots; and, of course, young musicians full of dreams.

Many of today's Malian stars have told me about their early musical revelations in the presence of the Rail Band. I imagined their intent eyes peering from the metal chairs alongside the bandstand, studying every move, charting their own paths to stardom. And why not? The Rail Band of the early 1970s had launched two of the most successful singers in African music, Mory Kanté and, especially, Salif Keita. Mory Kanté had landed a hit on the French pop charts in 1988, an unprecedented achievement, but Salif, the so-called "golden voice of Mali," had gone further still. To this day, he remains welcome in concert halls and recording studios from L.A. to Tokyo, Paris to Johannesburg. And it all started on the Buffet's humble bandstand.

The night's music at the Buffet began at around 10:00 and usually ended before 1:00 in the morning. There were no breaks. Around midnight, someone would bring the band a drink. Everyone drank soda except for me, Dirck, and Durango the percussionist, the only regular band member who would break ranks and join the Americans in drinking a beer. When the evening's music reached its peak, Dirck and I knew the incomparable sensation of turning inside the Rail Band's elaborate dance music engine. All the wheels, gears, belts, and spindles moved together, from the snap of the bass drum to the sway of the dancers. Djelimady's hands exploded with spectacularly clear and lyrical lines, and when he fell back into the music's deeper cycles, musicians and audience alike fell into a collective hypnosis. Time vanished. And then at a certain moment, when the crowd had thinned to a handful, Djelimady would reach back and unplug his guitar, and the world would fall silent but for the hissing of the trains. There were never any encores at the Buffet.

Djelimady generally packed up his guitar and headed for the Nissan within minutes of the show's end. Sometimes a friendly female face would be waiting for him by the stage, though she might simply want a ride back to Lafiabougou. I never knew, because for me and a few of the other musicians in the band, the end of the gig was in a sense the beginning of our Saturday night. Long after the last society couple sashayed off the Buffet's dance floor and went home to bed, other, seedier Bamako establishments boogied on, sometimes until 3:30 in the morning. Some of the most interesting live music I found in Bamako went on in those bars.

"So Banning. Dirck," Djelimady would say, shouldering his guitar bag and glancing at his watch. "What are you doing? It's late, you know." Djelimady might not have approved of our going out late, but he never complained. He warned that places like the Bar Bozo were dangerous, and he made no secret of his disdain for alcohol.

To be polite, Dirck and I would ask he if he wanted to go out on the town with us. "Come on, Djelimady," I might say, "work is over. Time to party." I suppose I liked to tease him a little, ever mindful of that moment when he had told Adama that I was "not like them." Djelimady seemed to get the joke, but he would just flash an ambiguous smile and

shake his head or dismiss us with a wave of his hand. In fact, I knew
that Djelimady would not have enjoyed nightspots like the Bar Bozo or
Le Segovien in Lafiabougou. This was a kind of father-and-son diplo-
macy. On the outside, I'd urge the old man to come out and play, while
on the inside I felt a mischievous excitement at the prospect of escaping his watchful eye.

Bamako closed down dead at night, and the sleeping city seemed
almost unfamiliar. During the day, the area around the Buffet was a car-
nival, with young boys hawking watercolor greeting cards, Bambara-
French dictionaries, maps, or cartons of music cassettes. Just beyond the
train station, in the street next to the American Embassy, blue-turbaned
Tuareg men sold huge, gaudy knives and swords with exotic leather and
bronze inlay and enormous sheaths. "Not expensive," they would say
in English. In the crowded central market just down Rue Mohammed
V, vendors displayed plastic bags of dry green medicinal leaves, blue rubber sandals, straw sweepers, beat up metal bowls full of nuts, grains, and
sulfurous dried *datu* plant, piled up slabs of rank fish, freshly butchered
sheep and cow parts, live chickens, coiled-straw pot scrubbers, shiny
white softballs of laundry soap, pyramids of metal cook pots and serving dishes arranged by size, towers of brightly colored plastic cups,
plates, bowls, and buckets, stacked lawn chairs, awnings shingled with
visor caps proclaiming Chicago Bulls, Madonna, Marlboro, and other
foreign interests, little piles of tomatoes, tiny onions, potatoes, roots,
oranges, melons, papayas, and mangos. And clothing: colorful cotton
shirts, mudcloth jackets, grand *boubous* for the men and tailored dresses
for the women, trousers, shoes, socks, underwear. All these things were
displayed and stored within rickety wooden stalls with sheet plastic walls
and corrugated tin roofs.

At night, only the stalls remained. Gone were the mountains of mer-
chandise, the hucksters, and the great army of shoppers. Abandoned,
the city was weirdly peaceful. Whatever dangers lurked amid the daytime crowds, I was more afraid to walk alone at night through those
dark, deserted streets, where if anything happened, no one would see.

One night after the gig, Barou, Dirck, Ali, and I walked from the Buffet across downtown Bamako to the Bar Bozo. As we turned onto the wide
Avenue de la Nation, street activity picked up, indicating that the bar was
near. By this late hour, the bitter, depressing stench of burning plastic and
rubber that descends on the city most afternoons had lifted, and in its
place came sweeter smells from the cook fires of Bamako's all-night food

zone. Green tea in the making gave off its distinct aroma, at once fruity and charcoal smoky. Chickens and beef brochettes, grilled atop steel oil-drum stoves, and stews simmered. Of course, underlying these savory odors, there was also the lingering fetor of the drainage ditches that lined all such large roadways, collecting a foul mixture of rotting fruit, stale wash water, and urine.

The dark, crowded Bar Bozo had clearly known an illustrious history before Dirck and I arrived in town to witness its last two months in operation. Depending on who you spoke to, Bar Bozo was either a sacred haunt for the Bamako clubber, the only place in town where you could have a gritty urban encounter with a live band, or else it was a perilous den of pickpockets, prostitutes, and drunks. I didn't see it as either. Perhaps, as some told me, I was just lucky not to have come up against a thug with a knife. Even Barou, whose sense of things I trusted, sometimes pointed out "bandits" in the crowd and warned me to steer clear of them.

As for the musical ambiance, Bar Bozo's boosters—the French producer Philippe Berthier prominent among them—did have a point. Three or four "bands" would take turns through the night, and some of them, like Lobi Traoré's Bambara blues rockers, Dounanke Koita's Malian variety band, or a locally based Senegalese *mbalax* group we chanced upon one night were as good as it gets in Bamako nightclubs. Others fell short. The groups that filled in between the main bands on any given night usually consisted of nameless collections of musicians who got up and sang cover versions of hits, anything from Salif Keita to Bob Marley. Whoever was playing had to cram onto a postage-stamp stage, an arc of dark, oily wood rimmed with protruding spokes that looked like the teeth on a cartoon dinosaur's lower jaw. Above the stage, track lights with few working bulbs cast a dim glow upon the musicians, and around the stage there was just enough space for ten or fifteen couples to dance rubbing close. A ceiling fan hung tantalizingly over the dancing area, silent and still. The dirty wall by the tables near the bar's entrance displayed a framed portrait of Martin Luther King and posters of American jazz artists: Satchmo, Bird, and Miles.

On this particular night, Dounanke Koita and his band were the featured act, which meant that whoever managed to coax or muscle their way onto the stage to do a few numbers, it would be Dounanke's job to get them off and continue his show.

Dounanke was raised in a family of musicians in a town called Tominian, east of Segu in Bobo country. He came to Bamako as a boy, and after many years of playing in wedding bands and as a support man in Manding and Bambara pop groups, Dounanke made his name at the age of thirty-five when he released his first cassette. The cassette was a rare recording of music from the Bobo, a people who straddle the borders dividing Mali, Cote D'Ivoire, and Burkina Faso. That first cassette was produced, like so many successful Bamako debuts, at Philippe Berthier's Studio Oubien, and it won Dounanke considerable play on radio and television at the time. But that was in 1992, and he hadn't followed up with a new release. "For now," he told me, "we do our work in the bars."

That was where I usually found him, playing after hours at Bar Bozo or Le Segovien—sometimes the upscale Akwaba, but other times the hidden Hotel des Arbres, Matignon, or other spots unknown to all but a few Bamakois. Dounanke's band was built around him and his three brothers, Soungalo on drums, Sekou on bass, and Siaka on percussion. While Dounanke himself cut a straight, friendly image, his brothers wore thin dreadlocks, not quite shoulder length, and lent the band a hip, slightly dangerous aura. When they did their percussion-based, pentatonic Bobo numbers, Dounanke and his brothers could really stir up the bar. It was a sound heard nowhere else in Bamako.

"Here we go," said Barou, when at last Dounanke lit into one of his Bobo songs. The drummer laid out a heavy, disco-style beat. Dounanke put down his guitar and slung a large talking drum over his shoulder, and the band built up a lively bed of percussion over which they chanted an occasionally repeating phrase, "Sinsinbo." The audience quickly joined in on this rhythmic refrain, which sounded to me like "San, san, BO!" with all the voices swooping upwards in pitch on the "bo." "Let's dance," said Barou, leading me into the thick crowd. "Watch my feet," he said, and when I looked down I saw that everyone was dancing a remarkable shuffling step. I studied Barou's feet as his right foot slid back and forth impossibly fast. Then he would shift his weight and shuffle the left foot. "Try it!" he shouted through a grin. I couldn't come close, but my efforts amused the patrons.

The band moved on to a 1930 Cuban hit, "El Maniscero" ("The Peanut Vendor"), probably the most widely covered song in West and Central Africa. Dounanke's rhythm section pushed the feel hard, making that old Latin warhorse gallop. Dounanke's rough guitar gave it a wild edge that distinguished their version from the limp takes tossed off by other bands, including the Rail Band, who invariably opened the night with this song. As the band played on, Dounanke kept changing instruments—bass, rhythm and lead guitar, lead vocal, talking drum, sometimes keyboards and trap drums as well. For all that, it was hard to spot him as the bandleader, since he rarely sang the leads and seemed content let others take the spotlight. "He's afraid of the mike," said Barou.

Before the band's first break that night, the Rail Band's bassist, Fotigui, and alto sax man, Ouedraogo, showed up, and with them bassist Djiby Camara. Djiby was the first Malian musician I ever played music with in a bar. During my first trip to Bamako, I had wandered into a bar called Cactus Bleu thinking I was going to see an up-and-coming Malian singer named Habib Koite. Unfortunately, I had been misinformed and sent to the wrong bar. Though I didn't know it, the band before me was not Habib's but Djiby's group at that time, District de Bamako. The band's music had been straightforward, and I'd noticed a guitar onstage that nobody was playing. Emboldened by a few beers, I had pulled out a guitar pick and waved it at Djiby—a complete stranger at the time—while pointing at the idle guitar.

"I thought, who is this guy?" Djiby would say when telling this story later. "And he wants to play guitar with us? So then he takes the guitar and he starts playing all these things. Zairean songs. Manding music. Cubano. Ooh la la!" Djiby made it sound like magic, but really the most difficult part had been getting up my nerve to wave that pick at him. Djiby was not a brilliant musician, but he was a born diplomat and everybody's friend—le chef de protocol—in all, a good person to have in your corner. When Dounanke's group took their next break, Djiby said to Dirck and me, "Come on. Let's do something."

By this time, Ouedraogo, the Rail Band saxophonist, had joined some friends in front, and as we moved toward the stage I saw him pouring back beer and laughing. Having known him only in the Rail Band, where he seemed a serious, studious musician, I was now seeing his alter ego. The Rail Band rhythm guitarist, Ali, also showed another side of himself in the bars after hours. When we reached the side of the stage, we found Ali already there, strapping on a guitar.

Ali had always impressed me with his gentle, confident manner and with the way he cheerfully abided brusque guidance from Djelimady during rehearsals. Djelimady complained that Ali wasn't serious, didn't practice enough, and so on. After I saw Ali perform with his friends at the Bar Bozo, I realized that the Rail Band was not his true calling. Ali wrote songs and sang in his native language, Mianga, and also in Bobo.

He had a song that joked about the Mianga people's reputed eating of dogs. In the song, Ali instructs a woman to sweep various items off his walkway—peanut shells, mango rinds, and dog parts. It's a lighthearted song about cleanliness, he explained to me. Listening to it without understanding Mianga, you would never guess the subject. It sounded like a peppy old R&B number, and Ali sang in a high, thin, lovesick tenor. His voice had a quality I associate with 1940s ribbon microphones.

Ali sang two songs and then called Dirck, Djiby, and me to the stage. Djiby took on Bob Marley's preachy rant "War," but he sang it in French, in the version popularized by Cote D'Ivoire's reggae star Alpha Blondy. The Bozo's patrons seemed to like having a couple of *toubab*s onstage, so we kept going. Confident with Dirck on bass, I risked a twelve-bar blues. Ali began improvising lyrics in Mianga into the microphone, and soon we were cooking. I noticed at one point that the drummer was playing exceptionally well. So many Malian drummers had seemed stiff and lackluster to me, but this man could fly. His playing was unconventional and a bit disorganized, but he got in some truly artful hi-hat work and his feel was great. He wore a hat and seemed very concentrated on his playing, but I eventually caught his eye to give him a nod of approval, and when I did, I discovered that this was none other than Samba, the Rail Band's number two vocalist. He flashed Dirck and me a smile, and we played on, happy in the knowledge that though we were in the raunchiest, meanest bar in all of Bamako, we were surrounded by friends and going over well with the regulars.

That was the only time I ever played at Bar Bozo. Its reputation for catering to Bamako's lowlife criminal element finally caught up with it when the owner refused to renew the lease at the end of that year. Luckily, there were other late night spots to discover. In fact, I continued to find new music bars right up until the end of my stay in Bamako. Not that they were plentiful, just hidden. In other musical African cities I have visited—Dakar, Harare, Kinshasa—bars make up the center of professional musical life. Hotels and dance clubs advertise proudly and musicians make or break their reputations on those stages. In Bamako, respectable music goes on in courtyards and concert halls. Those who dare to defy Islam and drink alcohol prefer not to draw attention to themselves. As a result, the bars are either elite establishments or else clandestine ones. Sometimes the only way to find out about an after-hours music venue is through word of mouth.

This situation has consequences for musicians. For one thing, most bars are impoverished dives that can't afford proper sound gear, drum kits, or even a real dance floor. Since these bars don't promote musical acts, they can't charge a door fee in order to pay the musicians. This in turn means that the musicians aren't working for money but rather to get discovered by a producer, or just to amuse themselves and jam with their friends. For me as a visiting guitarist, this made for lots of chances to get up with a band and try the waters. The only person apt to mind would be some local guitarist vying for the same guest spot. As much as I benefited from this casualness, I saw what a disaster it was for the musicians. For the bar bound, like Dounanke Koita, music scarcely seemed a profession at all.

"My parents figured, everyone in the family was going to play music," Dounanke told me. "So there was no need to send the kids to school. But now I've traveled a lot and I know that if I had gone to school, it would have been better. I don't know how to read. I can speak just a little French. Now, all *my* kids are in school. They can play music if they want, but they're going to school first."

The attitude of Dounanke's parents—that a musical vocation superseded the need to be educated—is something found only in griot families. Had Dounanke stayed in his Bobo village, he might have been able to live as his father did, playing weddings and naming ceremonies. As a pop musician in Bamako, where there aren't many Bobo, he found himself laboring in these dead-end bars.

The bars of Bamako have produced a few success stories. The most impressive has to be the eclectic singer/guitarist/bandleader Habib Koite. Back in 1993, I had been looking for Habib when I chanced upon Djiby at Cactus Bleu. I later heard the real Habib, with his band Bamadan, or "Mouth of the Crocodile," and I saw instantly that they represented a different order of musical talent and vision. A stolid, handsome fellow with short dreadlocks, Habib cradled a nylon string guitar that he played in his own way, evoking the ornamentation of griot guitar or the pentatonic melodies of the hunter's harp, but never according to traditional orthodoxy. Habib had studied jazz, composition, and classical guitar at Bamako's National Institute of Arts. He had absorbed Pink Floyd and Ten Years After along with Salif Keita's burnished international pop and all manner of Malian roots music. Habib had listened deeply and developed a personal guitar style that set him apart from all of Mali's other guitar geniuses. Similarly, he sang in a silky tenor that owed as much to American soul singers as to *jeli*s.

What's more, Habib had a steady band that rehearsed as regularly as the Rail Band, though no government checks came their way. Habib's drummer was solid, his bassist far above par for Bamako, and his talking drummer and balafonist, a *jeli* named Baba Sissoko, exceptional. The group was filled out by a second guitarist who also sang and played harmonica.

"I don't want to identify with a strong ethnic culture," Habib told me when I interviewed him. He told me he was born into a griot family in western Mali, near the Senegal border. But his parents steered him away from music, toward a career in business, law, or government. When he defied them and pursued music, he did so with a modern outlook, unencumbered by tradition. "Here, each ethnic group has its music," Habib told me, "and has to avoid other music. That's it. Their music, *not* other music. Those who play the Manding *balafon* think that people who play the Senufo *balafon* are savages. They're not intelligent. They have only five notes. Now me, I went to music school. I was curious about a lot of kinds of music. So today, I can play all the ethnic musics of Mali in my way."

In 1993, Habib became a one-hit wonder with a song called "Cigarette Abana." The song had earned him first prize in Radio France International's "African Discoveries" music contest and the chance to record in Paris. The resulting recording had made him famous back home, so famous that when he parked his motorcycle on a Bamako street, he was apt to be surrounded by children singing the catchy refrain to his song: *"No more cigarette! No more cigarette! Abana!"*

By the time I returned to Bamako, Habib had come of age. He and his band were touring and recording in Europe. When in town, they could skip the Bar Bozo and play in a higher class of establishment, like Le Hogon, a so-called "cultural space," or Akwaba, the bar where *today's* government ministers are apt to take their wives on a Saturday night. Habib and his band even played the occasional concert at Bamako's premier venue, the theater-style French Cultural Center, which caters to a sophisticated foreign crowd along with Bamakois flush enough to pay the ticket prices. Habib was the exception, but, as everyone knew, his career began in Bamako's neglected after-hours dives.

The most out-of-the-way venue I ever found in Bamako was called Ma Kele Kele. People were saying that Ma Kele Kele would inherit the Bar Bozo's mantle as the best after-hours spot on a Saturday night. Unfortunately, while Bozo had been located smack in the center of town, Ma Kele Kele was cached away in the far suburbs, beyond Lafiabougou and the Wayanko mesas where Samory had fought the French, over the bridge that begins the road to Guinea, and then down a winding dirt road unmarked by any sign.

Dirck and I failed in our first attempt to find the place. We went looking for it with Joyce Miller, a teacher at the American School of Bamako. Joyce had occasional access to the school's Jeep Cherokee, and she was forever in search of music with the energy she had learned to expect during her postings in Kinshasa and Rio de Janeiro. Joyce was often disappointed but always game to try again. That first night, we got no music at all. When we reached the dirt road to Ma Kele Kele, we concluded that no nightclub could possibly be nestled in the woods down such a road and abandoned the search.

"No, no," said Ali of the Rail Band when Dirck and I next saw him at rehearsal, "you have to go *down* that road. Trust me." It didn't seem possible, but Ali insisted that he and Fotigui, the Rail Band's bassist, had been out there a few times to play with Lobi Traoré, the so-called Bambara bluesman. Word was that Ma Kele Kele was fast becoming Lobi's home base and that he had built up a following there. We tried again. We reached the unmarked dirt road at around 2:00 in the morning, but this time we turned and followed its winding path for a few hundred yards. We took a sharp turn to the right, and there, tucked into the trees and the darkness, was a parking lot with some thirty cars and a number of mobilettes in it. Taximen lingered by their beat up yellow cars, waiting to ferry people back to town. We had found Ma Kele Kele.

Beyond the parking lot, the club itself centered around a big, circular dance floor, just a slab of concrete set in the middle of a packed-dirt clearing surrounded by umbrella-shaped mango trees. A bright fluorescent light, green and eerie, hung over the dancers, and lawn chairs placed around the concrete seated about a hundred customers. Two or three waitresses made the rounds serving Coke, Fanta, and beer in large and small bottles. The musicians gathered on benches behind the dance floor and the band played just in front of them along the edge of the concrete slab. Behind all that, a low, mortar block wall with the name Ma Kele Kele painted on it in tall white letters enclosed a pen filled with large pigs. Smaller pigs wandered freely through the crowd.

"Christians," said Barou, upon seeing a couple of these pink creatures asleep under a tree. I took no offense at the remark. Christians form a very small minority in Mali, as low as 1 percent by some estimates. Since the overwhelming Muslim majority does not eat pork, pigs too are few and far between. The thinking was: Where there are pigs, there *must* be Christians.

As we arrived, a group of musicians were playing electric Manding music, a stripped-down imitation of the Rail Band sound. We spotted Lobi on the bench behind the musicians. He seemed to be on a break and sat chatting with Rail Band members Ali and Samba, biding his time.

Lobi Traoré stood barely five feet, but he made up for his diminutive stature with an outrageous wardrobe. Rarely seen without his brown French beret, Lobi could fill out his look in radically different modes. Sometimes he played the proud Bambara hunter in patterned brown and black *bogolon* (mudcloth) robes. Other times he dressed in biker's leather or a lumberjack's plaid shirt and blue jeans. His kinkiest outfit included a matching vest-and-trousers combination made from a furry, bright green material probably designed for the linings of winter coats in France. Whatever way he went, the beret seemed to work. These outfits suggested a man keen to put on airs, but Lobi, who often dropped by the Rail Band rehearsal just to say hello and chat, struck me as about the most straightforward and modest musician I knew in Bamako.

Lobi descends from a long line of Bambara nobles in the city of Segu. Segu was the capital of the largest Bambara empire, which fell only in 1861, just decades before the French consolidated power in the region. When Barou took me to interview Lobi at his home, I asked how he fit into that history. Traoré is, after all, one of the key Bambara names. Lobi deflected my question without a thought. "It's the big *griots* who know that stuff," he said, "not me."

Lobi's professional career began when he came to Bamako to play guitar in a wedding band. "The group played only Manding music," he told me. "So I was at the side. I didn't really understand Manding music. My inspiration has always been Bambara music. So at home, when I'd take up my little guitar, I would play what I sing. In the beginning, it wasn't any good, but it got better. I started to understand pentatonic melodies on the guitar. So when we went with this band to play at weddings, sometimes I would ask if I could do a Bambara song. I would take the guitar and play a song, and everyone was happy with it. In the end, they would ask for these songs. 'Play a Bambara song!' they would shout."

A group hired Lobi for three months of work in Abidjan, and he stayed there for seven years. When he returned, he had developed a sound that would take him far. Lobi had heard plenty of blues and rock 'n' roll from America and England, and he had begun to incorporate the guitar phrasing he heard there into his own playing, especially when he took a solo. His moniker—the Bambara bluesman—led me to ask what he thought of the Malian blues connection, and I found his matter-of-fact answer revealing.

"When I was young," Lobi told me, "before I even knew I would become a musician, I listened to a lot of blues—John Lee Hooker and all that. Maybe I was inspired by it. Maybe the blues was inspired by Africa. Maybe the resemblance is just a coincidence. What I know is this: The music I play comes from my place. To me, blues is American, nothing but American. It wasn't me who came up with the idea of Bambara blues. People kept saying, 'Bambara blues, Bambara blues.' In the end, I accepted it. But I don't think the blues is our music."

During the 1980s, when Lobi returned to Bamako, there were already a number of artists recording so-called Bambara music. None of them did it like Lobi. Where the average Bambara act leaned heavily on electronic keyboards, harmonized vocals, and driving dance rhythms, Lobi's sound was simple, gritty, and full of open spaces. Lobi liked the bars and he built his early reputation in places like the Bozo. This strategy kept him a secret from most Bamakois, but it did bring him to the attention of producer Philippe Berthier.

Having just recently installed his recording studio, Berthier was eager to find new artists he could put his mark on, and Lobi fit the bill. Berthier recorded Lobi's first cassette, dubbing it *Bambara Blues*, and as Berthier had hoped, both the name and the music found an audience, both in Mali and in Europe.

By the time I met Lobi, he was living a double life. Once or twice a year he went to Europe to play the festivals and sell the CDs that Berthier had helped him produce. His international panache let him do an annual show at the prestigious French Cultural Center, where, like Habib Koite and Ali Farka Touré, he would play mostly for foreigners. For most Malians, Lobi remained an occasional voice on the radio. He had no big hits. He rarely played weddings or baptisms. I never saw him on the bill with lady griots or Wassoulou singing stars for big concerts at one of the two stadiums, or at the Palais de la Culture. But tucked away in the forbidden nightspots of Bamako where the beer drinkers gathered, Lobi performed more often than any of those bigger stars. Rarely did a Friday or Saturday night go by that Lobi wasn't serenading a throng of close-dancing couples somewhere.

Lobi came on for his last set just before 3:00 A.M., and if nothing else had justified our quest for Ma Kele Kele, this did. Lobi's reserve and poise set him apart. His singing had a deep soul quality about it—a little raspy and keening, but effortless. But his guitar playing was the hook for me. Lobi could play the silences like a Cool Jazz man—like Miles himself—unusual in this land of notey improvisers. Lobi's songs were laid back, brooding, and heavy. He used just two backing musicians, typically Ali of the Rail Band on bass and Fotigui or Samba on drums. Though the music was mostly slow, the crowd of working-class Malians soon filled the dance floor, and they stayed there through Lobi's last song.

Sometime before the end, Barou left on his mobilette. "The roads are dangerous now," he said. "Bandits string wire across the road to knock people off their bikes. My friend is leaving too. We'll ride together." I watched the two red tail lights jerking above the dirt road until they turned out of sight, while Lobi held me spellbound.

Joyce Miller dropped Dirck and me at our house sometime after 4:00 in the morning. The house was at the end of the road, just before the edge of the river-cut cliff where dogs congregated in the dark of night—rather like the beer drinkers of the bars, happiest when hidden. Sometimes we would find as many as fifteen of these scrawny curs lurking around our entranceway. Seeing us, they would shift cautiously away. On that December morning, we lingered by the sand pile where Djelimady's construction workers made their concrete by day. We savored the peace. Late at night, every incandescent light bulb in the neighborhood became a paint brush, working the inner surfaces of tree leaves and pouring over the rough, creamy facades of buildings. Nothing seemed to stir except us and the silent dogs. Soon a *muezzin* cried from a mosque, calling the faithful to prayer.

6

Storms

Ni san kulula, bee bolo be i kun: **When the thunder rumbles everyone takes care of himself.**

(Bambara proverb)

he Colonel didn't work on Sundays. I usually tried to sleep in, but even with fans to keep off the mosquitoes and cut the heat and earplugs to dampen the cries of children, I couldn't long escape the world buzzing beyond my cinder-block walls. When I did stir, I would find the Colonel hovering over his propane stove, ready to fix me a breakfast of sweet, milky tea and salty eggs—scrambled and laid into a section of French bread.

On weekdays, I would leave early for the Tounkaras' and see the Colonel only late at night. He was a night owl, and we always exchanged a few words before sleeping. As Djelimady had suggested, I gave the Colonel a little money from time to time. Cultivating his friendship began as a matter of security, but I soon began to appreciate the man on his merits. He listened well, often repeating the last few words of whatever I told him, followed by a decisive *"Oui,"* his French equivalent of the English butler's "Very good, sir." The Colonel offered advice on many subjects. He had no doubt about whom I should and shouldn't trust, how much I should pay for things, and who was in the right in any dispute. So, although his cooking was awful, I left the Tounkaras to themselves on Sunday mornings in favor of breakfast and conversation with the Colonel.

Horse racing was always a topic. For about a year, the new democratic government had been sponsoring a national betting pool on French horse races twice weekly. A few days before each race, the PMU, or *Pari Mutuel Urbain*, would publish its *Programme Officiel*, a single sheet of paper providing the date, hour, location, and length of the race, as well as details on the twenty horses that would be running. The program listed each horse's name, sex, age, stable of origin, total earnings to date, jockey, weight, trainer, owner, placement in last five races, and odds for the race. There was a short paragraph on each horse giving a bit of analysis on its recent performance, health problems, character, and so on. Most of the horses were also rated by the press as *Favoris, Second Chances, Outsiders*, or *Gros Outsiders*.

All over town, small pink kiosks bearing the painted insignia PMU-*Tiercé* sold tickets at 200 CFA each. The equivalent of the American trifecta, the Tiercé game required the bettor to predict the first three horses to complete the race. If you identified the right horses, but in the wrong order, you could win from 2,000 to 50,000 CFA, depending on the number of bettors and winners. If you got the order right as well, you could win as much as one million CFA. The PMU had caught on, and so provided a substantial windfall for the government, allowing it to pave roads and construct monuments and to claim that all this flowed from its democratic policies.

Madou Djan Tounkara had lost a lot of money on the horses. I used to joke with Barou that this was his roundabout way of repaying the money he presumably took from the government. Madou had finally been forced to concede that his brother Djelimady—too skeptical to be taken in by the PMU—had been right. "I'm through with the horses," he had told me. Barou, on the other hand, claimed to have made more than he had lost on the horses. Both he and the Colonel spoke as if the PMU were a job. If you took the time to calculate all the information correctly, they maintained, you would win.

The program for the second weekly race appeared on Thursday morning, and the race itself was run on Saturday afternoon. Thursday nights usually found the Colonel gathered with friends, drinking tea and sifting through stacks of old programs, compiling figures, scribbling out lists, and arguing. The cinder blocks piled up for Djelimady's new house became their desk, and they didn't stop until each had created a list, *"bien calculé,"* as the Colonel put it. The trouble was, the Colonel didn't always buy a ticket, and at breakfast on Sunday morning, the news was often grim.

The Colonel's actual job was with the public power company. On workdays he rose with the sun and traveled across Bamako to install and repair power lines. He didn't return until the evening, and for this he earned about 500 CFA per day, less than the price of three PMU tickets. Dirck and I were at first moved to give the Colonel money for the PMU, but his losses soon dissuaded us.

"Well, I bet on 11, 2, and 9," he would report over tea and eggs the next Sunday morning, "and the winning order was 11, 2, and 6. Now, I did have that one too. You see? I even wrote it down. But that's not the one I bet on. No. The one I bet on was 11, 2, and 9." I told the Colonel that if he didn't intend to buy a ticket, he shouldn't pick winners. "Don't pick winners. *Oui,*" he would say with a solemn but meaningless nod.

"Why don't you buy a ticket to go see Salif Keita?" I teased at one Sunday breakfast. "At least then you *know* you'll get something good for your money."

"Salif Keita. *Oui,*" said the Colonel, humoring me. He wasn't a music fan, but he was a Keita. "Me and Salif. Same family," he boasted. Between Sunjata Keita, founder of the Malian Empire, Modibo Keita, the first president of the Republic of Mali, and Salif Keita, the country's most beloved pop singer, there weren't many names more prestigious than Keita. At least the Colonel had that.

As Christmas approached, posters went up all over Bamako announcing a series of three concerts by Salif Keita. Salif had not brought his band to Bamako for nearly three years, and now he was billed to play with a world-class lineup of backing musicians from Mali, Guinea, Cameroon, and France. He would do three concerts, two high-priced shows at the French Cultural Center and one bargain-priced Christmas Eve blowout at the Stade Modibo Keita. Since the end of the summer, the airwaves had been crackling with Salif's new hit "Tekere," which means "clap your hands." The song was on television, on the radio, and in the discos. Children clapped and sang it in the street. Bar bands covered it. Griot singers even did versions of it at street parties. "Tekere" was an instant classic.

Salif had been living in France for most of the past decade, but he had spent a good part of that fall in Bamako. I knew this because shortly after I arrived, Djelimady, Madou Djan, and Moussa Kouyaté had taken me on an afternoon pilgrimage to Salif's home village, Joliba, about ten miles south of Bamako on the road to Guinea. Salif's father, a noble hunter chief, had died, and the Tounkaras wanted to pay respects. We had crossed paths with Salif on our way back to Lafiabougou. Everyone had gotten out of their cars and the Tounkaras had quietly offered condolences by the roadside. Djelimady had introduced me, and Salif had recalled our earlier meetings in Dakar and Boston. I had taken the opportunity to request an interview, and Salif had given me a local phone number and a date on which I could call.

Salif's story is a legend of world music. He was born an albino, a fate burdened with superstition in a sun-baked African country. In addition to near blindness and painful skin conditions, albinos are often ostracized, seen as harbingers of bad fortune. When Salif was born, his father reportedly summoned the family griot and asked, "What have I done to deserve this?" Salif was a direct descendent of Sunjata Keita and the son of a chief. But his choice of music as a career mocked that noble ancestry. It was a profound act of rebellion, and Salif paid a bitter price within his family when he ran away from home in 1968 and began playing his guitar in Bamako bars. With nowhere else to go, Salif used to sleep among abandoned stalls in the market at night.

"There were two ways I could go," he told me when I interviewed him in Dakar in 1992. "I could become a delinquent and practice banditry, or play music. There was no other way. Because I was a noble, it seemed better to play music than to become a crook. So I chose music. I was nineteen years old. I hadn't played music professionally before. I had two traditional pieces I played on guitar. There was a bar across from the market. When I had problems, I'd forget my cares by playing guitar and trying to sing. One day, the people drinking in the bar heard my guitar. Their juke box was broken, so they told me to come in. I sang a couple of things. I didn't really know how to play, but they were happy and they put money in my guitar. I made fifty Malian francs. The first money I made I sent to my mother because I wanted to recognize her. It was to show her that I had nothing else to give, but I never wanted to forget her."

From these sentimental beginnings Salif made his way, and just a few years later he became a founding member of the Rail Band. As the public gradually realized what a remarkable singer he was, things began to go his way. Before Salif, the legend goes, only *jeli*s could be accepted as professional musicians in Mali. After him, any child could dream not only of a career in music but of sensational success. Just the same, there are those in Salif's own family who have never forgiven his betrayal of ancestry.

Salif launched his second band, Les Ambassadeurs du Motel, at the invitation of a minister in President Moussa Traoré's government. When that minister was arrested in 1978, the band lost financial support and Salif came under pressure to back Moussa's dictatorship. Resenting this, and perhaps a little afraid, he fled with members of his band, taking a car and driving by night all the way to Abidjan. The coastal capital of Cote D'Ivoire was well on its way to becoming the recording hub of West Africa by then, and the songs Salif created there with the re-named Les Ambassadeurs International made him famous throughout the region. One song, "Mandjou," was paramount to his success. In "Mandjou," Salif assumed not only the regaling voice of a griot but the avocation as well. He sang the praises of Sekou Touré, the first president of Guinea, for his loyalty to African culture. After Touré died in 1984 and the horrific excesses of his paranoid regime became known, Salif faced questions about this song. He never backed away from it. In fact, he recorded a new version of his tribute to the dead dictator in 1995, scarcely changing a word.

Salif moved on to Paris in the early 1980s, and in 1987 he created what is arguably the most significant single recording in modern African music, *Soro*. By then, many African singers had tried to incorporate elements of mainstream international rock music to create a sound that would make the world take African music seriously on the contemporary scene. It had never really worked—until *Soro*. Salif fused the *jeli*'s wail with the unbridled freedom cry of rock 'n' roll. He became an African superstar.

Salif also affected Djelimady's life in a crucial way. In 1968, when a confused and dispirited Salif ran away from his village to ponder a life of crime in Bamako, he found Djelimady there. They were both young musicians raised in villages, now loose in the city. Djelimady was playing guitar in a state-sponsored neighborhood band at the time, and though he had not fully developed his guitar technique—the years of standing on one foot lay ahead—he was good enough that when Salif asked to hear Djelimady play his guitar, the music made an impression. The two boys became friends. Salif left the Rail Band the year that Djelimady joined it, 1972, but they have always remained close.

Everyone in Bamako seemed to know this history. I occasionally heard people wonder out loud why it was that when Salif became famous and able to put together any band he wanted, he had not called on his friend Djelimady, the best of Mali's great guitarists. There were, of course, reasons. To begin with, Djelimady did not like to travel and would have demanded more money than Salif wanted to pay a guitarist. Also, from Djelimady's point of view, being the guitarist in a singing star's band could never have offered the artistic freedom or the limelight that he had known in the Rail Band. But for all the respect the Rail Band had garnered, it could never match Salif's commercial achievements, and Djelimady knew this.

Adding to the sting, the guitarist who *had* landed the job with Salif, Ousmane Kouyaté, was Djelimady's protégé, one of those players my mentor claimed to have taught his approach to Manding music. When Djelimady talked about Ousmane, I sensed that he too had moments of regret.

Once while traveling in the north of Mali, I was pulled into a police station outside the city of Mopti. In a throwback to the clamp-down policies of earlier governments, the authorities in this region still demanded a local visa for travelers in nonurban areas. I had neglected to get one and so had to appear and account for myself. In the process, I found myself in conversation with the presiding police officer, an older gentleman. I mentioned that I was studying guitar with Djelimady Tounkara in Bamako and opened a floodgate.

"Djelimady never got his chance," the officer declared with unexpected passion. "He should have risen up with Salif Keita and Mory Kanté. He should have gone to Europe and made his own group. Now, look at him. He's working with the *griottes!* What is that? Ah, Djelimady. He missed his chance."

"He's still a great guitarist," I said. "He can still do those things."

"No," said the policeman. "Djelimady has gone down now. It's too late."

As talk about Salif's upcoming concerts rippled through Bamako, I recalled this encounter, and I began to wonder how Djelimady felt about his career and his lot in life. I had sensed hints of psychic storms brewing beneath Djelimady's jovial exterior. Most of the time, he was the picture of bonhomie. He adored his family, especially the children, with whom he carried on grandfatherly conversations. A smile from a baby could dissolve him in smiles, and he had told me how he couldn't take long trips because he needed his family around him. He seemed to possess a boundless generosity of spirit, and this made his darker moods disturbing to behold.

Early on, I witnessed ugly rows between Djelimady and Samakou, his eldest son. The first came when we were playing guitar one afternoon and

Samakou attempted to set up the TV to watch a kung fu film. Djelimady lashed out at his son. When Samakou dared to talk back, Djelimady exploded. A similar incident occurred a few days later in a fight over Samakou's unwillingness to surrender his keys to the new house. I knew that one explanation for the intensity of these clashes had to do with family structure. The relationship between a father and his eldest son is notoriously combative in Manding society. In addition, as a child from a previous marriage, Samakou had a necessarily rivalrous relationship with his half-siblings and his stepmother, Adama Kouyaté. Beyond all this, Samakou did keep company with a rough crew. Cut off from his family, he had found ways to compensate.

Samakou was by no means Djelimady's only bugaboo. He had health problems—chronic neck pain, insomnia, and regular bouts with malaria. Djelimady fretted over his health. When I met him in 1992, he was a heavy cigarette smoker. Now he had quit smoking, a proud achievement, but still poor health dogged him. Beyond this, Djelimady had secrets. One day at a Rail Band rehearsal, Karamogo, an ex–rhythm guitarist in the Rail Band who had moved to Calgary, Alberta, dropped by during a visit to Bamako. He delivered a cassette from a woman Djelimady had met the previous summer when the Bajourou trio had played in Canada. Djelimady showed me the cassette and said, "I have to bring this tape to listen to on your machine."

"It's from his girlfriend," Madou explained. "Adama Kouyaté must not hear."

That night we were out at the doorway playing guitars, and Djelimady instructed me to play on while he listened to the tape on my walkman. As he sat back with the headphones, he smiled, then laughed, then settled into closed-eyed reverie as he listened to the Calgary woman's voice on the tape. When he dropped me at home that night, he sat out with the Colonel on the verandah, drinking tea and talking softly in Bambara. The next morning Djelimady seemed distant, and that afternoon when we returned from town for lunch, he got into an argument with his wife. Again I found myself cursed with ignorance of Bambara. The rest of the family understood but, like me, they pretended not to notice as Djelimady and Adama tangled. Adama Kouyaté was a woman of directness and force. Though not a singer, she had a voice a *jelimuso* could be proud of, and an argument between her and Djelimady made a spectacle.

As usual, Barou proved the only person capable of giving me insight. "The wife of Djelimady wanted to go to a baptism," he told me. "Djelimady didn't want her to go."

"Why not?" I asked.

"Adama is a strong woman," Barou replied. "Sometimes she does things in ways that make Djelimady angry. She didn't ask him if she could go. She just said she was going. So he said, 'If it's like that, I'll tell you. You aren't going.'"

Aside from his personal struggles, Djelimady had to mediate other people's disputes in his complicated household. One afternoon I arrived at the compound for lunch and ate alone, while a group of women sat around the TV under the shade of the compound's main verandah. As I started into my watermelon, angry words broke out among the women. Six or more soon entered the fray, shouting, crying, and prancing about the compound. Young Sambry Kouyaté was instructed to take the children out to the street. Some obeyed; others stood at the ramp, looking up bleakly at their unraveling elders. Tareta, the most glamorous of Djelimady's daughters, became so exasperated that she flung herself to the ground, rolling on the concrete and making a sound strangely suspended between sobbing and laughter. Even Djelimady's mother was drawn in. She shuffled up to the verandah wall and began incanting a menacing phrase over and over and pointing accusingly at one of her granddaughters.

Djelimady and Madou arrived in the midst of this. Djelimady quickly joined the battle while Madou paced, his worried expression deepening. Now and then Djelimady would cast a glance my way, telegraphing concern that I should be seeing this but also a certain bemusement at my confusion. He had no intention of explaining what it was about. Barou arrived near the end of the scuffle.

"What was going on?" I couldn't resist asking later, as I perched precariously on the uncushioned rack at the back of Barou's purple motorbike.

"I just heard the end," said Barou. "I don't know."

I pressed him, knowing that he had heard one particularly passionate speech by the woman on the verandah. "What was that woman saying at the end?" I shouted over the wind.

"That the daughters of Djelimady were wrong."

"About what?"

"I don't know. But it's the wife of Djelimady who starts these things."

"That's odd," I said, "she didn't seem to be involved."

"She says a few things to get her daughters started," Barou explained. "Then she sits back."

Many angry conversations at the compound flew past me without explanation. Everyone seemed to know that I must be curious, but no one wanted to explain. In anger, people said things they might regret, things nobody wanted to repeat. When so many people live so close together, privacy is protected by trust and silence, not closed doors or secluded spaces.

One evening, Salif Keita dropped by the house after dinner. Dirck, Djelimady, and I were out on the street playing music when a shiny white Peugeot swung around the corner. Before the car had even stopped, its passenger door swung open and out bounded Salif in a white *boubou*.

"Cocha!" he shouted at Djelimady.

Before Djelimady could react, Salif swung around and looked directly at me. "You know his name?" he asked, pointing at Djelimady.

"Djelimady," I said dumbly.

"No!" bellowed Salif. "It's Cocha! Ask the women about that. They know." Later, Djelimady would explain to me that *cocha* is a Manding word for a man who uses his musical instrument to seduce women.

As Salif's brother and a driver looked on from the Peugeot, Salif and Djelimady began slapping one another like old football buddies and bantering in Bambara. We made a circle of chairs and everyone sat. I took the opportunity to show off a little by picking up my guitar and playing "Sunjata," praise song to the Keitas. The effect was immediate.

"That's *my* song," said Salif as if I had stolen something from him. I nodded and kept playing, hoping to build up to the more elaborate variations before someone seized the guitar from me. I didn't get far. "Give me that," said Salif. He cradled my guitar with the neck pointed high in the air and played an elegant Manding riff. He began to sing quietly, and soon I discerned the words and melody of "Tekere," the bouncy pop hit that had played like a nonstop soundtrack to my Bamako experience. Here was the song stripped to its essentials.

The visit didn't last long. Salif left as suddenly as he had come, telling us that he was about to fly to Paris. "Tomorrow?" I asked, still keen to set up an interview.

"Tonight even," he replied.

"He's a liar," Djelimady said with a laugh as the Peugeot pulled away. "He's not going to Paris tomorrow or tonight. He's going to Lake Debo." Djelimady explained that Salif was going to participate in a ceremony of fishermen. I didn't understand the nature of the ceremony, except that at the height of the event, everyone throws rocks into the water. "He likes that sort of thing," said Djelimady.

Talk turned to "Mandjou," Salif's tribute to the Guinean dictator Sekou Touré. I asked Djelimady if it didn't bother people that Salif was still singing praises for a man who had imprisoned and killed thousands of his countrymen. Djelimady offered a roundabout defense of the dictator, mostly on the basis that Touré had stood up to the French and that he had defended and nurtured his country's music culture. Madou shook his head. "Sekou Touré killed a lot of people. Intellectuals and artists too," he reminded his brother.

"Is it true that Sekou Touré had Fodeba Keita executed?" I asked. Fodeba Keita had been an influential musician in Guinea, the founder of the world-renowned Ballet Africains. Many African artists I had interviewed over the years had cited him as an inspiration. Keita had even given Ali Farka Touré his first guitar lesson back in 1956. Sekou Touré had always revered Fodeba Keita, and as president, Touré had named him Secretary of the Interior, a post the artist held until his execution for treason in 1969. I didn't understand how this relationship could have ended so badly.

"It was personal," said Madou. "Fodeba Keita was known and loved by all the people. Sekou Touré was jealous."

"But Salif still sings about him as a hero," I puzzled. "Why?"

Madou shrugged, puffed on his cigarette and said, "Sekou Touré loved Salif. Salif used to spend weekends at Sekou Touré's resort home." He paused again to smoke. "Sekou Touré was more than just a dictator. He was a killer, just like Hitler."

Ignoring this, Djelimady began chuckling to himself and then said, "Salif says he wants to record three songs with me. He and I on acoustic guitars, Ousmane Kouyaté on bass, and two chorus singers. That's it."

"Sounds great," said Dirck.

"So I asked him," Djelimady continued. "I said, 'Salif, are you going to pay me for that?' 'Oh yes,' he said. 'A lot?' I asked him. 'Naturally,' he said." Then Djelimady snickered. "Oh, Salif," he said. "What a liar!" Djelimady seemed more tickled than annoyed. He longed for Salif to be as good as his word, but he couldn't let himself believe it.

I did eventually interview Salif Keita at his mansion-like house in Djelibougou. He was in the process of returning to Bamako to live, and he had been working on the house. A sixteen-track digital recording studio—probably the best recording facility in the whole country— adjoined his bedroom. When at last we sat down to talk, Salif showed none of the flare and bombast I had seen when he visited the Tounkaras. He had almost nothing to say.

Where I had hoped to hear Salif's reflections on the mythic arc of his relationship with his father, I got, "He was my friend. I miss him." Where I had hoped to hear Salif's evocative impressions of Bamako during the '60s, I got, "It was a good time. I was young and discovering life." And where I had hoped for a wealth of stories about Salif's early days with Djelimady, I got a moving testimonial—"Djelimady is more than a friend. He is a brother. He marked my youth."—but little more. By the time I asked about "Mandjou," the praise song to the dictator, I wasn't expecting much. "Now everybody says Sekou Touré was bad," Salif scoffed, and went on to make his refusal to change the song a point of honor. "Why should I, a small musician, change my song because people say this or that?" When I was a guitarist palling around with Djelimady, Salif could joke and be my friend too. But when I became a journalist aiming a microphone at him, he had little to gain from candor.

Dirck and I bought Djelimady a ticket to the opening night at the French Cultural Center, and Salif gave a masterful performance. Dressed in hunter's regalia and bathed in golden light, he knelt on the stage while his band filled the theater with majestic sound. Salif rose and sang with closed eyes, sang from a place so deep within him that his soul seemed to shimmer in the sound waves. Salif could be as maddening as any puffed-up prima donna pop star, but he deserved his mantle as the grandest musician in Mali.

The last Saturday before Christmas was a gray day, cool and windless, thick clouds hanging low over the city. It was the height of *harmattan*, the season when clouds of Sahara Desert dust, high in the atmosphere, linger over West Africa, creating an orange haze and the coolest weather of the year. At lunch in the compound, Djelimady gave the sky a rueful glance. For ten days or so, he had been spending time with his best friend, a businessman named Douga Sissoko. They had been preparing for this day. Working out of Douga's house in the Hippodrome neighborhood, they had organized an event to help launch a new bank in the

Kayes region of Mali, the region that borders Senegal. Douga had called a series of meetings with Djelimady and also a host of griots from Kayes in order to plan a fund-raising concert. The concert would publicize and raise money for the new bank, which would in turn bring money and development projects to the Kayes region. The concert was to take place that afternoon at the smaller of Bamako's two stadiums, Stade Mamadou Konaté. Now, in addition to hasty publicity, the event would be hampered by poor weather.

As we left for the concert at around 3:00, the darker clouds were actually producing a light spatter. The moisture brought a gritty aroma to the air, an exotic sensation after months of dryness. But Djelimady was vexed by it.

In the stadium, there were nearly as many musicians and griots getting ready to perform on the stage as there were spectators in the bleachers. Adama Tounkara and Sayan Sissoko were there with their *ngonis*, along with two other guitarists, a *kora* player, a bassist, various talking drummers, and a guy playing a Yamaha electronic rhythm box with his fingers. Tuning and feedback marred the first few songs, but the parade of *jelimusow* began anyway. As one woman sang, the others would dance in circles and lines before the stage, swinging their arms and pressing them forward, constantly sitting down and then rising again for a brief, unhurried dance. Soon the griot men joined them, prowling the stage like exotic birds in sunglasses.

Oddly, no money changed hands. I took this to mean that the proceeds would go to the bank. But despite the cast of stars and the presence of television cameras, the crowd that turned out could scarcely have offered much return. The event had failed, and Djelimady was glum. He complained about the sound, the lack of rehearsal, and the inadequate publicity. "We'll have to do this again," he said when it was over. There were too many of us to fit in Djelimady's car, so Dirck, Sayan, Madou, and I rode with him, while Adama and Moussa Kouyaté walked off to find a *bashée*.

When we reached the compound, dinner was underway. Dirck, Madou, and I took our seats before the television and began tossing around some Bambara. Barou arrived and took a seat with us. Dirck had learned a Bambara proverb from the Colonel and was showing off his ability to recite it. The proverb said, "No matter how long a piece of wood floats in the river, it will never become a crocodile."

"Very good!" said Barou.

"Dirck," echoed Madou, "you are intelligent."

Dirck had applied himself to Bambara and was showing me up. I quickly wrote the proverb in my notebook, but not out of competitiveness. This particular proverb struck me as a good metaphor for two American musicians playing music with the Malians. The next time someone said to me, "Banning, you have now become a Malian," I would have a clever rejoinder, for no matter how long an American plays guitar in Bamako, he will never become a *jeli*.

As we talked, we could hear behind us the sound of Djelimady arguing with his wife. It was rancorous, though nothing like the fight I had witnessed a few weeks earlier when Adama had insisted on attending a baptism against Djelimady's will. I didn't pay much attention as they went into their bedroom. But then Adama emerged, still arguing, and she entered the compound even as Djelimady shouted at her from the bedroom door. Adama spoke to him in a strange voice. It was not loud or angry, rather quiet and vaguely song-like. The tone was unlike any I had heard from her. It carried an unmistakable feeling of fearless, willful defiance, but also a kind of desperation. Djelimady responded with fury.

Still in his white trousers but with his shirt off, Djelimady stormed into the courtyard. Adama was now seated in her place on the other side of the doorway from us. The compound was full, with some ten or more children gathered on stools close to the television, the old ladies on the verandah, and a number of girls and women in the dark cooking area. Without warning, Djelimady approached Adama and struck her hard on the face with the back of his right hand. Madou and Yéyé Tounkara leapt to their feet and moved in to stop him, but before they could restrain their brother, he had popped off two more forceful blows to either side of Adama's head. Madou, Yéyé, and others had to drag Djelimady away from his wife, who was by now wailing, her argument still flowing with her tears.

Some of the women escorted her into one of the back rooms. Djelimady made one more effort to break free of his brothers, but failing, he seemed to regain himself. Dirck and I stared ahead at the television, then showing a cartoon of Conan the Barbarian dubbed into French. The children remained glued to the program, and I wondered whether this event was familiar to them. There was shouting. The old women scolded Djelimady, who continued snarling in rapid Bambara. Barou went into the back room to see Adama Kouyaté.

When Djelimady joined us for dinner, he knew he had to explain himself. "You must excuse me," he said rapidly. "But Adama was gone the whole day and she did not tell me where she was. Among us, wives do not do that."

"I guess not," Dirck muttered in English. We ate in silence. Soon Moussa Kouyaté and Adama Tounkara arrived from their *bashée* voyage. Moussa quickly homed in on the food, but the griot didn't take long to sense trouble. Though he had eaten only a few bites of millet paste and peanut sauce, he washed his hands and went to work, listening first to Djelimady and then to protests from the old women.

Djelimady went into the bedroom and his wife emerged, dressed in red, her head wrap draped over the sides of her face. She sat not in her customary place but on a tiny wooden stool between the television and the bathroom. She removed her white shoes and pressed her feet together, tucked under the stool. Miriam, her youngest daughter, went to comfort her as Djelimady passed them on his way to the bathroom, still muttering angrily. Adama made no effort to avoid him. Yayi, a little girl of three, brought Adama a shot glass of gunpowder tea.

At the Buffet Hotel de la Gare, Dirck and I had reasonable success playing with the Rail Band in the cool of that December night. Both of the saxophonists were absent. Kabine Keita, the elder one, had spilled ignited gasoline on his hand and burned it badly. And the younger player, Ouedraogo, whom we knew from the after-hours bars, had been sick for more than a week. Without horns, the band avoided the Cuban numbers and stuck to Manding music, the most interesting part of the repertoire for Dirck and me. But whatever pleasure the music brought us that night was tainted. Djelimady did rise to do his prance a few times and seemed to get caught up in the music, but now we watched him through new eyes. The guitar king, with a smile for everyone and a spirit that stretched to the Sahara, was also capable of brutality.

On Sunday, we did not see Djelimady all day. In the evening, we passed by Barou's house to get his impressions. Barou said that Adama Kouyaté had insulted Djelimady in front of the whole family, using dirty language. It had been more than he could take. The fight had begun in the bedroom when Adama asked for permission to go to a wedding. Djelimady had said no, claiming that she had been going out every day. It wasn't good. A wife needs to be at home sometimes.

"Among us," said Barou, "when a husband tells his wife no, it's no." Adama had kept arguing, and when she had come into the compound, she had insulted her husband with shocking words. "I've seen him shout at her plenty of times," he said. "Many, many times. But in all the years I've known Djelimady, I have never seen him hit her until last night."

Barou offered more. He spoke about the time when Djelimady first came to Bamako in the mid-'60s, the very time that Salif had been

unwilling to recall for me in our interview. "Djelimady was an apprentice tailor when he came here," said Barou. "He had only been in school
a few years. You must have noticed that he still can't speak proper
French. That's why. He was never really educated. When Djelimady was
young, in the village of Boudefo, they thought he was a mental defi-
cient. He couldn't speak well, and he drooled. Other children were
afraid of him. Just like his young son now, Balla."

Balla, a timid young boy in the compound, did bear a resemblance to
Djelimady. I had not known he was Djelimady's son, but I had noticed that
something was not right with him. He rarely spoke, and the twins led him
around and watched after him, though he was probably thirteen and they
just ten. I tried to imagine Djelimady like that, a quiet, aloof boy. It did-
n't fit. The Djelimady I knew was more than just adequately intelligent.
He might believe a lot of nonsense—that AIDS was just chronic malaria,
for example—and his French might have been rough, but he was not slow.
In fact, little seemed to get past him. What could have changed him so?

"When Djelimady came to Bamako," said Barou, "he played only one
song on the guitar, 'Sunjata.' He wasn't a guitarist yet. He planned to
support himself as a tailor."

I recalled Djelimady's own description of how he became a guitarist.
"Everyone thought I was crazy," he had told me. "I used to lock myself in
my room for days and practice. They had to bring me food. I wouldn't
even leave my room to eat. I did that for years."

Djelimady used to make this speech to show that understanding his
tricks on the guitar was useless without the commitment of long hours
in practice. Now I saw something new in it. If Barou's story was true,
Djelimady's withdrawal into music had allowed him to reinvent himself, like Sunjata the invalid boy and like Salif. Djelimady and Salif had
been outcasts together, and though they had found new lives through
music, old wounds remained within them.

On Christmas Eve, The Rail Band played under the colored lights and
the hanging metallic frills. With Salif Keita performing at the stadium
and every club in Bamako open for business, the Buffet Hotel de la Gare
managed a modest but lively crowd. Djelimady's powerful friend Douga
Sissoko made a grand entrance, shouting praise to the musicians, including Dirck and me. Singers Samba and Damory had worked out a syn-
chronized dance, turning together to the left and then the right. Unfortunately, the down jackets they wore to ward off the cold made their

choreography into a comedy. Near the end of the night, Salif's guitarist Ousmane Kouyaté turned up at the Buffet, fresh from Salif's stadium concert. I gave him my guitar and he sat in with Djelimady for a couple of songs—the old master and his successful protégé.

Dirck and I declined the traditional bar crawl, as he was succumbing to one of those vague illnesses the African traveler inevitably encounters. When Djelimady dropped us at the house, I felt hungry. It was almost 3:00 in the morning, but I knew I could still find something to eat down the street. The main bar near our house, Le Segovien, was overflowing with customers despite the late hour. I decided to step into the relatively quiet alternative, Le Perroquet, two doors down.

Bands do not play at Le Perroquet. The only time it ever sees a crowd is on mornings when they distribute new PMU programs there. In the evenings, the bar plays quiet music, Cuban songs, old Manding recordings, sometimes reggae or jazz. I suspected that the bar's business had more to do with prostitution than with music or beer, for I had sat on the open verandah there before and watched the same woman escort one man and then another out of the bar and to his car or mobilette and return alone. Across from the verandah, corrugated iron roofs and wrecked cars recalled squalid corners of the Caribbean or a poor American city. Under the palms with the Latin music tickling the ears, the place had a casual charm.

Most of the bar stools were full, and as I squeezed in to give my order, a plump fellow in a white T-shirt and red cap looked straight at me and asked, "What are you doing here?"

"Getting a beer," I replied.

"No, not in *this* bar," he said. I looked at this man to evaluate whether he presented a threat. Once he had my eye, he held it, staring from his craggy, white-whiskered face and slowly rephrasing his question. "What is a white *European* doing in Mali?"

"I'm a musician," I said.

"You are *not* a musician."

"Yes, I am." I protested. "I play with Djelimady Tounkara in the Rail Band."

By now, I was close enough to smell the man's beery breath. "I know you," he said, his tone shifting to intimacy. "I've seen you at the Buffet." Then he stood up quickly from his bar stool, and spread his arms wide in a clear invitation to an embrace. I resisted, but soon found myself hugging this odd little man. I felt his whiskers scratching my neck as he planted a moist kiss there.

Then his tone turned menacing. "I know what you think," he said. "You think you're better than your soloist. You sit there with all your European tricks. Djelimady doesn't know those tricks. *You're* the professor."

"No," I insisted, "Djelimady is the professor."

"You know," he said pointing an accusing finger at me, "you can never trust a European who says nice things about Africans. You want guitar. I play guitar and I can show you the *real* guitar. What you have seen so far is. . . " He spat at the ground to complete his thought.

"What is your name?" I asked.

"J. C.," he replied.

"J. C.?" I asked, amazed at being accosted by a stranger named J. C. on Christmas morning.

"J. C. Jackson," said a man seated at the bar.

"*Not* Jesse Jackson," my accuser protested.

The man at the bar repeated himself merrily. "J. C. Jackson! J. C. Jackson!" he chanted.

"Never Jesse Jackson," the little man blustered. "*Je n'aime pas Jesse Jackson. Je ne suis pas d'accord avec Jesse Jackson parce qu'il mange les derrières des blancs!*" With this, J. C. stuck out his ass and pointed at it, telling me that Jesse Jackson was fit to be found there.

I laughed, and J. C. seemed to warm to me again, his rant easing to a lecture. He told me that white people with their technology were responsible for the destruction of the earth. He said he had lived in Europe for twenty-two years and he knew what he was talking about. "I know the European," he said. "*Il est méchant!*"

As I broke away with my beer, J. C. turned abruptly and walked out of the bar. I never managed to correct his notion that I was a European. Then again, I didn't learn much about him either. Later, Barou would tell me that J. C. was a Liberian who had lost his family in the civil war there and was now writing a book about it. For the next four months, I would visit Le Perroquet at night every so often, hoping to find J. C. again. I never did. He remained an apparition, a ghost of Christmas present, though I never forgot his words. I was the professor. Other people I met in Bamako probably had similar thoughts; they were just too polite to say so.

I walked back to the house, rehearsing in my head Dirck's Bambara proverb. As always, I found the Colonel standing outside his door, as if waiting for me. I gathered myself and out it came, in Bambara: "No matter how long a piece of wood floats in the river, it will never become a crocodile."

The Colonel smiled and answered in French, "*Joyeux noel.*"

1

Return of the Diva

What makes *jaliya* difficult
It is finding a worthy patron
And what makes *jaliya* pleasant
It is finding the right patron

From the griot song "Lamban"

ay after day, money problems needled Djelimady. Construction on the new house had almost stopped, and the Nissan sounded worse than ever. I offered $200 to replace the shock absorbers, and everyone thanked me for the gesture. Djelimady seemed almost embarrassed to accept my money and resorted to his familiar refrain. "Without Solo and Yayi around," he said, "I have to pay for *everything*." Solo, or Souleymane Tounkara, was Djelimady and Madou Djan's younger brother. Yayi Kanouté was Solo's wife. Yayi's renown as a *jelimuso* had been sufficient to get her some festival gigs in Canada the previous summer. With Solo on guitar and Cheick Hamala Diabaté on *ngoni*, Yayi and Groupe Lamban, as she and Solo called their outfit, had left Bamako in July. They had yet to return, and they had sent no money.

I first heard the music of Yayi Kanouté when I picked up her debut CD during a research trip to Paris in 1991. At the time, my Paris informants had touted Yayi as something of a sensation in Mali, especially for her song that spoke up for jilted wives, candidly condemning infidelity. I had found the recording good, but unexceptional. All that changed, though, when I visited Djelimady's house in Bamako a couple of years later and recorded Yayi, Solo, Djelimady, Adama, and Cheick Hamala performing together with acoustic instruments in Solo and Yayi's living room.

On my tape, Yayi sings in a dry, robust voice. It creaks and threatens to go airy but persists with a kind of burliness and builds to a satisfying griot gale, rough and ragged, like Tina Turner after Ike. Perhaps the arid fragility of that voice would eventually have touched me anyway, but listening to my own recording so many times had burned Yayi's sound into some deep recess of my psyche.

Yayi and her group had been delayed in their departure for the Canadian festivals. By the time they actually got off, they had missed one of the key events, the Montreal Jazz Festival. They had performed at the smaller Francofolis festival in Montreal and had found a little work in Ottawa and Toronto. Then, after a month in Canada, they had moved on to Washington, D.C., to stay with Tounkara relatives there. I had spoken to Solo by telephone just days before my departure for Bamako. His querulous voice at the other end of the line had reminded me of discussions over the years with African musicians at a loss in America. Abandoned to inexperienced promoters, such artists had a way of finding my name and calling me for help. Solo and Yayi were in the hands of a cousin who worked in the Malian Embassy. He had hoped to arrange concerts all over the East Coast. I had tried to sound encouraging on the telephone, but it had sounded like folly to me. Even with a professional agent behind her, Yayi and her griot pop would have been a tough sell in American nightclubs and concert halls.

Once settled in Bamako with the Tounkaras, I heard occasional reports on the progress of Solo and Yayi in America. Sometimes Solo would telephone and a child would run over from the Logo Hotel to say he would call again in ten minutes. By then, Madou or Djelimady would be there to take the call. These calls always boiled down to a simple piece of news for the benefit of everyone at the compound. Solo and Yayi had gone to New York. They had played a successful gig there. They had returned to D.C. They had played the Kilimanjaro Club there. David Gilden, the American *kora* player—who, like me, once lived with the Tounkaras in Bamako—had visited with his *kora*.

These reports always had Solo and Yayi happy, working hard, and unsure when they might come home. To me, the upbeat bulletins made them seem further away than ever, since I assumed things to be far worse than the news let on. We heard nothing about long days spent sitting in a Washington apartment waiting for something to happen. Nothing about dwindling earnings. Nothing about being deceived by shifty club owners. Nothing about the miseries of winter.

I had met Solo and Yayi just once. I probably would not have recognized either of them on the street. However, I was now coming to know them through their four-year-old son, whose real name was Badra but whom everyone at the compound called Colos, as in the Latin word "colossus." It was a funny name for such a small child. The only things colossal about Colos were his protruding belly button and his ego. Whenever I arrived at the compound, Colos would rush forth with his hairless head and round eyes and stick out a small hand to shake. A clown, a ham, and a natural dancer, Colos charmed all visitors to the Tounkara compound, despite competition from a clan of charming children. Along with the twins, Lasine and Fuseini, Colos seemed destined for the entertainment world. He memorized comic sketches from the television, down to precise inflections. Sometimes Colos would dance through the courtyard in his tiny *boubou*, holding a stick up to his chest as if it were an *ngoni* and making a show of hopping abruptly every so often—a child's rendering of the jerky griot's dance.

"Solo was just like that as a child," said Madou once, "always dancing and clowning." When Madou had left Bamako some twenty years earlier, Solo must still have been a boy. Watching Colos seemed to take Madou back to that lost time, and he stared at the child with fascination.

After Christmas, Solo sent 100,000 CFA, about $200, to Madou to buy a cow for a friend's wedding. The gesture mystified me, for I still imagined Solo to be all but starving on his slim earnings from the Kilimanjaro Club in Washington. Everyone knew of the Kilimanjaro's reputation for taking advantage of musicians. Solo and Yayi must have played a weeknight there, I reasoned, since only well-known stars and Zairean or Cameroonean dance bands played the Kilimanjaro on weekends, when the African embassy crowd circulated. Yayi's name on the Kilimanjaro marquee couldn't have brought the group more than $500, I reasoned. And yet, this showy gift from Solo.

The arrival of money bolstered the Tounkaras' fond notion that Solo and Yayi were soaking up riches in America, and the idea began to seduce even me. I had heard tales of wealthy West Africans sponsoring lavish soirées for visiting musicians in New York and Washington. Perhaps they would stay indefinitely. But on New Year's Eve, as Djelimady, Dirck, and I were heading off to play the year-end gala at the Buffet

Hotel de la Gare, Djelimady made an announcement: Solo and Yayi would return that night. Sure enough, as the Rail Band tore into the first song of the new year, the Manding ballad "Mansa," I caught sight of a dandy in a light-colored, double-breasted suit and a felt hat with a black ribbon band. He climbed onstage, beaming, and shook my hand right in the middle of the song. Djelimady pointed at him and shouted over the music, "Solo!"

Yayi was there too, and I recognized her dimly. Based on cassette jacket photos I had seen, she seemed to have put on weight in America. She had a soft, doughy face and hungry eyes, as large as those of her son Colos. Before the close of the New Year's celebration, Yayi sang with the Rail Band. A flood of emotion overcame me on hearing that rough, relaxed voice once again.

When Dirck and I next entered the Tounkara compound on the afternoon of New Year's Day, something had changed. "The Americans," as Solo and Yayi were then being called, had returned with a haul. Solo's trunk alone could hold three times what mine did. A black, leathery affair with brass corners, it was nearly three feet deep and at least six feet wide and was filled with fancy clothing. In addition, the couple had traveled with two guitar amplifiers, two new electric guitars, and four suitcases containing more clothes, as well as cooking pots, a cordless microphone, guitar effects pedals, a boom box, and small gifts for everybody in the compound. It looked to me like over $5,000 worth of merchandise. In addition, Solo said he had paid $1,000 in overweight charges and 50 percent of the customs due on arrival in Mali.

That day I watched Solo hand Djelimady 250,000 CFA ($500) to help with construction at the new house. "This will buy the bricks for the second floor," Djelimady told me. A few days later, Solo bought a used car, a sporty white Honda. The car ran roughly and had a gear shift that you could change by breathing on it. Rather than invest in mechanical work, Solo had the car painted fire-engine red, as if to announce to all of Bamako that a new day had dawned for the Tounkaras. Ten days later Djelimady announced that he and Solo had to go to the airport because Solo and Yayi's "sound system" had arrived. They returned with an eight-channel Peavy mixing amplifier and two speakers big enough to regale a large wedding audience. My own offerings to Djelimady were dwarfed by this infusion of new technology.

How was this possible? Solo showed me a video of the Kilimanjaro gig, in which an African man places a $100 bill on the stage before Yayi.

"After the show, he came backstage and gave us $1,000," said Solo coolly. But this hardly explained all these acquisitions. After all, three people—Solo, Yayi, and Hamala, who had not returned with them—had all had to eat for six months, and two of them had flown home to Mali. The group had played no big concerts, made no record deals or television appearances. Yet they had returned with the sort of trappings African stars purchase at the end of a twenty-five-city tour.

With Solo and Yayi back in town, Dirck and I played our first street wedding. It happened unexpectedly. Djelimady drove us straight from the Rail Band rehearsal to a street in the downtown Dravela neighborhood where Solo and Adama Tounkara were setting up to play. Ina Tounkara was the *jelimuso* for the occasion and Sambry Kouyaté was along to play button-punch electronic drums. Djelimady strapped up and plugged into Solo's new American rig. Dirck and I sat in the shade and watched at first, but after lunch Solo told Dirck to get his keyboard from Djelimady's car and Dirck insisted that I bring my guitar, too. "I'm not going up there alone," he said. So we plugged in our instruments and began playing along with griot songs we had been learning in our sessions with Djelimady—"Kaira," "Dene Kenyiba," "Bajourou," "Lamban," and many versions of "Diaoura."

For all their variations, these songs usually build around simple repeating parts. If you know two or three of these, you can play along without disrupting the improvisations of the singer and soloists. As we played on, Ina collected 500 and 1,000 CFA notes. All the money went into Solo's hard-shell guitar case. We played for about three hours and then Solo opened the guitar case and set about counting the salad of bills it contained.

I asked him, "How much is a lot of money to make at one of these things?"

"Oh," he answered, "sometimes you get a lot, lots of gifts. Fabrics and *boubou*s. All that."

"That's *not* what he asked," said Djelimady. Eventually figures came forth. Solo said that the range for a wedding was $50 to $200. That day's haul was small, about $70. Half of the money went to Ina, since it was her contract.

"It's tough," said Djelimady, shaking his head and pocketing his share. Solo gave Dirck and me each 1,000 CFA, two dollars. The money was inconsequential, but the event was important. From that point on, whenever there was a wedding, we were expected to come and play.

Most weddings took place on either Sunday or Thursday, but during the approaching month of Ramadan, Muslims were expected to devote themselves to fasting and prayer; street parties and concerts were drastically curtailed. In the meantime, the pace of weddings rose week by week. The following Thursday, we played another wedding, this time with Yayi at the mike. The combination of a larger, more serious audience, an early start, and Yayi—fresh from America and a hot item with the public—added up to a steady flow of cash. Yayi gathered fistfuls of bills, which Solo or Sambry crammed into an electric guitar case on the ground. We played from 11:00 A.M. until 3:00 P.M. and then stopped to eat. Four different plates arrived and we gorged ourselves, reaching down toward the ground to dip into metal bowls for sinewy chunks of beef, sections of fish, and hot potatoes boiled in spicy juices.

Solo kept a small, programmable keyboard in front of him and from time to time he would shift its beat—faster, slower, backbeat funk, rock, Latin clavé—each groove as wooden as the next. Locked into this rhythmic treadmill, musicians were robbed of any ability to stretch or condense the time, normally powerful techniques in African music. I made no secret of my disdain for these electronic rhythm devices, and Solo listened, more entertained than convinced.

As for the sound itself, Solo and Yayi's new gear did reduce the amount of distortion, but it also raised the overall volume, and as Yayi continually turned back and demanded that Solo boost her microphone level, feedback wailed louder than ever before. Also, with the amplifiers arranged in a row and musicians seated on either end, no player could hear everything. Each fished into the sea of muddled sound seeking a current into which he could jet his stream of notes. As the long day wore on, occasional moments of spectacle would rouse Dirck and me from the delirium of our repetitive duties. I stared at a woman as she abandoned herself to mad, flailing dance. When she stopped, her face glowed with purgation and release—a reminder that this was ritual, not performance. My aesthetic judgments about the music were irrelevant. For the *jeli*s, the flow of money was the measure of success.

We played for more than six hours that day. In the warm orange light of dusk, Djelimady and Solo backed the guitar case against a wall and counted out more than 100,000 CFA. Dirck and I earned 2,500 each, the most we would ever receive for our participation at a Bamako street party.

During Ramadan, we learned, the Rail Band members would take their annual vacation, suspending rehearsals and concerts. Djelimady was determined to complete the arrangements the band had been rehearsing before the break, so Buffet rehearsals found Djelimady driving the band to play them over and over again without error. One morning, Djelimady directed the band to move all the equipment to Bamako's central television station to record two songs with a pair of blind Bambara singers. Barou had announced at the last moment that he needed his keyboard, and Solo's keyboard proved unplayable, so Dirck was forced to sit out the session. At the end, Djelimady asked Dirck what he'd thought of the music.

"It was fine," said Dirck. But as he spoke, he raised his left hand, held it flat and wobbled it. Djelimady watched the hand.

"Ah, Dirck," he said, chortling. "He's an American. He doesn't want to wound, but he doesn't want to lie. He says it was fine, but his hand says something else."

That hand waver instantly entered the realm of Tounkara humor. It was a way of invalidating whatever tactful thing you happened to be saying, and it had many applications. At the time, though, Dirck had been genuinely annoyed, particularly at Barou for suddenly announcing that he needed his keyboard when it was too late to make other arrangements. The fact was, we had seen little of Barou since Solo and Yayi had arrived. We decided to pay him a visit. We found Barou's living room packed with family and friends watching a "Kickboxer" film on the VCR. Barou stepped out beyond the curtain and spoke to us in the shaded verandah.

"Solo has all his things from America," said Barou testily, when Dirck asked about the keyboard. "If I had gone over there, I would have brought back a *good* keyboard." Barou looked at us, working his thin eyebrows nervously and reading the puzzlement on our faces. "You know I was supposed to go to America with them, don't you?" he asked.

"No," we replied in unison.

"Okay," said Barou, "I will tell you the story." We stepped away from the doorway, and Barou began. "Before this tour, I was the bassist in Yayi Kanouté's group. It was Yayi, Solo on guitar, Cheick Hamala *and* Adama on *ngoni*s, Seydou Diabaté on *tama*, and me on bass. We were six. First they cut Seydou, then Adama, then me. But it was *me* who arranged all the visas in Abidjan. They could never have done it without me." Barou had demanded a contract and a guarantee of reasonable pay. "I told Solo and Djelimady, 'I am the head of a family. I can't go along just to *discover* Canada. No. I need to know what the terms are going to be.' I suspected that they were going to leave me. The tour was not well planned. Life is expensive in Canada. How could there be enough money for everybody? But they needed me to arrange things right up to the last minute. So they didn't tell me what they were thinking. I even went to Solo and said, 'Everyone in Lafiabougou thinks I'm going to Canada. If I don't go, they're going to think I'm just a talker. My reputation is at stake.'

"'No, no,' Solo said, 'You're coming. Don't worry.' Then, on the night before they were to leave, they called me to the house and told me. 'We're sorry. There isn't enough money. We can't give you a contract. We can't bring you.' Djelimady offered me 100,000 CFA as thanks for my help. At first I refused it, but Djelimady came to me later and put the 100,000 CFA in my pocket. He wouldn't take it back."

Barou said that despite what we had heard in Solo's telephoned reports, nothing had been organized in Canada. The tour had been a disaster.

"But Barou," I broke in. "Then how did they come back with all these things?"

"They were lucky," he replied. "They met Babani Sissoko there."

Babani Sissoko. There was that name again. I kept hearing it invoked like some ethereal force that hovered over the affairs of men somewhere between the president of the Republic and Allah himself. Babani Sissoko. His mere mention raised eyebrows and quieted listeners. Babani was the miracle man. The money man. The instant he entered a story, fortunes changed, and the impossible became possible.

"Solo and Yayi found Babani in America," said Barou, "and he gave them money for everything."

Babani stories always seemed to end this way, with a breathtaking stroke of the man's transforming generosity. Babani was a Malian, but he apparently lived abroad and hadn't actually been to Bamako for some years. His doings had never much concerned me before, but now I was getting interested.

"Who is this guy?" I asked Barou.

"You know Douga?" asked Barou, "Djelimady's best friend?"

"Sure," I said.

"That's Babani's younger brother. Same mother, same father."

Now I began to understand. The first time I had ever heard of Babani was when Salif Keita's father had died and we had driven to Joliba to pay respects. The following day, I had been away from the Tounkara compound when Douga had arrived with 1 million CFA in cash, a gift from Babani to Salif's family on the occasion of the patriarch's death. Salif had once recorded a song about Babani, and the money was a kind of acknowledgment for that. The moment Babani's gift arrived, Douga and Djelimady had hopped in the car and headed back to Joliba. They had arrived at the height of a hunter's wake for the fallen chief.

"Oh, Banning," Djelimady had tormented me afterwards. "You should have been there. All the hunters in their *bogolon* danced around fires. Salif danced with the hunters. He had tears rolling down his face. My God, it was beautiful."

This missed opportunity had been so painful to learn about that I had barely stopped to consider Babani's role in the story. Babani's gift to the Keita family had seemed large, but understandably so. Salif was Mali's greatest singing star, and his father, Sina Keita, was the village chief who had learned to accept his son's musical calling even though it violated tradition. The two men were icons of Mali's modern age. At these mythic heights, the ordinary merges with the miraculous. Why couldn't a Malian magnate honor the Keitas with a conspicuous gift on hearing of Sina's death?

"But Barou," I asked, "why would Babani help Solo and Yayi?"

"He is one of the wealthiest Malians," said Barou. "I mean *really* wealthy. And he loves to give things to musicians, especially to griots. He once gave Kandia Kouyaté an airplane so she could fly to his village and entertain him. When Solo and Yayi found out that Babani was in Washington, they rushed to his house and played for him immediately. He gave them money and that's how they came home with all this stuff.

"Anyway, it's over now," said Barou. "I'm glad I didn't go to Canada with them. And now I don't want anything to do with Solo and Yayi. Have you noticed something? Solo cannot look me directly in the face. When he shakes my hand, he looks down at the ground. Have you noticed that?" We hadn't. "I don't like the people in Djelimady's family," declared Barou. "They are not honest. Djelimady is the only one. The rest. I don't like them." Barou added bitterly that even Djelimady wasn't calling him to play gigs with his keyboard anymore. "Now he calls little Sambry with his push-button drums instead. If that's what he wants, okay. I'll leave it."

Then Barou asked, "By the way, how much did Solo pay you for the wedding you played?"

We told him. He smiled. "Every time I ever played with Solo and Yayi, there were fights about money. *Big* fights. Solo thought that as the husband of Yayi, he deserved an equal share, and they would argue about this after every gig. Next time you play," said Barou, "try asking Solo to add just a little more. You'll find that at the next wedding, he'll say, 'We don't need you this time.'"

One evening Dirck and I found ourselves eating dinner with Moussa Kouyaté, the family griot. We asked him if he had interceded in the matter of Barou and the North American tour. He said he had. Moussa told us that when the matter had arisen, he had listened to both sides. As griot, Moussa served as a kind of judge in the family, and in this case he had judged Barou to be wrong. "He demanded a contract," Moussa told us. "But how can you give a contract? It was Yayi's first tour. They didn't know what they would find, how well they would do, what would happen. How could they give a guarantee in advance? Barou should have understood that if you want to go to America, it is a risk. He did not want to take the risk. So he did not go." Moussa brushed off the matter of Barou's efforts to secure passports and visas. He had been compensated. He had no complaint.

Dirck and I continued to play street parties with Solo and Yayi, and we did not take Barou up on his challenge by asking Solo for a raise. Barou's story was unsettling, but I also felt grateful to Solo for breaking us into the street party circuit; Djelimady had never asked us to play at these events before. The truth was, I liked Solo. Like Madou, he was solicitous of my needs and loved to chat. His smile had an unctuous quality about it, quite different from Djelimady's, which always seemed sincere even when he used it to manipulate. Solo was an operator, but it was hard to see him as mean or heartless.

On the night Solo and Yayi's public address system arrived from the airport, I took the opportunity to probe Solo on the subject of his earnings during the tour. Even if I had not heard Barou's account, the facts raised obvious questions, so I asked them. "You can't have bought all these things with money from concerts," I said casually. "You must have had friends over there, right?"

"We had good luck. Yes," Solo allowed. He then showed me the business card of one Dr. Ibrahima M. Fofanah, senior executive officer for public affairs, HRH Prince Mohammed Faisal El Saud. Fofanah was the man who had placed the $100 bill before Yayi in the Kilimanjaro Club video. Solo told me that Fofanah had given them $1,600 during the show and another $1,000 later. "Then we also met Babani Sissoko," said Solo, as matter-of-factly as he could. Solo quietly confirmed Barou's story: Babani had given them $10,000.

As soon as Solo and Yayi settled back into the Tounkara compound, they began talking to me about making a recording. Yayi spoke first. She came to me one morning at breakfast and bossily announced that I was to bring my recording gear and make a recording of her singing. Yayi's French was minimal, like that of many female vocal stars I met in Bamako, and her simple language added bite to her brusque manner. "Tomorrow," she snapped after giving these instructions. "Okay?"

But nothing happened. The Rail Band rehearsal went on as usual. The next night, Yayi repeated her demand, but again nobody—other than me with my gear—seemed to pay any attention. After a week of this, Solo explained things to me. Now that Yayi had returned from America, he told me, she needed to record a song to perform on television as a way of announcing to the public that she was back on the scene. She needed to do her song on the most widely viewed music program on Malian television, Top Etoiles.

Every Friday night at around 10:00, all Bamakois within range of a television watch Top Etoiles. If you walk through any Bamako neighborhood during that hour, you can hear it playing in courtyards and houses. Televisions are often moved out to the street and set on chairs so that large audiences can gather in front of them. I sometimes caught the show in snatches as I drove or walked through town, passing television after television tuned in to ORTM.

For a foreigner, the Top Etoiles format takes some getting used to. During an hour, some twelve or thirteen artists perform one song each. The show's MC, a tall, smooth-talking fellow named Adama Koité, introduces each artist. Koité always has a special guest whom he interviews in brief segments throughout the show. That artist gets to do two songs, one near the beginning of the show and then a big closing number. When Top Etoiles began in 1992, the producers tried to have groups play live on the air. But the task of recording so many groups, often with faulty or inadequate equipment, proved arduous, and they soon went to a "playback" format. Each artist had to come to the show's taping with an audio cassette of his or her song. Then, before a live audience, the song would play over loudspeakers and the artist would make an entrance and then lip-sync and sometimes dance to the playback. If an artist had enough money to produce a complete video, Top Etoiles would accept that instead.

MTV it was not, but Top Etoiles had the power to boost careers and to end them. It provided the perfect venue for Yayi's return to the

Bamako public stage. And no old song would do—not after six months in America. Yayi needed something new for her public, and this was the recording I was to make for her. We began seeing a television promo for Top Etoiles that ran during the evening news. The promo touted "the return of Yayi Kanouté after her six-month tour of Canada." It showed an archival clip of Yayi dressed like a Fulani bride, with colorful baubles in her hair, huge gold-plate earrings, a pleated dress like a seven-layer cake, and a grin cutting deep into the powdered hills of her cheeks.

That Saturday, after dinner, we went to work. We set up in Solo and Yayi's living room at the back of the compound, the same room where I had recorded them during my first visit and where I had recorded Ina Tounkara's praise cassette. Yayi's song was a reggae arrangement of the *jeli* standard "Kedo." It was a good idea, but the recording we made that evening was a failure. I had persuaded them not to use the drum machine, a small triumph, but when we heard the tape back on speakers the following day, Yayi's lead vocal—the most important element—sounded weak. We would have to try again.

The following Monday morning, Dirck and I arrived at the compound to find Yayi fully in charge. We were going to the Rail Band practice room at the Buffet to record the song with real drums and backup singers. Djelimady rushed ahead to alert the Rail Band musicians. Dirck got lured into a fooz-ball game with the children. When it came time to go, he was busy washing grease from the metal handles off his hand. Yayi snapped at him mercilessly, "Dirck, you're making us late!" Simmering with irritation, Dirck joined Yayi, Djelimady's daughter Tareta, Ina Tounkara, and me in a crowded taxi destined for the Buffet. Near the Lafiabougou terminus, Yayi spotted Seydou, the talking drum player, by the roadside. "Seydou!" she bellowed from the taxi window. We pulled up next to the percussionist and Yayi thrust a 500 CFA note into his hand and commanded him to get his *tama* and go to the Buffet immediately.

At the Buffet, the Rail Band went along with the plan. I played producer, positioning musicians and amplifiers around my stereo microphone, running sound checks, listening back, and then repositioning people to get the right balance. When it came time to record, Seydou had not appeared. Durango's congas would have to do. The recording we made in the Rail Band practice room sounded more normal than our first effort, more like a band, thanks to the addition of real drums and bass. The unmistakable concrete room echo gave the track a garage band quality. To my ears, it did not sound good enough to play on television, especially for Yayi's grand return, but everyone else seemed happy with it.

That night, Barou told me that a very pleased Seydou had arrived at his house that morning to announce that he had eaten a fine breakfast on Yayi Kanouté.

The next day, Yayi dressed in pearly hues and lace for the videotaping of Top Etoiles. Both of the Tounkara cars and two taxis filled up with Tounkara women as well as Solo, Sambry, Dirck, and me. The entourage made its way across the river to the Hotel Colibri, a club and restaurant in Badalabougou, just across the Niger River from downtown Bamako. Sambry, Dirck, and I were the last to arrive, and failing to talk our way past the ticket collector, we summoned Solo, who hesitantly reached into his pocket to pay the cover for Dirck, me, and a somewhat indignant woman who glared at him like a jilted lover. I paid for Sambry and we entered the open-air pavilion where an audience of 250 or so sat in an arc around a round dance floor with a shallow stage behind it.

Professional Betamax cameras, bright halogen lights, an elegant public, and the smooth MC delivery of Top Etoiles host Adama Koité did little to disguise the shoddiness of the production. Adama and his special guest, Malian reggae star Oumar Koita, sat at a plastic table before the stage. First they struggled with malfunctioning wireless microphones, but giving up on that they switched to a single microphone that they passed between them during the interview segments. Oumar's big entrance was compromised as he had to wrestle the microphone cord free of a chair leg. They did not re-shoot the scene.

As the show taped, artist after artist took the stage, faking through performances of their chosen songs. I tried to imagine the settings under which the other songs had been recorded. Some sounded decidedly more professional than ours. Others sounded worse. Virtually all of them had programmed drumming, which gave them a phony veneer that marred good singing. Oumar Koita's reggae opener won him polite applause from the 80 percent female audience, which resembled the crowd at a large wedding or baptism party. Some stars brought their backup singers on stage, adding visual flare to their segments. Habib Koite brought his whole band before the cameras. They danced together, performed convincing mock performances on guitar, *tama* and *balafon*. This group had plainly learned a lot about showmanship during their tours in Europe.

Then Benogo Diakité, a master of the small hunter's harp or *kamalé ngoni*, did a Wassoulou number, undistinguished except for the astounding rubber-kneed dancing by a ten-year-old boy clad in hunter's *bogolon*.

At last Yayi stepped into the spotlight. Her pearly outfit had just been a teaser for the live audience, because by the time she went on camera she had changed into a New York cowgirl look, complete with a full-length, fake leopard skin coat, rhinestone-studded black cowboy hat, leather boots, glitter, and red eyebrows arching across her shiny, shea-buttered forehead. Our reggae recording seemed to sell. The garage band ambiance made a refreshing change from thin-sounding drum machine songs, and its contrast with Yayi's presentation was bizarre enough to be genuinely entertaining. Flanked by Tareta and Ina Tounkara, Yayi mouthed her way through the song, and during Djelimady's guitar break she fetched Solo from the audience. Dressed in black with a cowboy hat of his own, he completed the picture of the returning "Americans." The Tounkara women in the audience leapt from their seats applauding and shouting and successfully attracting the roving television cameras.

At the end of the program, Oumar Koita performed a moody rap song on the subject of AIDS. In basso profundo, Oumar chanted over and over the song's catchy English-language refrain: *"What you gonna do? What you gonna do to stop AIDS?"* Most of the artists returned to the stage to dance in this peculiar finale. As Sambry, Dirck, and I slipped away early to avoid a crush at the *bashée* stand, I saw Habib and Yayi arm in arm seeming to chant along with Oumar. I wondered if Yayi knew what she was saying. As we headed for the main road, we saw people outside who had climbed into the trees around the club to peer over its ten-foot walls.

The program aired that Friday. Ironically, we couldn't watch it because that was the night that Djelimady and Douga Sissoko had rescheduled the fund-raiser for the regional bank of Kayes. This time, with heavy television promotion, the show went on at the Palais de la Culture, and unlike the first, pre-Christmas attempt at the small stadium, this event drew an audience. The television spots promised a mega-concert with twenty-four *jelimusow*. Unlike many of Bamako's over-hyped spectacles, where you might expect half of the advertised artists actually to appear at the show, all twenty-four singers made it to the performance. They clustered in the shadowy right wing of the Palais's enormous stage, regally dressed, each one waiting her turn to sing just a single song.

Solo had invited Dirck and me to join in Yayi's first public performance, to play her reggae version of "Kedo" at the Palais de la Culture. The show began around 10:00 P.M. with *jelimuso* Backo Dagnon singing a slow, incendiary "Sunjata." Her performance came off with operatic grandeur and set a high standard that each successive singer would strive to match or exceed. All the *jelimusow* used the same opening gambit, and since each sang only one song, the routine was repeated again and again throughout the night. The singer would wait for the music to set the mood before revealing herself. She would start singing offstage through a cordless microphone. Then, on the second or third line of the song, she would march into the spotlight with sweeping steps, as if propelled by a higher force. Occasionally this device achieved the desired effect of producing a surge of support from the audience. But its predictability carried risks. If the audience sat silently during the entrance, the singer could look absurdly self-important.

Songs dragged on and the waiting cadre of *jelimusow* became restless. Audience enthusiasm waned audibly as the parade of griots continued. Dirck and I sat with Ina, Tareta, and Yayi near the back of the wing area, almost into the last row of curtains, where we could smell the sharp odor of urine wafting in from the dank, filthy artists' toilets and mingling with the *jelimusow*'s perfume. Fighting off sleep, I made frequent tours around the periphery of the Palais. During one, I caught the end of Top Etoiles, which was then airing on a black-and-white TV behind one of the concession stands in the lobby. It was the final number, and all the artists were onstage, dancing to Oumar Koita's AIDS song in brighter-than-life light. On television, that sleepy restaurant looked like a modern TV studio.

Meanwhile, backstage, Yayi seethed with impatience. Fifteen *jelimusow* had performed, it was well past midnight, and Yayi was ready to sing. She summoned Douga. Then she sent for the evening's MC, an older gentleman in white *boubou* and professorial glasses. Each man received a hissy tongue lashing from Yayi, but neither gave ground, insisting that she wait her turn. Yayi's celebrity was working against her. Fresh from America, she was *the* attraction. The promoters feared that once she sang, people would leave. They were saving her. Yayi's mood lifted briefly when Ina Tounkara sang. She clapped in big, slow griot claps—lots of arm work, not much sound—while Ina sang with another woman who was dressed and made up to look exactly like her. This fashion twin seemed to be part of Ina's developing stage act. As the audience applauded and, once again, Yayi was not called, her mood sank anew, and the vigil continued.

The best singers left the spotlight clutching fistfuls of bills donated by their fans in the audience. I saw at least one resist as Douga came to collect the money—after all, this was a benefit. The woman's fist maintained a tight grip around the notes as Douga pleaded with her and worked to pry her fingers loose.

Yayi sang sometime after 1:30 A.M., nearly four hours into the spectacle. Fotigui Kouyaté, the Rail Band bassist who had played on the Top Etoiles recording, manned the drums. Solo, Djelimady, and I all played guitars, and Dirck played keyboard. Sayan Sissoko joined in on ngoni, along with a *tama* and a *doundoun* player and a guy tapping on an electronic drum, even though none of these extras had rehearsed the song. The chaotic griot reggae that resulted did have a certain charm, especially with Sayan doing his customary wriggling, twitching dance and Djelimady prancing forth for solos. At one point, Solo plugged my guitar cord into his effects pedal so I could step forward on the enormous stage to take an unrehearsed solo of my own. The crowd, now directly before me, emanated approval. Yayi belted and beamed while Ina and Tareta swayed on either side of her. After all the waiting and despite the thrown-together band, the song played well.

I rode home in the newly painted red Honda with Solo and Yayi. Solo did his best to maintain good humor, savoring the triumphant mood. Yayi was fuming, not about having played her song with a ragtag team of unrehearsed jammers but about being held until the end. Apparently she blamed Solo for this. At last he ventured a few mild words in defense of the strategy, and instantly they were fighting angrily in Bambara, just as Barou had told me they did after every gig. Solo switched on the radio, then in the midst of a Voice of America news report. The refreshing chatter of American news anchors mingled with Yayi's bickering and Solo's soothing murmurs. The diva of the Tounkara compound was home. Life in the family would now be sweet again.

8

Faith in Shadows

Allah ma ko kelen da: **God has not created only one thing.**

(A favorite refrain of the *jelis*)

Within days of Yayi Kanouté's return to the Bamako stage, the fast of Ramadan began. For a month, practicing Muslims would forgo all food and drink from the first light of morning until sunset. Though I knew that Ramadan would interrupt musical activities, I had awaited it with curiosity, hoping it might reveal more about the spirituality of the city and people around me. Bamako's religious life had mostly eluded me. I had heard the *muezzins'* calls. I had witnessed the spectacle of midday prayer on Friday, when whole streets in the downtown area filled with supplicants dropping to their knees in unison. I had learned to speak familiar blessings. "May Allah bring you good health." "May Allah awake you on a good day." But behind these routine displays, there was an emptiness, a sense that important things remained hidden.

In the Tounkara compound, no one, aside from the two old women, ever went to the mosque or prayed with any regularity. Djelimady's eldest daughter, Bintouba, had married in a religious ceremony in December, but the ritual had mystified me. Djelimady and a few other men had stayed home. Everyone else had walked to the mosque at the Lafiabougou terminus to pray. Bintouba's new husband had not attended the ceremony or even the party afterwards.

121

"That's the tradition at a religious wedding," Moussa, the family griot, had told me. A "religious wedding," as opposed to a "civil wedding," produces no official documents. If the husband dies and his family refuses to support the wife, she has no recourse in the courts. In the religious ceremony, the bride's uncle, not her father, oversees the marriage, and the groom stays home while his friends and family celebrate. Was this the prophet Mohammed's Islam, or was it an African innovation? Was the choice of a religious wedding simply a way to skirt civil laws, as some suggested, or did it have spiritual significance?

West Africa, it seems, has adapted Islam broadly but not deeply, especially in the southern interior, away from the coasts and the Arab lands to the north. The traditional Muslim cleric, who preserves and teaches the religion's doctrines, has become the African *marabout*, a sage who can combine Islamic learning with the magical powers of a medicine man from the old animist religion. But whenever I asked what exactly *marabout*s could and could not do, I got muddled answers.

Djelimady spoke about the spread of Islam through Africa as though it were a sporting event. He would rattle off statistics reporting the increasing dominance of Islam throughout the region. Eighty percent in this country. Ninety percent in that one. Djelimady was proud to call himself an African, a Malian, a Manding, and a Muslim, but it was hard to connect any part of that pride to the beliefs and practices of Islam.

Djelimady had a favorite rhetorical question, a kind of gauntlet he liked to throw down to the West. "I can never understand," he would say, "how Western countries who have everything, who are superior to us materially, technologically, intellectually, politically, and even morally, can kill their own people the way the Nazis did or the way they are doing in Bosnia. Here in Africa, we have Liberia, Somalia, and Rwanda. These are disasters. No question. But at least you can understand them. The people in these places have *nothing*. In Liberia, they barely even have a culture. They know only pressure. They think they have nothing to lose, so they go mad and slaughter one another. But in Europe, people have all the advantages. How can they throw that away?"

Implicit in this question was the assumption that nothing like this could happen in Mali, and that Islam was at least part of the reason. "Here in Mali," Djelimady liked to say, "we have tolerance. If there's a fight between two families, or an accident where someone is killed, the families come together. They sit, they make tea, they discuss. And then they let it go. That's tolerance. Even if someone has died, Muslims take it as God's will. Nobody has to be blamed. We don't need to have a lawsuit. That is our strength here in Mali. We tolerate. We go on. We do not hold on to bitterness from the past."

Djelimady told me that many years earlier he had been driving through Bamako when a little girl had run out from between two parked cars into his path. His car had struck the girl and injured her severely. "I offered to pay her hospital bills," he told me, "but the girl's father said, 'Djelimady, we've known you for many years. We've come often to the Buffet to hear you play. You are a good Muslim. The child ran in front of you and there was nothing you could do. It was God's will. We cannot accept your money.'"

Djelimady's claim to a culture of forgiveness fascinated me, but I wondered how much it had to do with Islam. For me, the bond between Muslims in Bamako felt more like a fraternity than a faith or philosophy.

On the first morning of Ramadan, I asked Djelimady if he would be fasting. "No," he said with a pained face. "I can't do that. My stomach is too fragile. The doctor says I shouldn't." Djelimady told me that he had worked hard in the past year. He had taken the Rail Band to Europe and they had made an ambitious recording. He had also toured abroad separately with the smaller Bajourou group, and after returning to Bamako, he had worked all sorts of concerts and street parties that he would normally have refused. He had done this because Solo and Yayi had not been there to contribute to family expenses. Now the Rail Band was well on its way to having enough material for the next record, Solo and Yayi had returned, and for Djelimady, Ramadan would serve as a well-deserved vacation.

"A lot of people develop stomach problems during Ramadan," said Barou. "Especially musicians." Barou estimated that no more than 20 percent of the people in Bamako actually observed the daylight fast. "There are people who fast at home, and then they go into town and gorge themselves at a restaurant. At night when they are allowed to break the fast, they come home and pretend they haven't eaten all day."

"Who do they think they're fooling?" I asked.

"They think they're fooling God," said Barou, laughing at the idea. Barou told me he planned to give up alcohol for the month. A strict Muslim would not drink alcohol in the first place, but Barou made no pretense of being devout, and he had a rationale. The idea of Ramadan, he said, was to experience desires but not to act upon them.

As I circulated among the musicians, I heard about a variety of ailments that prevented individuals from observing the fast. Many felt compelled to offer some excuse. Others, like Yayi Kanouté and Solo and Adama Tounkara, made no pretense of honoring the fast. Adama in particular felt that Ramadan posed an unfair obstacle to musicians. "Other people can work," he complained. "Why not us?"

Adama was finding it difficult to provide for his twin sons. He tended to skulk around, hangdog more often than not, complaining about all the obstacles his fiancée's family threw in his path. Now he had to sit and do nothing for a month. As my life had grown busier, I had had less time to linger at my house playing music with the neighborhood *jelis*, and Adama seemed to take it personally. He rarely offered music lessons anymore, and his greetings now led directly to requests for money. "It's Ramadan, my friend," he would drone, lifting his moony eyes at me. "I haven't eaten since last night. I don't even have money for cigarettes. Why don't you give me 500 CFA?" Once I had been his "best friend." Now we had come to this.

The *jelis* suffered during Ramadan, for the daytime street parties they relied upon really did grind to a halt. Bar musicians, on the other hand, proceeded apace. Dirck and I made a few excursions to Ma Kele Kele, where we found the pigs mingling among the patrons and the Rail Band sidemen sitting in with Lobi Traoré before healthy crowds. Dounanke Koita had recently asked Barou to play keyboards in his group, and they were working little bars every weekend. "Under Moussa Traoré, it wasn't like this," said Barou. "You couldn't buy a beer anywhere during Ramadan. Even restaurants were closed." Perhaps Djelimady was right in claiming that Mali's Muslim population had risen to over 80 percent, but in the capital, the religion's hold on people's lives was declining in the era of democracy.

With the Rail Band on vacation and Djelimady in repose, I took up an offer to work with Toumani Diabaté, master of the twenty-one-string harp/lute, the *kora*. Just thirty years old, Toumani had already traveled the world playing solo *kora* concerts, a form unprecedented in Manding music. He had made his first record in England in 1988 and began releasing his music in Mali only after he had achieved recognition abroad. Toumani had further surprised Malians by making two records with a "new flamenco" group, Ketama, and another with an orchestra of Japanese musicians. Toumani was a product of tradition, but he had chosen a maverick path.

I first met Toumani in 1991 when he performed at the New Orleans Jazz and Heritage Festival. Short and slim but muscular, and blessed with a slyly attractive smile, Toumani requires a crutch in order to walk; one of his legs has been atrophied from the knee down ever since a bout of polio he suffered as a child. I remember him making his way through revelers in the narrow New Orleans streets, lingering outside zydeco dance bars to listen, then leaning on his crutch and swooping ahead in his blue *boubou* while his Belgian manager hovered.

Toumani descends from seventy generations of *kora* players, a line that leads back to the musical city of Kita and before that to Guinea Bissau, where Toumani says the *kora* was invented. Toumani's father, Sidiki Diabaté, was born in the Gambia, where *kora*—not *ngoni* or *balafon*—dominates Manding court music. Shortly before Mali achieved independence in 1959, Sidiki came to Bamako and pioneered the development of Mali's own *kora* tradition. The *ngoni* remains the indispensable accompaniment for *jeli* singers in Mali, but thanks to Sidiki and his contemporaries Batourou Sekou Kouyaté and Djelimady Sissoko, the *kora* is now well established among Malian griots. By the time I returned to Bamako to study, Toumani had inherited his father's mantle of cultural importance. He enjoyed a complex identity as a jewel of *jeliya*, a musical renegade, and a handsome Casanova.

On the musical side, Toumani rarely played street parties or appeared on television, and he avoided Bamako's mega-concert cattle shows. He arranged his own contracts for the most part. A downtown Lebanese-owned pizzeria and a restaurant called Fast Food were regular haunts. Toumani played solo concerts on request, but most in demand was his all-instrumental Manding super-trio with Basekou Kouyaté, the young *ngoni* wizard from Segu, and Keletigui Diabaté, grand old man of the Manding *balafon*. Bamako's music press regaled Toumani's trio as trail-blazers in griot music. Toumani's musical forays may have upset traditionalists—including, at first, his own father—but they had seduced the critics, perhaps dangerously so.

When the trio performed at the French Cultural Center early in my Bamako stay, radio and television commentators joined the public in over-the-top praise. The act of breaking *jeli* tradition by eliminating the singer and moving the improvisation in a jazz direction was so revolutionary that few could really evaluate the music. Any clever feint—like Basekou's penchant for quoting the flute call from the American Western "The Good, the Bad, and the Ugly"—seemed like genius, no matter how often repeated. I felt that the trio's performances and its one recording lacked intensity and sounded as though the musicians were still playing for diners at a restaurant. I knew they were capable of more. But in the face of such adulation, what would inspire them to reach for it?

Toumani exemplified the difficulties of keeping up a band in Bamako, especially a griot band. His partners in the trio were forever being offered other work, and they required substantial pay for their presence. So, on the side, Toumani had put together a loose-knit cadre of musicians he called the Symmetric Orchestra, a name borrowed from Toumani's Japanese project. The group included two guitarists, a bass player and drummer, various percussionists and singers, Toumani's brother Ladji as a stand-in on *kora*, and, whenever possible, his two partners from the instrumental trio. Unfortunately, none of the regular players in the Symmetric Orchestra was in the same league with Toumani, Basekou, and Keletigui. In trying to maintain both groups, Toumani found himself squeezed. He wanted to help the young players in his band, but when high-paying work came along—a foreign tour or a showcase performance at the French Cultural Center—it went to the trio. The players in the Symmetric Orchestra complained that Toumani always let them down when it counted. Meanwhile, powerful people kept whispering in his ear, urging him to abandon the Symmetric Orchestra altogether in favor of the trio. Toumani tried to please everyone, but it was an impossible task.

Early in my stay, Toumani invited me to visit him at his nighttime hangout, a place he called *"le grin."* A mere lean-to hut in the middle of a construction site alongside Rue Kasse Keita, *le grin* symbolized another of Toumani's idealistic ambitions. He planned to build a music school on the site, and when he arranged for students to meet him there for daytime lessons, he referred to it as "the *Kora* Center." At night, though, *le grin* became Toumani's court, the place where he received visitors, much as Djelimady did at the Buffet Hotel during Rail Band rehearsals.

Barou led me to *le grin* one night. He was nervous. "The police watch this place," he told me as we threaded our way through dried mud alleys. "They know people smoke marijuana there. It's dangerous."

We found Toumani with his *kora* and a few friends, chatting in the light of a full moon. "Hey man," he said. "You finally came. I don't believe it."

Toumani had learned English during his travels. Sometimes he peppered his talk with the sort of crude speech that American or European musicians might use among themselves but that no respectable Malian would utter publicly. Toumani's easy language, his need to experiment musically, and his candid demeanor all gave the impression that he understood Western ways better than the people around him did. That assumption had proved treacherous for Toumani's foreign representatives. More than once, when all the arrangements for a tour had been made, Toumani had failed to get on an airplane at the appointed time. It was hard to say whether he understood the havoc he created by not arriving to play well-promoted concerts. His own reasoning remained obscure, shrouded in sometimes illogical explanations. Toumani had angered many with these gambits, but in time they always seemed to forgive him and try again. After all, nobody plays the *kora* the way Toumani does.

We sat and talked for an hour or so at *le grin* that night, and eventually Toumani reached for his *kora* and began to play. The first thing that struck me was the sound of his instrument. The low notes seemed to bubble up from beneath the earth, and the high ones floated above, warm and crystalline, nothing like the edgy sound that shocked the airwaves when Toumani plugged into an amplifier to play with a group. A *kora* player uses four fingers to pluck at two facing planes of nylon strings. In Toumani's case, each finger makes a voice, distinct and eloquent. As he went along, he added complexity, developing internal rhythms, counter-themes, greater and greater density. The flow of ideas veered steadily toward a resolution that came some twenty minutes later. Toumani played his *kora* in the moonlight as grandly as Keith Jarrett embarked on one of his solo piano improvisations in a European concert hall.

I badly wanted to work with Toumani, but events always seemed to conspire against it. On weekdays, the Symmetric Orchestra practiced in the morning, in direct conflict with Rail Band rehearsals. And whenever I visited Toumani at his home on the weekend, we spent the time eating his wife's cooking and listening to CDs on his stereo. Talking and exchanging ideas seemed to come first, music later.

In addition, Toumani was undergoing personal changes during my stay in Bamako. He was distancing himself from the rowdy lifestyle of the musicians in the Symmetric Orchestra and dedicating himself more seriously to Islam, especially to its intellectual tradition. He was studying Arabic with an instructor and spent hours in prayer. When I arrived to visit, I would wait in his sitting room with its hanging tapestries and French-style armoires full of porcelain knickknacks. I would sit on a colorful leather hassock until Toumani completed his lesson or his prayers.

It was hard to reconcile this man of devotion with the roguish fellow I had met in New Orleans years earlier. Toumani was a puzzle, its pieces still falling into place.

My musical opportunity came when I learned that the Symmetric Orchestra would continue to work during Ramadan. Dirck and I told Toumani we were free for the month, and he encouraged us to come and work with the group.

Nine months pregnant, Toumani's wife Fanta Sacko swept into the Diabaté compound practice room with a mission. She wore a lavender gown, and the aroma of flowery perfume embraced her. Fanta glared at the bony girl singing in the session, and the girl gazed back with doe-eyed helplessness. Fanta had sung *jeliya* since childhood but had put her career on hold to bear Toumani's children, yet another departure from tradition, in which, normally, *jeli* husbands manage and play instrumental accompaniment for their singing star wives. I could not understand a word of Fanta's Bambara, but I sensed she was telling the singer to assert herself. "Sing it like you mean it, girl!" I imagined Fanta to say. "You're supposed to be regaling kings, for God's sake. You sound like a chorus girl."

The Symmetric Orchestra's project for the month of Ramadan was to record a demo for this young singer, whose name was Kanjoura Camara. Camara, as everyone called her, sang well enough, though she lacked the *jelimuso*'s self-possession. To my ears, her voice sounded thin, and I wondered how she had earned the right to work with the Symmetric Orchestra. Whatever the explanation, such largesse could not be refused, and now Camara had to endure the vagaries of Toumani's world.

For the first couple of days, Toumani never entered the practice room. He left us to work on our own, and in a chaotic way we began to arrange and practice three or four songs. When Toumani did arrive and plug in his *kora*, the work became focused. Toumani liked to arrange songs with frequent transitions, requiring all the players to come together on a short phrase or melody. His ideas were demanding and reflected his personal sense of phrasing. Perfect execution required that every player catch every cue and respond correctly. Since nothing was written, this called for good memories. It taxed the abilities of everyone there, and Toumani ran the material over and over, hoping for mastery that never quite materialized.

Near the end of the second week of our Ramadan rehearsals, Toumani announced the first recording session. We would go to the French Cultural Center the following Saturday and record three songs. The session went poorly. Keletigui and Basekou—stars of the super-trio—arrived to record, but since they had not rehearsed the songs, they had to be coached on detailed arrangements. The oldest musician there, Keletigui was observing the holy fast and was cranky about everything. Also fasting, the drummer had a hard time keeping tempos up to speed. Christian, the French engineer, labored to get sound for the large group despite frequent prayer breaks. All the sound went through the house system and into my digital tape recorder; there would be no chance to remix or fix errors. Predictably, the result disappointed Toumani, and everyone left feeling dejected.

Over that weekend, Fanta gave birth to a son, her third child by Toumani, and that night Dirck and I turned up at the bass player Djiby's house for a celebration. We found most of the Symmetric Orchestra there—though not Toumani—drunk on little airline bottles of Scotch whiskey and English gin.

When we turned up at the Diabaté compound on Monday morning, the mood had changed. Kanjoura Camara's father had died, and she would not be coming to practice. The band made an attempt at rehearsing but soon broke up and headed home. I found Toumani in his bedroom.

"I am not happy," he said woefully. "What should I do? These guys don't want to work. I play my *kora* for two hours every day. Every day. Why can't they do that with their instruments?" We spoke for a while, and eventually Toumani came to the point. "I'm calling off the rehearsals," he said. "When they're ready to be serious, we can start again."

At the time, it seemed like a moment of truth. But later, when I had moved on to other things, the Symmetric Orchestra reconvened and recorded an imperfect demo tape for the singer Camara. The group went back to their regular gigs at the pizzeria and Fast Food. A couple of months later, the French Cultural Center arranged a Central African tour for the trio, angering the Symmetric Orchestra players who would be left behind. But their anger was for naught in the end. Mysteriously, Toumani didn't make the plane, and the tour was canceled.

During Ramadan, dinner at the Tounkara compound took on added drama. For observers of the fast—including Djelimady's wife Adama Kouyaté, his half brother Yéyé, and the two old women—the moment after sunset, when eating was allowed, came like rain after a drought. In the fading light of evening, Djelimady's wife sat back in her spot by the doorway, faint with hunger, her spiked hair pressing against the

back of her chair. Before her, a fourteen-year-old girl fidgeted with a
baby, bouncing her, snuggling and whispering to her. Behind them,
three women attended to the fires while Djelimady's mother squatted
before a metal bowl and splashed water over her face. Over by the well,
Djeneba, the servant girl, hauled water, while another girl pounded millet, occasionally releasing the pestle and clapping her hands together
quickly while it hung suspended in air above the wooden grinding bowl.
Madou and Solo sat in conversation on the verandah. I took my customary seat and watched the tide of children that swept in and out of
the main doorway from the street. When at last darkness fell, the fasters
ate first. Then the women served the non-fasters, first the men, then
the children, and finally the other women.

One night at dinner, I sat alone with Barou. Ramadan had inspired
so many discussions about Islam that I found myself wondering about
the spirituality that preceded it, about animism and the spirit world. I
knew that Barou feared people who commune with spirits, but he
seemed at least willing to discuss the subject, so I pressed him for information. Barou told me about a special kind of *marabout* called a *soma*.
These men work with fetishes and can perform powerful and dangerous magic. Worse still, said Barou, they encourage and play upon people's paranoia. If you come complaining about a mysterious pain, they
ask questions about your enemies, planting seeds of suspicion in people. Barou viewed these practices with respect and disapproval. He had
told me that both Adama Tounkara and Djelimady visited *soma*, but
that neither one would speak of it, not even with him. Barou said he
knew about this because he had seen the *marabout*'s fetishes hanging
behind the doors in their bedrooms.

Djelimady's teenage nephews, Sambry and Harouna Kouyaté, had
recounted with adolescent glee the sordid pleasures of magical
vengeance. Sambry once explained to me that if you want to kill an
enemy, you need only take a chicken and write the person's name on its
skin. Then tie the chicken up and place it on a nest of carnivorous ants.
When the chicken is dead, said Sambry, your enemy will be too.

All I could glean from my friends were scraps such as these. The
occult lives of the people around me proved still more elusive than their
ties to Islam. Long after returning from Bamako, I would discuss Islam
and animism with the Malian anthropologist Kassim Kone, and his com-
ments would prove more revealing. Kassim believes that the coming of
Islam boosted the power of the *jeli*s in Manding society. The two tradi-

tions fed off each other and that elevated the *jelis* above the blacksmiths, touted for their occult powers since the time of Sunjata. I told Kassim that I never saw evidence of animistic practices among my *jeli* friends.

"But they must have been using fetishes," Kassim replied. "Traditional medicine is strong among the *jelis*. Djelimady probably rubbed himself down with special oils and potions before going out. This is very common. It's true that they don't discuss it. But I can tell you that the most Islamic person in Mali is only 85 percent Islamic. The Muslim religion spread in West Africa because it did not take anything away from the traditional religion. It only substituted and added things. People may pray to Allah every day, but when they are in trouble, they go to a *soma*. People say that Islamic prayers are like perfume; God inhales them and wants to breath in all he can get. Traditional prayers are like shit; God takes one whiff and wants to deal with whatever is causing it immediately. When you are in trouble, you go to a *soma*."

Dirck left Bamako near the end of Ramadan. "Ah, Dirck," said Djelimady as we watched my friend disappear down an airport corridor with his banjo in hand. "Back at the house," said Madou Djan, "the old women are still talking about him."

The next morning I stopped by Barou's house on my way to the Tounkaras'. Soon his mother, a friendly woman of sixty, stepped through the doorway. Her slow movements and hunched bearing told me something was wrong. From beneath a white veil, she said, "Our friend is gone."

"I know," I said, a little surprised that she would take Dirck's leaving so hard. Their most memorable interaction had come when she had called Dirck "*toubabou*" and he had responded "*farafina*," meaning black African. Madame Diallo had dressed him down for the remark. As a Fulani from Burkina Faso, she considered herself Arab, *not farafina*.

"The son of my sister," said Barou's mother, shaking her head. I turned to Barou in puzzlement.

"Ouedraogo," he said softly. "He died this morning."

I had heard of many deaths in Bamako, but they had never been people I knew. Mamadou Ouedraogo, the tall singer and alto sax player in the Rail Band, had been a friend. We had played music and raised beers together at the Bar Bozo. He must have been about my age, around forty. Ouedraogo had not played with the Rail Band since mid-December, when he first checked into Gabriel Touré Hospital. No one had seemed to know how sick he was. Just after the start of Ramadan, Barou had gone to visit

Ouedraogo and had returned with the news that he was suffering from yellow fever and losing weight fast. Barou had shamed Djelimady into visiting his band-mate, and Djelimady had returned with a grim assessment. "Ouedraogo," he had said. "He waited too long to get help. He should have gone to the doctor sooner. Now, I don't know what they can do for him."

Later Barou would tell me that Ouedraogo had died of sclerosis of the liver, not yellow fever. But Djelimady would continue to blame yellow fever, claiming that Ouedraogo had mistakenly taken the treatment for malaria. "You must not drink or make love to a woman if you have yellow fever," Djelimady would assert with his usual confidence. "If you do, you die." There seemed no point in trying to sort out the discrepancies.

In Bamako, bodies are disposed of quickly, usually within twelve hours of death. That afternoon, musicians arrived at Ouedraogo's house near the Lafiabougou terminus for the interment. The entire Rail Band was there, along with Lobi Traoré, Dounanke Koita in an electric blue *boubou*, and his brothers with thin dreadlocks popping out from beneath white painter's hats. The Imam was among the last to arrive. He descended from a car in white robes, a maroon fez, and sunglasses. His disheveled attendant collected the Imam's shoes as he stepped onto a mat at the edge of the street. When the corpse arrived, people moved into the street and organized themselves into lines. An embroidered black blanket partially covered the body. After a short prayer, cars and motorbikes formed a procession to the cemetery, which looked up into the Wayanko pass where Samory had tormented the French. The sun, descending toward the mesas there, poured golden light over dry cliffs, cemetery walls, and a hastily assembling crowd.

Pallbearers carried Ouedraogo from a pickup truck to his grave, a shallow hole dug no more than three feet deep in the red, clay-like earth. Beyond the hole, for a long way, rows of earthen mounds marked fresh graves. Most of them did not have names on them, just sprigs of what looked like mango trees stuck into the dirt. The older, harder graves bore simple nameplates at their heads, and some of the sprigs had filled out into small trees.

The black blanket came away, and as Ouedraogo's body was placed in the ground I caught a glimpse of his legs, thin as doweling and wrapped in a white shroud. Djelimady joined the musicians and family members nearest the grave. Men took mud bricks and placed them in the hole to cover the body. Handfuls of wet clay followed, and then shovel loads of dirt. The mourners helped. I saw Barou handing off a shovel to Fotigui, the Rail Band bassist. Damory, the singer, stood atop the dirt pile and heaved earth onto his friend's body before passing the shovel to Djelimady. A cloud of dust rose, and behind it the pallbearers scrubbed their hands over buckets of water.

The crowd returned to the house to hear final words from the family griot, and the interment was over. As we walked away, I asked Barou, "What do Muslims believe happens to a person when he dies?"

Barou said, "Muslims believe that as soon as the people leave the cemetery, spirits descend on the grave with a thunderous noise and remove the dead man's spirit. They then ask the spirit, 'Who do you serve?' and if the person has been a good Muslim, he answers directly, 'I serve only Allah.' Then he goes to a very nice place, where he is never alone, and he and the other good spirits relax, discuss, and wait for the day of judgment. If the person gives a different answer, he is returned to the earth and then he is taken out again and returned to the earth, over and over, until judgment day."

Barou said that for Muslims, the final judgment was still some fourteen hundred years away. "That's a long time to spend waiting under the earth," I said.

"Yes," he agreed. "But if the judgment is bad, waiting under the earth is the good part." Barou chuckled, and I wondered whether he believed what he was telling me. I wondered what those mourners believed. It was dark as we walked toward the Tounkara compound, where the women were breaking fast for almost the last time. Ramadan was ending, but the old emptiness lingered. The spiritual life of Bamako remained hidden.

9

Mali's Favorite Son

The hero . . . is someone with special powers used to work against the stabilizing and conservative forces of his society; he is someone who, in pursuing his own destiny, affects the destinies of others. He is the agent of disequilibrium.

From The Mande Hero, Text and Context, by Charles S. Bird and Martha B. Kendall

Ramadan ended with festivity on February 20, but my life with Djelimady and the Tounkaras never returned to its earlier patterns. "The Rail Band is going to privatize now," my guitarist mentor told me one morning at breakfast. "As soon as we work out the terms, we won't rehearse and play at the Buffet anymore. We're talking to the French Cultural Center. Things are going to be better. You'll see." As word passed around town that the Rail Band was about to end its twenty-five-year partnership with the train station hotel, most people took the news as a death knell. Djelimady bristled at the suggestion that the Rail Band was through. People were just jealous, he insisted. Once the Rail Band shook off the last vestiges of its socialist past, the music would flower anew in the rich soil of Malian democracy.

Whatever the fate of the Rail Band, I knew I was entering a period of flux. A British record label had arranged to fly Djelimady to Cuba for ten days of recording. Djelimady had haggled over the terms but had eventually signed on. Cuban music was part of the Rail Band's roots, after all, and

134

in the early days of the Malian Republic, Fidel Castro had initiated cultural exchanges with Mali. Djelimady and the Rail Band had actually played in Havana years earlier, and this new recording was to be a homecoming of sorts. In addition, I was expecting a visit from Sean Barlow, the producer of Public Radio International's program *Afropop Worldwide*, coauthor of my first book, and my partner in earlier African travels. We would be traveling and recording sessions for the show—all further distractions from my work with Djelimady.

I did not foresee the event that would most significantly transform life among the Tounkaras. Babani Sissoko, the multimillionaire who had rescued Solo and Yayi in Washington, D.C., was about to pay a long overdue visit to Bamako. Djelimady underplayed Babani's arrival so much that I don't recall when he first mentioned it. In a sign of what was to come, Babani's brother Douga Sissoko turned up at the compound one evening driving a new Opel Monterrey road cruiser. He arrived in the midst of my evening lesson with Djelimady, which he interrupted by blasting over the car stereo a cassette of Djelimady performing in Paris during the 1980s. "That's the *real* Sunjata," said Madou Djan. Children gathered around the shiny deep green vehicle to hear the loud strains of Djelimady's guitar calling from the past. Douga sat back, bemused, and sipped tea. As he was leaving, he handed out crisp 1,000 CFA notes to all the children.

"Babani will come this weekend," Djelimady said afterwards. "That's what Douga came to tell me." We went back to our lesson, our last for a long time, as it turned out.

When I reached the compound on the Monday morning after Babani Sissoko's Sunday arrival, I found Djelimady just waking up, looking as ragged as I had ever seen him. He'd been up with the welcoming party until after five in the morning and had slept barely an hour. I heard him telling Barou that even the Rail Band would have to get by without him for a while, as he would be busy helping Babani get settled.

"When was the last time Babani came to town?" I asked Barou.

"Eight years ago," he said.

"Eight years?" I asked. "Where's he been all that time?"

"Hard to say," Barou went on. "At first, he disappeared. Then he turned up in Dakar. Morocco. Then, for a long time, people said he was in Dubai, working with the sheiks. Then last year, I heard he was in America."

"And now he's here," I said. Barou nodded. He could see that I did not fully grasp what was happening. He warned me not to expect much from Djelimady for a while.

"How long do you think Babani will stay?" I asked him.

Barou shook his head, unwilling to offer encouragement. "God only knows."

"Come on, Banning," said Djelimady, emerging from the compound in a sky-blue *boubou*. "We've got to get into town."

That meant taking a taxi, for during Ramadan the old Nissan had given out entirely, this time with a blown head gasket. Coming on the heels of two expensive repairs that had taken scarce funds from the construction project at the new house, this breakdown had been a bitter blow. Djelimady had had the car towed to his mechanic, and two weeks later it still hadn't been repaired. Now, when he needed to go somewhere, he sent one of the children for a taxi.

"Babani came with four airplanes," said Djelimady as we rode along Sheikh Zayed. "727s."

"He's a good friend of yours, isn't he?" I asked.

"Yes," growled Djelimady with deep certainty, "since childhood."

"Well, maybe he'll help you fix your car," I suggested.

"Maybe," he said distantly.

"By the way," I asked, "how did Babani get so rich?"

"Ahhh," said Djelimady. "That is a great mystery."

"You really don't know?"

"No," he said. "Nobody knows."

"Nobody but him."

"Nobody but him," Djelimady agreed.

As we arrived at the Buffet, I handed Djelimady my customary Monday food contribution, 10,000 CFA. "Oh," he said, hesitating. "Listen, Banning, if you want to wait, you can give that to me later. I mean, if you need it."

"No," I said, puzzled by this reluctance. "That's our agreement. Go ahead and take it." Djelimady took the bill and whisked it into the big front pocket of his *boubou* as he headed into the Buffet garden. We found the musicians at the practice room door, and Djelimady began talking to them in quick, excited Bambara. He produced the key and opened the door. We set ourselves up and began to play, but after a few runs through the arrangement we had been working on before Ramadan, Djelimady abruptly ended the rehearsal. He explained that he had to go to the airport to help retrieve Babani's things from customs.

Djelimady did not return to the compound until dinnertime, at which point he boasted that he had helped to clear more than five tons of goods without paying duty. He said that Babani had shipped over fifty new vehicles into the country, and that he *had* paid duty on them. Throughout dinner, the conversation went like that, all numbers and statistics—so many refrigerators, so many vans, so many American cars. Djelimady reported these things with boyish enthusiasm. I had never seen this side of him before—so impressed with everything. No sooner had Djelimady washed and eaten than he rushed off again, this time to the Hippodrome neighborhood, where Babani was setting up shop in a newly built mansion near Douga's place.

After dinner, I dropped by Barou's compound and told him the news. He laughed when I reported Djelimady's hesitancy in accepting my money. "When he left the house this morning, Djelimady showed Sambry a wad of bills," said Barou. "Five million CFA! Your ten thousand was nothing to him."

"That must have been for the customs charges," I surmised.

"Probably," said Barou, "but with Babani, every favor brings its reward. So, tell me. Did the Rail Band rehearse this morning?"

"Yes," I said, "but not for long."

"They're nervous now," said Barou, clucking. "They know what's coming."

"What do you mean?"

"Once, a number of years ago, Babani called Djelimady to Paris and kept him there for over a year," said Barou. "The Rail Band couldn't play. The other musicians were so angry with him that they decided to throw him out of the band. Then Djelimady came back with all this new equipment. You know those big Ranger amplifiers they play through now? Babani paid for them. It was funny. The musicians were ready to kill Djelimady. Then they saw that sound system, and it was all hugs and kisses. 'Oh, Djelimady, we missed you so much!'" A toot of falsetto laughter burst from Barou's throat.

Barou listed for me the gifts Babani had made to Djelimady over the years. There was a car, subsequently wrecked by Djelimady's oldest son, Samakou. There were trips to Europe, Dakar, Abidjan, and Lomé, beautiful clothing for Djelimady and his wife, and also cash gifts. Barou said

that Babani had even paid for the land on which Djelimady was building his new house. Djelimady's generosity toward me, it seemed, had
grown directly from Babani's generosity toward him.

"Babani gave Ami Koita her house," said Barou, and he reminded me
about the airplane given to Kandia Kouyaté. These two singers were
among the top *jelimusow* in Mali. I had never met the younger Kandia,
but I had visited Ami at her enormous house with its circular courtyard,
a space made beautiful by elegant stone masonry and well-tended gar-
dens. "The place was already furnished for her," said Barou. "One day,
Babani just handed her the keys."

Everywhere I went, people were talking about Babani. I had begun
playing guitar informally with a Wassoulou singer named Sali Sidibé,
and I now found her working up a praise song to the returning magnate. Back at my house, the Colonel could speak of nothing but his
youthful experiences with Babani. It turned out that the Colonel's older
brother had married Babani's aunt. My friend insisted that I come into
his room and look at photographs. One showed the aunt and the young
Colonel in Babani's home village of Dabia in the 1970s. The men wore
short Afros and white elephant pants. "Babondo was my friend," said
the Colonel. For some reason, he called Babani "Babondo." "I'm sure
that if he saw me now, he would give me lots of money. *Oui.*" The
Colonel nodded with his usual solemnity.

Toumani Diabaté explained to me that in the early 1980s, Babani had
returned to his home village of Dabia, a dry, lonely gold-mining town
in the Kayes region, near the border with Senegal. Babani had apparently ordered the village razed and had embarked on a massive rebuild-
ing project. He had reconstructed every house with electricity, air con-
ditioning, running water, and a television. He had built a power plant
to supply the town and had transformed the lives of the 1,100 families
living there. Toumani told me that during the construction, Babani had
flown musicians out to Dabia to entertain him continuously, sometimes
keeping them there for months at a time. Babani had rewarded them.
"He bought me my car," said Toumani. "But now, I never hear anything
from him. Not for a long time."

"There was a problem after the Dabia project," Barou told me.
"Somehow Babani spent more money than he had. The airplane he
gave to Kandia Kouyaté actually belonged to the president of Gabon,
and he wanted it back. All of a sudden, Babani owed people money and

he couldn't pay them. So he disappeared. I guess he must have found some more money and paid them after all. Because now he's back."

In the fall, when Babani had sent money to Salif Keita's family following the death of Salif's father, I had not grasped the significance of the gift, but in our interview, I had asked Salif about it. "Salif," I had said, "people tell me that though you are not a griot, you sometimes do griot's work. Why did you sing about Babani Sissoko?"

"I didn't sing about Babani," Salif had said. "I just thanked him." He didn't elaborate.

It struck me that Salif and Babani were two sides of the same coin. Salif was a noble who had transformed himself into a kind of griot. Babani, it turned out, was actually born to a griot family, but he had never practiced *jeliya*. Instead, he had transformed himself into a virtual noble—the man who gives to the *jeli*s. Both were great boosters of Malian traditions, and yet each had broken the rules in fundamental ways. They were heroes in that distinctly Mande sense, "agents of disequilibrium."

Everybody had a theory as to the source of Babani's wealth. The Colonel claimed that Babani first went to Gabon, where he got rich as a gold trader. Djelimady confirmed that there had been a friendship between Babani and Gabon's longtime president, Omar Bongo. Babani had even married Bongo's niece. But this hardly explained Babani's millions. Some speculated about criminal activity. Drugs, arms dealing, and counterfeit money topped the list. I heard talk of illicit dealings in architectural relics in Sierra Leone and of diamonds illegally mined in Mobutu's Zaire. Djelimady denied all such charges. "When Babani was in the United States," he reported, "the FBI followed him around. They couldn't figure out how this Malian guy was so rich. Whenever he spent money, they would check to see if the bills were counterfeit. They were real."

Still others claimed that Babani had supernatural powers. They spoke of *maraboutage*, that slippery word that suggests both Islamic learnedness and also a way with the spirit world. "Babani performs miracles," said Madou Djan Tounkara flatly. "There is not another man like him in the world." The notion of African presidents and billionaire Arabs turning to a Malian *marabout* for magical cures, mystical knowledge, or even the elimination of enemies, titillated the imagination but demanded confirmation that no one I met could provide.

"Babani has lots of money, but nothing in his head," an older Bamako musician once told me. "He is the Malian Rockefeller, not a *marabout*. A fetishist, yes, but no *marabout*. And certainly no devil."

"Even his family doesn't know how he got so much money," said Madou Djan when I questioned him yet again. "Not even his own brothers." It was almost as if Babani's benefactors didn't want to know where the money came from. His patronage was all the more wonderful for the mystery that surrounded it.

Babani's affection for Djelimady posed no mystery, given the rich man's love of music. In four months in Bamako, I had heard some world-class instrumentalists, but I had not found a guitarist to rival Djelimady. I used to joke that Babani and I apparently shared the same taste in guitarists. I naturally wondered how the friendship between Djelimady and Babani had come about. As time went on, Djelimady became reluctant to discuss Babani with me, and he would never speak about him into a tape recorder. But one evening at dinner, I asked him how he got to know Babani in the first place, and he told me this story.

In the early 1960s, when Djelimady was still a young player in the National Orchestra, he used to perform at street parties around Bamako with a singer called Tiekoro Sissoko, Douga and Babani's cousin. Then as now, Tiekoro and Douga were fast friends, so when the young Douga first came to Bamako, he soon met Djelimady and became smitten with his guitar playing. Douga began to study with Djelimady, and over the years he has become a reasonably good guitarist. I could still see remnants of the old teacher/student relationship. When Douga dropped by the Tounkara compound, he would sometimes pick up a guitar and play something to surprise Djelimady, still looking for approval from the master.

"When I met Douga," said Djelimady, "Babani was running a coffee stand in Kayes. He was a poor kid, not yet twenty years old. His family considered him a failure. Sissoko is a good griot name, but Babani didn't want to be a griot. And how was he going to get anywhere selling coffee by the cup? Then Babani moved to Dakar, where he went into business selling used items. He had a little success there. That was where he first started inviting griots to come and play for him. In the early '70s, Babani's father took ill and came to Bamako for treatment."

By then, Djelimady was the lead guitarist in the Rail Band. Like his brother before him, Babani became fascinated with the band and the new sound they were creating. Babani particularly loved the combination of Djelimady's guitar playing and Mory Kanté's singing, especially when they interpreted Manding classics like "Sunjata," "Janjon," "Lamban," and "Diaoura."

"Babani went through all his money," Djelimady recalled. "He spent it taking care of his father. I used to pay his price of admission at the Buffet, so he could come in and see the Rail Band. That's how we became friends. His father died in 1974, and after that Babani disappeared. Nobody knew where he had gone or what he was doing for about five years. When he came back, he had millions."

"Is Babani a *marabout?*" I asked Djelimady.

"No," he said. "I spent a year in France with him. We lived in the same apartment and I never once saw him reading a book. I don't know how he learned English, Spanish, and Arabic. Do you know he even speaks Hindi? I myself never knew him to talk much at all. He could never do griot's work. That used to frustrate his father. My God, it made him angry, but Babani just couldn't do it. And you know, I understood that, because my father wanted me to learn all the histories too. He was really disappointed that I showed no ability or interest in all that."

I found myself believing Djelimady that night. The puffery and boosterism fell away as he recalled those early times, paying Babani's admission to the Buffet and sharing the pleasure of music with him. It was a moment that you hope for in interviews but that rarely comes, a moment when the person being interviewed is possessed by a memory and tells a story simply and honestly. But the more curious I became about Babani, the less Djelimady wanted to discuss him.

Sean Barlow arrived in Bamako at the pitch of Babani Fever, and during his brief stay we managed to meet the famous man. Given Djelimady's closeness to Babani, this might seem no great feat. But Babani never visited the compound. He adored Djelimady but his affection did not extend to the Tounkaras in general, let alone to hangers-on like myself. Babani the man seemed to me as remote as his implausible legend.

Then, at the close of a particularly active day, Sean and I arrived for a late dinner at the Tounkaras'. Instead of the usual hubbub of cooking, visiting, washing, and arguing over the din of the television, we found a ghostly void. Only Djelimady's eldest daughter, Bintou, the two old women, and the children remained. Everyone else had gone to Babani's "to play music," we were told.

We decided to make the pilgrimage to Hippodrome ourselves. We hurried to Barou's house and told him what we had in mind. Barou would not have undertaken the trip on his own, enticing as it was, but escorting foreign journalists and personal friends of Djelimady's to Babani's compound just might work.

We set out in a taxi. Bamako's taximen had always struck me as shockingly ignorant of major sites around the city. I used to joke that they might as well be immigrants from Haiti. This one, however, knew exactly where Babani was staying, and when we saw the house we understood why. Babani had set himself up in a large, cream-colored villa just beyond the nightclub Akwaba on the Route de Koulikoro. Outside the house's tall surrounding walls, a crowd of cars and people were gathered, as they had apparently been doing, more or less steadily, since Babani's arrival in town ten days earlier. Six or more military men guarded the entrance, roughly fending off suppliants seeking entry with one story or another. Barou made our plea, saying that we were with the musicians. I produced my business card. Over the wall, off in the distance, we could hear Djelimady's guitar being played through the wah-wah pedal that Sean had brought him as a gift from New York.

The guard disappeared within the compound and soon returned and admitted us. Barou flashed me an excited smile as we passed through the gate. Inside, two spanking new road cruisers like the one Douga had brought to the Tounkara house were parked in the driveway. A further crowd of extremely well-dressed people sat in chairs or stood along the wide front of the house. More paramilitary men controlled entry to the building itself. We walked past the land cruisers and around to the back of the house, where Yayi, Solo, Djelimady, Adama, and another *ngoni* player were getting ready to play on a round, thatched-roofed bandstand nestled into the garden at one end of a long swimming pool.

It must have been 11:00 P.M., and the musicians were still working out their sound, tuning meticulously, ferreting out small buzzes and imperfections. Solo, forever vexed by the failures of his electronic American spoils, was struggling with Yayi's cordless microphone, which had unhappily chosen this moment to die. Yayi stood by, hissing.

"We waited for you," said Djelimady, deflecting blame lest I feel slighted at being left behind.

"We decided to come and see for ourselves," I said, letting him off the hook.

"*Voila,*" he rumbled. Djelimady was nervous. When I asked if Sean could record a bit of sound for his radio program, Djelimady said no. "*Le patron* wouldn't like it," he told us. Meanwhile, Madou Djan stood out front holding up a boom box to record for himself, and the inevitable video cameraman soon showed up and went to work. The message was plain: Visiting *toubab*s should count their blessings, not push their luck.

I watched one Sissoko inspecting the bandstand. "Too many Tounkaras," he muttered to a friend. Douga lingered by his land cruiser, talking on a cellular phone.

"You mean everyone important isn't already here?" I quipped to Barou.

"Alpha Oumar?" mused Barou, referring to Mali's president.

Peering through windows, I noticed that Babani had not yet had time to furnish his new home. People stood around in large, empty rooms, some of them eating off styrofoam plates or drinking canned sodas. I looked into the kitchen and spotted Djelimady's wife amid the new refrigerator, oven, freezer, and dishwasher. A woman accustomed to cooking with an iron pot placed atop three rocks and a fire, she looked uneasy and stood off to the side. Outside, other Tounkara women—Madou's wife Fanta and Djelimady's daughter Tareta—also kept to themselves.

From the moment the musicians began to play, it was clear that this would not be the usual street party blowout. For one thing, there would be just one person for the griots to praise. That person knew and loved music and oratory and expected a real performance, so gone were the drum machine, the exaggerated guitar effects, the distortion, the microphone feedback. The Tounkaras came together with a tightly unified sound, Solo using his octave pedal to play dignified bass lines on guitar, Djelimady reining in his leads, and the two *ngoni* players gingerly filling in the cracks. Though electrified, the music bore the elegance of the very best acoustic sessions I had heard at the Tounkara compound.

Babani offered the guests in his compound good music but little else. No food or drink was served to those outside the house. After an hour of standing around in the evening heat, Sean and I were overwhelmed with thirst. Samakou Tounkara, Djelimady's son, offered to take us out to hunt for a drink in the neighborhood. Samakou had plenty to report—Babani had received twenty-six new cars that week and would surely give Djelimady one of them within days—that sort of thing. Now, Samakou said, assuring us that Babani had gone out and would not return soon, would be a good time to go and find a drink. But just as we reached the gate, Samakou stopped abruptly, seeing that Babani himself was pulling up to the driveway in a new Mitsubishi Pajero.

Tall, thin, dressed in a white *boubou* and smiling warmly, Babani stepped out of the car and was quickly surrounded by military men and white assistants, some of them apparently Americans. I noted in particular a tall, muscular Frenchman dressed in a Malian *boubou*. "He's a commando," said Barou.

"A commando in a *boubou*," I noted.

A few of the guests managed to get to Babani during his brief walk from the car to the house. He greeted them, very relaxed and friendly, but moved quickly and vanished behind the heavy glass front door. Babani did not emerge for over two hours, by which time men had carried fuzzy, dark green couches out from the house and set them up in a line facing the musicians. These remained empty while the guests placed their own chairs or found a bit of ledge on the musicians' side. Their positioning made it clear that Babani, not the players, would be the real entertainment.

When at last Babani swept out the back door of the house and took his place on one of the couches, the musicians tore into their instruments. Two *funéw*—talking griots—began a lengthy presentation of tag-team flattery, for which each was rewarded with a thick stack of 10,000 CFA notes. Military men guarding Babani placed their riot helmets along the edge of the slowly filling swimming pool, folded their arms, and watched the action.

Yayi sang at length, followed by Manian Damba, the *jelimuso* with whom we had traveled to Kita back in December. I took advantage of a lull to approach Babani with a copy of Sean's and my book. The transaction was completed in seconds, but everyone noticed. Babani Fever was spreading.

"What did you give him?" asked Madou Djan when I returned to my spot at the side of the bandstand.

"Our book," I answered.

"That is *very* good," said Madou solemnly.

It was after 2:00 in the morning, and Sean and I were exhausted. I had seen Djelimady's blank expression and wasted eyes at breakfast on many mornings. I knew how long these soirées could go on. "Babani doesn't sleep!" Djelimady would complain. I found Barou and suggested that we might want to leave before the end. He was shocked.

"But Babani is going to give money to *everyone* at the end," he said.

"Who told you that?"

"Bouba Sacko," he replied. I looked over at Bouba, the thin, nervous guitarist who had been Djelimady's foil in the small Bajourou group. Forlorn without his instrument, Bouba was standing as close as possible to the Tounkaras onstage. Next to him, brothers Sayan and Sekouba Sissoko and also the old balafonist Keletigui Diabaté huddled in as well, fighting to stay awake, doing their best to look like contributors, while on stage, Djelimady, Solo, and Adama Tounkara danced and played in a kind of altered state.

There must have been 150 or more guests spread throughout the compound on either side of the house. None of them were leaving, despite the late hour. They all looked hungry and tired. "Barou," I finally asked. "Do you really think Babani is going to give money to all these people?"

He relented, and we taxied back to Lafiabougou. The next morning, Samakou told us that Babani had handed out 3 million CFA ($6,000) to each musician at the end of the night. He also said that after the party, Babani had proceeded directly to the airport and flown to Nigeria. "He's coming back in a week," reported Samakou confidently, "and when he does come, he'll bring a new car for Djelimady." I learned later that the musicians had in fact been given 3 million CFA to divide among them. As usual, Yayi had claimed most of it. At the compound, life seemed strangely normal. There was nothing to suggest that riches had ever flowed through that shabby concrete doorway.

I had planned to visit Dakar with Sean while Djelimady worked in Cuba. By the time we learned that the Cuba project was being postponed, I had already booked a ticket. But it didn't matter. Old concerns about interrupting my work with Djelimady were now irrelevant. Dakar, with its press of urban energy, felt like New York after months in sleepy Bamako. As Sean and I hustled around the sophisticated oceanside Senegalese capital, I found myself appreciating the city's comparative polish. The taxis had working doors and meters. The people spoke excellent French and often English as well. The restaurants served gourmet African cuisine. Best of all, the nightclubs had real sound systems, paying customers, and razor-sharp bands with rhythm sections unimaginable in Bamako. Senegal, the first and most solid of France's West African colonies, had kept its edge.

Even there, musicians were talking about Babani Sissoko. We dropped in on Baaba Maal, one of Senegal's biggest stars, and he reported that Dakar too had enjoyed lengthy visits from the eccentric Malian. "All the griots go crazy when he comes," said Baaba in English. "Babani likes *too much* the music."

I flew back to Bamako on a Sunday when no trash fires burned and a wind had cleared off the hovering haze. From the plane window, I could see the sweeping meanderings of the Niger River, the twin spires of the Great Mosque, and the outlines of Bamako's taller buildings, all sharply etched in clear light. The city that had seemed all darkness and dust when I'd flown in three months earlier now felt like home.

As the plane landed, I spotted two unmarked 727s off to one side. Babani had returned. "From Nigeria, eh?" I asked Djelimady, whom I found relaxing at the compound.

"No," he said, "Lomé, Togo. You should have seen it when he landed. The entire airport closed down. All the workers left their posts to try and meet him. He was afraid. They had to take him out in a fire truck." Djelimady told me that when Babani had arrived at his house in Hippodrome, he had distributed 3 million CFA in small bills to the crowd outside his gate.

"He's encouraging them," I said. "He must like the attention."

"He likes it," said Djelimady. "But then it becomes too much."

Samakou had been wrong about the money, wrong about Nigeria, and also wrong about the new car. The Nissan still languished with the repair man, and no shining steed had replaced it. Djelimady still rode taxis, which meant that I would still ride the *bashée*s and Sotrama minivans. The Tounkaras had been invited back to play another soirée, and Babani's largesse had continued. He had presented Yayi Kanouté with a one-kilogram bar of gold. She got it out and showed it to me. She told me that the shiny slab, about the size of a deck of cards, was worth between 6 and 7 million CFA.

"That's over $12,000," I exclaimed.

"Eeh!" said Yayi, snatching the gold bar back from me and then adding, "He gave *three* to Tata Bambo Kouyaté." She glared at me. "Three!"

Djelimady seemed to have adjusted to his new life as part of Babani's entourage. The edginess I had observed in him since the rich man's arrival had given way to the old cheer and confidence. He speculated that Babani might finance the solo record he had long dreamed of making, the one in which he would trace the road between Manding music and jazz. "I'm going to call it *La Nuit des Manding*," said Djelimady. "Because, you know, Sunjata won the war at night."

That evening, I found Yayi in the compound. The men had gone out, but she was reworking her look. Her hair, unattended, stuck up in that dry crown of fuzz that Malian ladies sport between hair preparations. "You missed a great wedding last night," she said to me in Bambara, leaving Barou to translate. I expressed my regret at missing what Yayi would consider a great wedding.

"But Yayi," I said, "I'm surprised you even bother to play weddings with Babani in town. They don't really pay well enough, do they?" Barou translated. Yayi laughed politely and changed the subject. "Banning!" she barked, switching to her rudimentary French. "Tomorrow morning at the Buffet. Recording. For Segu Top Etoiles. I'm the invited guest."

I reluctantly agreed. Our first recording session together had been an ordeal, and the prospect of another round with Yayi at Studio Rail Band didn't excite me. "You know, Yayi," I said, risking a joke, "the recording has gotten kind of expensive since the last time."

"Eeh!" she said again, her eyes flashing like headlights. "Well, okay. But you'll have to pay *me* to play weddings with us from now on." Tightfistedness was second nature with Yayi, but given what was to come, she would have been well advised to splurge on a real recording studio, now that she could afford it.

Over the course of the next week, Yayi coerced me through a painful series of recording sessions. First we worked with the Rail Band, but after two stressful days of rehearsal and recording, Yayi pronounced the resulting tape unsatisfactory. "*Cassetti pas bon,*" she declared. "*Les coeurs sont petits!*"

A second attempt failed when the recording studio Yayi had lined up was unavailable and her musicians refused to wait around. The recording that ultimately aired on Segu Top Etoiles was made at Carrefour de Musique, a ramshackle, four-track cassette studio belonging to two nineteen-year-old twin brothers. Yayi recruited musicians on the spot, and they arranged the music as they recorded. Once underway, the session did take on a certain magic—blue-painted walls, orange incandescent light, a shaft of golden, dusky sunlight pouring in through a small window, and a roomful of passionate, sweating griots making music to the lashing pulse of a drum machine. As they taped the final vocals, Adama and Sambry danced joyfully and coached the chorus, and everyone's faces shone with sweat. It was as though they had planned it this way all along.

When the Tounkaras went to Dabia, I blamed myself for not having better understood Djelimady's friendship with Douga back in the beginning. I kept remembering the evening during my first week in Bamako, when Djelimady had taken me to Hippodrome to visit his friend. "Douga plays guitar too," he had said. "Bring him a set of guitar strings." Douga had appreciated the gift, but for me the evening had been dull, a matter of sitting in front of someone else's television in a shadowy compound, listening to strangers speak Bambara. After that, whenever

Djelimady had said he was going to see Douga, I had told him I had something else to do. Eventually he had stopped asking me to come along. Could it all have been different, I now wondered? If I had cultivated my own friendship with Douga, might I too have ridden the private plane to Dabia with Djelimady, Solo, Yayi, and Adama Tounkara?

As it was, I came to the compound a couple of days after Yayi's Segu recording to find a chauffeur-driven, double-long Toyota pickup truck parked by the Tounkaras' doorway. Djelimady and Solo were hurriedly loading amplifiers, instruments, and suitcases into the truck bed. Ami Koita sat impassively in the passenger seat, filing her painted fingernails. I instantly recognized Mali's most beloved *jelimuso* by the beauty mark on the side of her nose. The truck would take them all to the airport, where one of Babani's planes was waiting to fly them to Dabia. I asked Djelimady how long he'd be gone, and his face wriggled. He was flirting with telling me something reassuring, when the truth was he had no idea.

I went back to my house to practice and found Mimi Konaté, the mother of the small tenant family, there as ever, tending her cook fire. I told her what had happened. "You must see Dabia," she said to me with a funny passion in her voice.

"Well, I would have liked to...," I began.

"No, you *must* see it," Mimi insisted. "You cannot believe what that man did for the place. Those people were living like *savages.*"

"Really?" I said, taken aback by the word.

"Savages!" she repeated, "In the truest sense of the word. They had no religion, Muslim or Christian. Babani civilized them. He built a mosque. He built a church. He is a real citizen of Mali, even if he is a criminal like some people say."

I went into my room, started up the fan, and sat at my small wooden table, the only piece of furniture there. I decided that if Djelimady was going to be gone for a while and the Rail Band out of commission, the best way to continue my work with Manding music was to study the tapes I had been making. I got out one of the recordings I had made of the Rail Band at the Buffet. Christmas Eve. I listened until the tape reached one of Djelimady's solos. I paused the machine, got out my guitar, some music paper, and a pencil and started transcribing. It immediately became clear that I would be many hours writing down a solo that Djelimady had played without a thought. Then I would have to learn to play it. The prospect of real work buoyed me.

Absorbed in the transcription, I heard a tap at my door. It was Bintou, a young, unsuccessful *jelimuso* who had taken a romantic interest in me. Reluctantly, I let her in. Bintou reclined on my bed and began to gossip. She told me that the three biggest *marabout*s in Mali were Babani Sissoko, Sherif, and a man called Djiné, which means devil. Babani, she claimed, knew nothing except *maraboutage*—magic and fetishes. Outside of that, claimed Bintou, he was an imbecile. Sherif, on the other hand, possessed a small measure of worldliness. They were all overrated as far as she was concerned.

Bintou told me that a *kora* player she knew had stopped going to the musical soirées at Babani's house because he had gotten sick of the way Babani doted on Djelimady. "Djelimady likes to show off in front of his master," said Bintou, and she went on to mimic the *kora* player's impression of Djelimady. "No, no, no. Don't play it *that* way. You must play it *this* way."

Bintou picked up a copy of Sean's and my book and inspected the photograph of Baaba Maal on the cover. "Baaba Maal," she said scornfully.

"You don't like him?" I asked.

"He's a bluffer," said Bintou.

"What?"

"He's a bluffer," she repeated, as if no explanation was needed.

Bintou flipped to the Mali section and spotted the signature next to Ami Koita's photograph. "Who signed this picture?" she asked. "Because I *know* it wasn't her." About this much she was right; Ami's husband had signed the book for her.

"How did you know that?" I asked.

"Because Ami Koita can't write," said Bintou. "She's not educated."

Ali Farka Touré, the Grammy-winning guitarist from northern Mali, got the treatment next. "Ali Farka will tell you he's a noble," said Bintou. "It's not true. He's also a bluffer. All those people from the north sing in those weak voices, and they dance their delicate little dances. They do that because they fancy themselves nobles. They don't want to sound like griots, screaming for money. They're very unfriendly people. All they care about is their gold and jewels. They think everyone else is inferior."

Bintou claimed that Wassoulou star Oumou Sangaré had destroyed her reputation with Malians by singing in bad French. Yayi Kanouté's voice was too shrill to please, and she and Solo had bought bizarre, even awful, clothes in America. They had made fools of themselves by wearing them on television. Had Bintou come by only to share her acid opinions, I might have treasured her friendship. Like J. C., the old fellow in Le Perroquet on Christmas Eve, she said things that others were too polite to say. Unfortunately, Bintou always brought her visits around to a request that I father her child, and I always had to throw her out.

"You're mean," said Bintou, heading for the door. I snatched my key from the table and followed her.

"That's right," I agreed. "I'm *mean.*" We walked to the road in silence.

That night, the air was moist, almost cool, after the sweltering day, rather like a perfect midsummer evening in New England. At the compound, Adama Kouyaté served millet porridge, *tow* with *datu,* that thick, slimy sauce that smells sulfury and rank in preparation but is oddly nice to the taste. I ate alone and assessed my situation. Djelimady had gone to Babani's native village. No telling when he would return. I had my tapes, but working in my oven-like house would leave me prey to Bintou and other unwanted visitors. Toumani remained in an uneasy stand-off between his trio and his band, and having extricated myself from his world at the end of Ramadan, I hesitated to reenter it. There was no doubt about it. I needed a new project.

PHOTO 17
Toumani Diabaté (kora).
Photo by the author.

PHOTO 18
Basekou Kouyaté (ngoni).
Photo by the author.

PHOTO 19
Foutanga Babani Sissoko with members of the Miami Central High School band, just after he gave them $300,000. ©*The Miami Herald/Maurice Cohn Band.*

PHOTO 20
Hunters' dance. *Photo by the author.*

PHOTO 21
Sali Sidibé, Harouna Samaké (kamalé ngoni), and Dirck Westervelt (banjo) *(front row)*, the author (guitar), Sali's daughter Sanata, and her husband Modibo Diabaté *(back row)*. *Photo by the author.*

PHOTO 22
Harouna Samaké with his 8-string kamalé ngoni. *Photo by the author.*

PHOTO 23
Hadja Soumano serenades Balla Sissoko at the Palais de la Culture. A Sissoko bodyguard (in boubou) watches. *Photo by Mamadou Traoré.*

PHOTO 24
Sayan Sissoko (ngoni).
Photo by the author.

PHOTO 25
Sadio Kouyaté performing at
the Palais de la Culture, money
at her feet. *Photo by the author.*

PHOTO 26
Oumou Sangaré performing at the Houston International Festival in 1999. *Photo by the author.*

PHOTO 27
Ali Farka Touré.
Press photo by Jon Mided.

10

A Woman of Wassoulou

In the forest the anguished bird sings a song
Full of distress the bird sings deeply.

Oumou Sangaré, from the song "Djôrôlen" ("Anguish")

amadou Jatigui Diarra, a hunters' chief, topped the grandest claims of the *jeli*s. "The Malian hunter is the beginning of a civilization," he told me. "He is the continuation of a civilization. He is the consequence of a civilization. The hunter's tradition has no beginning, and it will have no end."

At a New Year's Day hunters' party in 1993, hundreds gathered in a field to eat *kola* nut and celebrate with Mr. Diarra and his clan. The hunters wore pelts, hooves, feathers, claws, and *bogolon* robes and danced in a lazy circle. They cradled archaic rifles, and occasionally one of them stepped to the center to discharge his weapon with a bang and a shower of sparks. Deep melodies boomed from *doso ngonis*—hunters' harps—and the rhythm loped to the metallic scraping of the *karagnan*. The music was darkly exotic, but it conjured familiar associations: work songs from the slave plantations of the Old South; the bass line from "Smoke on the Water." After nightfall, smoke from leaping fires hovered above the crowd. The jolt of *kola* nut and gunfire sustained the celebrants.

"Man at his awakening understood that nature gives him his nourishment," Mr. Diarra told me, "and the hunt was his first activity on earth." This was as close as I came to hunter's

157

culture in Mali. I had missed the funeral of Salif Keita's father, and I never visited the southern Wasulu* region, with its woodlands, game, rural pageantry, and magical cults. Mr. Diarra had told me that life in Wasulu was "a festival of nature." But I knew the region only through its reflections in the capital: *bogolon* fashion; the sensuous dances that Djelimady's oldest son Samakou danced with his male friends around a boom box at night; and, especially, Wassoulou music. Wassoulou songs peppered the Bamako airwaves with a brashness and carnality rare in the music of *jeli*s. American musicians like Dirck and me could engage the pentatonic Wassoulou sound easily, because it bristles with connections to our own blues and funk. No other Malian music style—except Bambara music—makes a better case for rock 'n' roll's African ancestry. And no other style has so challenged the musical supremacy of the *jeli*s.

"What's to learn?" asked Djelimady when Dirck and I arranged a session with a Wassoulou guitarist. "It's always the same melody." Djelimady had acknowledged that hunters' musicians were the forebears of the griots. He had no quarrel with Mr. Diarra's rhapsody about the timeless wisdom of hunters. But when it came to the musical judgment, Wassoulou pop was mostly *"monotonie"* as far as Djelimady was concerned.

Back in the 1960s, when a Wasulunke boy named Alata Brulaye built the first *kamalé ngoni*—literally "young boy's harp," a child's imitation of the *doso ngoni*—calamity followed. Hunters' songs were meant for the spirits. To play or even to *hear* them under improper conditions might upset the balance between the human and spirit worlds. Brulaye constructed his six-stringed instrument smaller and tuned it about a fourth higher than the revered hunter's harp, but the resemblance scandalized elders. They called Brulaye's instrument *samakoro*, Bambara for "bed lice," suggesting that when it bit, you could not ignore the itch. *Kamalé ngoni*-wielding boys began writing songs of love and satire to play at recreational dances.

"In a village, when the *kamalé ngoni* played," Wassoulou music's biggest star Oumou Sangaré once told me, "everyone went out. Nobody worked. Even if the parents did not want the kids to go, they went anyway. With us in Africa, when parents speak, you don't oppose them. So

---

*I use the spelling Wasulu for the region, as it appears that way on most maps and in historical texts. I use the spelling Wassoulou for the music, as that has become the industry standard.

the *kamalé ngoni* became known as *samakoro* because young people used it to aggravate old people." The *kamalé ngoni* craze was probably no more stoppable than the rock 'n' roll that was upsetting British and American elders around the same time. "Naturally," added Oumou, "this instrument *had* to be exploited."

And it was. When I lived in Bamako, Alata Brulaye was an old man living in obscurity in Wasulu. He has since died, but he must have taken satisfaction in knowing that some of Mali's most successful pop stars built their careers with his instrument. Oumou Sangaré used *kamalé ngoni* music and her own nightingale's alto voice to purvey songs demanding women's rights in Africa. Her lyrics used ideas from the Koran to attack long accepted practices of arranged marriage and polygamy. Oumou electrified and infuriated the public. She released her first cassette *Moussoulou* ("Women") in 1990 at the age of twenty-one and instantly became the most talked-about star in Mali.

The truth is, only a handful of modern African singers have been brave enough to create genuine controversy and weather the heat. The late Fela Anikulapo-Kuti was brutalized for decrying the excesses of Nigeria's thuggish leaders, among other things. Thomas Mapfumo went to jail for singing freedom songs in Southern Rhodesia, and even when the country became Zimbabwe and embraced him as a hero, he criticized the new government for its corruption. Oumou Sangaré was not the first Malian singer to demand respect for women, and she has not faced physical danger for questioning African social order. But her courageous and beautiful music has altered Mali's cultural landscape. Through the *kamalé ngoni*, Oumou summoned the power of the hunters to her cause. She became impossible to ignore.

Oumou's success must have stung the *jeli*s. In Mali, she nipped at their heels by winning popularity that only they and Salif Keita had known before. Abroad, she buried them with unprecedented record sales. A wave of new "women of Wassoulou" sprang up in her wake. Suddenly every upstart kid with a *kamalé ngoni* was earning a spot on Top Etoiles, and unlike griots, Wassoulou singers—almost all of them women— could sing about anything they liked. In the early '90s, as democracy dawned in Mali and argument became the order of the day, Wassoulou songbirds made the *jeli*s seem hidebound in tradition.

Ethnicity too plays a part in this rivalry. Wassoulou stars are not Manding like the *jeli*s. Most of the people in Wasulu were originally Fula (also called Peul, Fulani, or Fulbe). Some say it was the nomadic ways of the cattle-herding Fula that led them from northern Mali south to live among the Malinke and Bambara. Others argue that the first Wasulunke were members of a Fula brigand army during the time of Sunjata. However they came, the people of Wasulu have spoken Bambara since at least 1800 and now rub shoulders and intermarry with surrounding peoples. In Bamako, the Fula of Wasulu do not stand out like the northern Fula, with their colorful turbans, copper skin, and Arab facial features. It takes a keen ear to pick out the lyrical Wasulunke dialect, but family names—Sidibé, Samaké, Sangaré, Diakité, and Diallo—reveal Fula origins.

Djelimady adored Oumou Sangaré, whom he called "one of the three best singers in Africa along with Salif Keita and Baaba Maal." Djelimady could also play pentatonic guitar styles, including Wassoulou music, as well as anyone. He told me that in 1973, he had lifted the guitar part from James Brown's "Sex Machine" and made a sensation for the Rail Band with a Wassoulou song called "M'Foli." *That* was originality. Today's field of Wassoulou artists—Oumou and a few others notwith-standing—is a creative wasteland by comparison. Interestingly, Was-soulou music's boosters made the identical criticism of the *jeli*s, who, they said, had been reworking the same fifteen songs for more than *eight hundred years.*

Two faiths. As long as I remained with the Tounkaras and the *jeli*s, excursions into Wassoulou music circles would be tricky. This became clear early on when Dirck and I met up with a Wassoulou guitarist I had befriended years earlier during my first visit to Bamako. Madou Bah Traoré arranged, produced, and played guitar for his vocalist wife, Djeneba Diakité. We found them both at a Wassoulou showcase in the concert hall at Modibo Keita Stadium in January.

The hall was one of those peculiar venues the colonial period had left behind. About the size and shape of a large high school gymnasium, it had banks of bleachers to one side and a large, empty space with a painted floor opposite. Pale blue and yellowish-tan paint covered everything from the concrete floor up to the steel girders that held up the roof. The room was an acoustical nightmare. Even if the show's promoters had owned a proper sound system, they would only have produced a louder cacophony of echoes.

Despite the music's popularity, few big Wassoulou concerts went on in Bamako, so the lineup that night had drawn well. The bill included both Sali Sidibé—the Black Pearl of Wassoulou—and Djeneba Diakité, as well as thirteen other artists. Oumou Sangaré was still touring in

Europe at the time, but even if she had been in town, the queen of Wassoulou had no need to put herself through such an ordeal.

Sali Sidibé had organized this concert as a tribute to Kagbe Sidibé, another veteran Wassoulou singer, who had died the year before. Madou Bah would later tell me that he had suspected from the start that Sali's true purpose was not to honor Kagbe but to promote Sali. His wife Djeneba had persuaded him to do the show, but after watching Sali stroll onstage in her polka dot dress to smile upon, kiss, or otherwise ostentatiously recognize each artist who sang, Djeneba concluded that her husband had been right. More than this, sound problems and long pauses hobbled any momentum the evening might have gained. Sali, Djeneba, and a few others performed bravely, and Madou Bah's feathery, animated guitar lines held me each time he played. A small man with a shaved head and an overlarge gray jacket, Madou Bah had style. He danced with his guitar, soloing and weaving among the players like a nervous elf. But this was hardly enough to rescue the night.

The show stopped abruptly around 1:00 A.M. Dirck and I puzzled at its complete lack of shape or pacing. Joyce, the American schoolteacher, said that the best part had been watching the singers primp in the ladies room. "Do you know those ladies change their shoes before *every* song?" Joyce exclaimed. "Right before they go onstage, they step out of their house shoes and into their tiniest high heels. It's a wonder some of them can stand up in those things."

Madou Bah found us in the dispersing crowd and insisted that Dirck and I pay him a visit with our instruments. Our first session seemed promising. Madou Bah was keen to play with us and excited about the banjo. He played us Djeneba's latest cassette, fresh from a studio in Abidjan. I mustered the courage to tell him that the music was good but that the drum machine spoiled the effect.

"I know," he agreed, to my surprise. "But the producer down there insisted. From now on, everything we do in America will go through *you.*" Madou Bah told me that he had planned to go back to Abidjan to begin another project but now that he had found Dirck and me, he would stay in Bamako as long as we did. This was part flattery and part desperate hope on Madou Bah's part. I explained, as I often had to, that I was not a manager or agent, but it didn't matter. I was an American musician and I was his friend. Anything was possible.

Madou Bah had two wives—both singers—and many dependents. He was nowhere near as successful as Djelimady and so had to take work as a guitarist, producer, arranger, or concert organizer wherever he could find it. "Both of my wives are pregnant again," he told us fretfully as we left that first day.

"Guess he hasn't got Oumou Sangaré's message on polygamy," said Dirck as we made our way to a *bashée*. One justification for polygamy is that the religion of Islam bars sex between a man and his wife during pregnancy and nursing, which can last for more than a year. If this had had anything to do with Madou Bah's rationale in taking a second wife, bad luck had dogged him again.

Madou Bah kept promising us that he'd put a group together to play with us, but the musicians never materialized. Even if Madou Bah had produced a band, Djelimady's attitude toward this project doomed it. As it turned out, Madou Bah had played rhythm guitar for the Rail Band briefly during the '70s. "I taught him how to play," said Djelimady one night after we'd returned from Madou Bah's place. "Did he tell you that?" I hesitated. "You see, that isn't good. When someone helps you, you should be grateful. You should show respect."

After Dirck left Bamako, I visited Madou Bah at his "office." This was just a bench under some shade trees next to the Maison des Jeunes, a hostel where homeless youth and touring musicians stayed. Madou Bah wanted to play blues that day. I showed him some scales, riffs, and chord forms that could work with Wassoulou songs. He brightened, as though we had broached a bold musical frontier. For me, the bridge between blues and Wassoulou was almost too obvious to provide much of a thrill all on its own. But I loved the songs Madou Bah showed me.

An ex-guitarist from Super Biton de Segu—Mali's most popular band throughout most of the '70s—sat listening to us that day. At one point, he broke in and spoke harshly to Madou Bah. "He was telling me not to teach you things," said Madou Bah, as we left. "'Why are you showing this white guy your music?' he said. 'Don't you know he's going to go back to the U.S. and make money with it?'" Madou Bah made a sour face. "That's the way these people think. They can't open themselves. That's why they can't advance."

Ouedraogo, the Rail Band saxophonist, had died two days earlier, and Madou Bah wanted to pay the family a visit in Lafiabougou. We shared a taxi. The sun had almost set when we reached the road. As we drove out Sheikh Zayed, the smoky air that engulfs Bamako at night descended in force, suffused with the cotton candy pink and tangerine light of sunset. The near, rocky hills looked faded and distant. I dropped Madou Bah at Ouedraogo's house. "When will I see you?" he asked, but the taxi was already pulling away. I didn't answer. A few weeks later, I stopped by the office and learned that Madou Bah had gone back to Abidjan. It was good news. It meant he had given up on me.

To operate as a musician in Bamako, you have to negotiate social and professional circles. Djelimady had his set of *jelimusow* who called him for weddings. The Rail Band shared musicians and socialized with Lobi Traoré's and Dounanke Koita's bands. When opportunities came along, word spread within their circles, and the rewards went to those with the right connections. Djelimady had disapproved of Madou Bah, but he had not forbidden me to work with him. I had been lucky to be with Djelimady, for he was big and well loved enough to rise above the petty insecurities that plagued lesser musicians. He shared his opinions freely, but he never set limits on my activities. Still, I let everyone know that my work with Djelimady took precedence over all else. This is why his departure for Dabia with Babani Sissoko left me at such a loss. Without Djelimady, my life in Bamako had no center. I was in no circle at all.

One morning, Samakou pulled up beside me in Solo's red Honda as I was walking along the road. "Get in," he said. "Sali Sidibé wants to see you." Sali lived near the Tounkaras, and I had befriended her *kamalé ngoni* player, a twenty-something boy named Harouna Samaké. I had visited them occasionally and Sali, Harouna, and I had played informally on the roof of their house during a few sunsets. This had posed no problem with Djelimady, in part because Sali lived in the neighborhood but also because Djelimady liked Sali and considered young Harouna the best *kamalé ngoni* player in Bamako. I had never entertained serious thoughts about working with Sali, but now things had changed. Sali was about to begin work on a new cassette, her first in over two years. Speaking through her husband Modibo, Sali invited me to play on the recording. With Djelimady away in Dabia, her timing could not have been better.

I liked Sali from the moment I met her. Most of the Malian women I knew kept up a cool front with me. The *jelimusow* were regal and distant—like Ami Koita—or else bossy, like Yayi. The Tounkara women loved to joke among themselves, but their jokes always seemed to have victims. Sali's joy was different, like something she couldn't control. It flashed in her sharp hazel eyes. It sprang from her cherub cheeks. It always gave me a lift. At the same time, I knew that Sali's smile hid pain and worry. She was heavy and often complained about soreness in her legs and puffiness around her eyes. Doctors had seen her but had not helped.

Sali's career was in a rut, and rescuing it was slender, mild-mannered Modibo's responsibility. This was normal for the husband of a singing star, but, being a good ten years younger than Sali, Modibo had a hard time conveying the manager's requisite air of authority. If Sali's smile hid pain, Modibo's hid insecurity.

Modibo set up for the first rehearsal in the semi-enclosed pale blue verandah between their bedroom and the courtyard. He brought out a standing fan, a number of chairs, two small amplifiers, and the enormous powered speaker used for Sali's voice and Harouna's *kamalé ngoni*. Musicians began to arrive. Barou pulled up on his lavender mobilette with Dounanke Koita perched on the back cradling a guitar and keyboard. Close behind came Bakari the *djembe* player and Mamadi Kondé, who played guitar and bass in Dounanke's band. A plump, fortyish man with small eyes, Kondé sat in a chair during Dounanke's shows, perfectly deadpan, a man doing his job. Kondé was a surefooted musician in all the Malian styles, but he always wore the expression of a man in whose lap a baby has just vomited.

Harouna emerged from his room with an eight-string *kamalé ngoni*, his own creation. Sanata, Sali's daughter, and the other girl chosen to sing backup lingered off to the side. And finally, outdressing everyone there in a sapphire grand *boubou* with gold embroidery cascading down its front, came Amadou Traoré, the arranger for the recording project and a veteran of many Bamako bands, including the legendary Malian *salseros*, Maravillas du Mali. Amadou, I was told, went by his stage name, "Adèze."

"*Bon,*" said Adèze, holding his transverse flute aloft and addressing the musicians with a professorial air. "Today we begin the newest recording of our hostess, Salimata Sidibé. As you know, Sali has not released a cassette in Mali since 1991. With this album, Sali will reclaim her reputation as the Black Pearl of Wassoulou. We have selected all of you in order to give this recording a new sound, something to win the attention of Sali's fans around the world. We have contracted with our producer, Saky Kouyaté, whose studio is right here in the neighborhood, and we hope to begin recording within two weeks. That will depend on us, my friends. It is not a small project we undertake today. Sali has selected eight songs for this cassette. So without further ado, let's go to work."

Adèze's formality took some getting used to. A lifetime in government bands had marked him. Right away, I could see he wasn't going over well with Dounanke and Kondé, whom I caught sharing skeptical glances as Adèze laid out the plan. Sali, on the other hand, was tickled.

She slouched back in her chair and chuckled at Adèze's jokes, fairly glowing as he took every opportunity to laud her. Once the rehearsal began, however, Adèze proved himself. He took charge. He mediated disputes. He kept things moving. There was none of the tentativeness of sessions with Madou Bah Traoré nor the anarchy of rehearsals with Toumani's Symmetric Orchestra. Only the Rail Band's well-oiled, time-tested machine and Habib Koité's disciplined team could compare. By the end of that first two-hour session, we had worked on three songs. I found myself believing that we really *were* going to make a record.

Sali's singing was a thrill. When she stood up and raised the microphone to her lips, the merry housewife fell away. Her voice matched those of *jelimusow* in force, but where they wailed from the heavens, Sali summoned her spirits from the earth. In heavy, liquid tones, her melodies meandered over the shuffling shoals of hunters' rhythms. She went out of tune now and then, and I had the sense that singing was not easy for her. But when the mood and the music were right, Sali rose above the rough edges and soared.

All through the session, Modibo's brother, a wiry boy of fifteen, prepared shot glasses of green tea, which he distributed with systematic fairness. Ten musicians jammed into such a small space generated heat in the March afternoon, when Bamako temperatures can break 100 degrees. That tea, brewed strong to the point of bitterness, sweetened to excess, and then poured through the air from glass to glass until it produced a head of brown foam, refreshed like cold beer and kicked like espresso.

When the music ended, Modibo pulled me aside and asked me to stay around. He wanted to ask if I had any advice about the recording. I made two suggestions: Vary the instrumentation from song to song, and use live percussion rather than a drum machine. I argued that if they did these two things, they could make a tape that would stand out from the legions of indistinguishable Wassoulou cassettes. Modibo translated for Sali, who nodded approvingly.

"So Djelimady has gone to Dabia with Babani," Modibo then said pointedly. Some weeks earlier, Modibo had suggested that I explore with Djelimady the possibility of arranging a soirée for Sali at Babani's compound. I had chosen a relaxed moment to float the idea with my mentor.

"Babani likes Wassoulou songs," Djelimady had said. "He might invite Sali. But if she goes, she should not bring a large group, just four or five musicians." At the time, I had taken this to mean: *They* can go, but *you* shouldn't. Sali had subsequently written a praise song for Babani and recorded it on a cassette. Modibo had taken the tape to Douga's house in Hippodrome just two nights earlier, on the eve of the Dabia excursion.

"I saw Djelimady there," said Modibo.

"Oh?" I replied.

"He was a little funny with me."

"What do you mean?"

Modibo said that Djelimady had suggested I should pay Sali when I visited her to play. Djelimady had already told me the same thing, and I had taken to ending my visits with Sali by offering her a little money, which she made a show of refusing and then accepted. But Modibo seemed more interested in my loyalty than in my money. After all, he had argued that I should be paid like all the other musicians, an offer I had refused. Modibo's point seemed to be that Djelimady was not looking after my interests. Lest I misunderstand, Sali jumped in, her eyes twinkling with revelation. "Djelimady," she said, and then in Bambara that even I could understand, "he's bad!"

"Perhaps he is jealous that you are working with us," Modibo ventured. "It's Africa, you know. We're all a bit egotistical."

Salimata Sidibé was born and raised in Yanfolila, Wasulu. Sali told me that her father, Fasse Koro Samaké, was a *marabout*, indeed the Imam of their village. He was also a sand diviner, a kind of prophesier who works by whispering into a handful of sand and then casting it before him to discover future good and evil in the patterns of the scattered grains. In Wasulu, lives can turn on such divinations.

Sali's father refused to let her sing, though in her nightly dreams she had been singing since the age of three. In the morning, she would tell her parents her dreams, worrying them. "If you are a noble, you don't sing," Sali reminded me. "But it was God who gave me this ability, and since it was a gift from God, people from around the village went to my father and told him to let me sing."

Sali continued, "There was this commandant, an administrative authority of Yanfolila. He took me in with him and I stayed there for five years. I was just a little girl, but every time there was a ceremony, he would sit me at a table and I would sing. Everyone thought it was marvelous, and they applauded me. My father became even angrier. He has never to this day said it was okay for me to sing. Song, for my father, is the work of Satan."

Another intercession allowed Sali's career to advance in spite of her father. In the early 1970s, when the state-sponsored Ensemble Instrumentale du Mali (EIM) was in its heyday, the group recruited its first artist from Wasulu. EIM's mission was to help build a sense of nationhood by bringing together artists from every region of Mali. Coumba Sidibé had become the first to sing Wassoulou songs for a national audience, and she had done well. Eager to recruit another singer from the region, EIM eventually heard about the young girl who stayed with the commandant of Yanfolila.

"The national director of youth came to our village," Sali told me. "He came to my parents and asked, 'Is Sali here? We need her to sing in the Ensemble Instrumentale.' My parents knew where I was, but they told the director I was not there, that I had gone to Cote D'Ivoire. He had an idea what was happening, so he went to the governor of the region. They went together to see my father with gifts, fabric for *boubous* and 100,000 CFA. They pleaded with my father. They could not force him. They couldn't take his daughter, but they could ask, saying that the Ensemble needed her. So after lots of discussion, my father's younger brother, who was there, had understood. He knew that everyone has their destiny. He said, 'Take her and let her sing.' This was against my father's wish, but there was nothing more he could do. That is the law of our society. If the younger brother of the father says yes, the father cannot say no."

Sali came to Bamako. She worked with the Instrumental Ensemble over the next nine years. She formed her own group in 1985 and began recording cassettes and building her audience. Sali played clever politics in the capital and managed to become the singer of choice for Mali's armed forces. She played all the army dances and dedicated her first cassette to the country's men in uniform.

Her next break came when a British musicologist named Lucy Durán came to Mali to film musicians for the BBC. By this time, Lucy had spent over a decade researching and writing about West African music. She had recognized Toumani Diabaté's genius when he was still a teenager and had brought Toumani to London to record his landmark solo *kora* record, *Kaira*. Though deeply inside the world of the *jelis*, Lucy was just discovering Wassoulou music when she arrived in Bamako with a BBC film crew.

Lucy and Sali bonded instantly. Sali took Lucy to her village, where Sali's father cast sand and made predictions about the personal lives of people in the film crew, some of which eerily came true, impressing everyone. Lucy helped to arrange a tour for Sali and her group in Europe. By then Oumou Sangaré had burst onto the Malian scene. Lucy helped to prepare a compilation of Wassoulou songs called *Women of Mali: The Wassoulou Sound*, which made a strong showing internationally. Wassoulou music had dawned.

Then, in 1990, during the last, bleak days of Moussa Traoré's regime, Sali wrote the song that would mark the peak of her career. "It was a story about gold," Sali told me. "We had a minister of finance here by the name of Zoumana Sacko. There had been a problem between some powerful foreigners involving gold. It was a question of fraud. They were exporting gold from Mali, and Minister Sacko stopped them. I had never met this minister, but I liked what he did. It showed that he loved his country, even though it angered the ministers who were working with the foreigners. So then I was invited to sing at a reception for the minister of defense. There were nine other ministers there as well. I sang this song 'Naka Gnami,' which means 'When Things Get Messed Up.' It says that when Mali's gold disappears, *Malians* should be the ones selling it, not foreigners. When I sang that, it did not please the minister of defense. He came right up to me and said, 'Why did you sing that about our gold? You must not sing that!' The ministers were very angry. Another politician had to intervene and tell them to leave me alone."

Perhaps those ministers already knew their days were numbered. In 1991, after Moussa Traoré was arrested and Mali's democratic era was at hand, Sali released her cassette *Naka Gnami*. It played like an anthem of the new patriotism.

"Singers began coming to me," Sali told me, "asking if I would sell them the rights so they could do their own versions of it. But I refused. Fodé Kouyaté came and asked, and I said, 'Fodé, if you record this song, it will be war between us for the rest of our lives.'"

It seemed that Sali had arrived at last in Mali. But musical careers in Africa are fragile, and from this height things unraveled quickly for Sali. She took a band to Gabon in October 1992. She had been invited there by a promoter who had planned performances for her throughout Central Africa. Gabon went well, but when the group moved on to Brazzaville in the Republic of Congo, they arrived just in advance of major civil disobedience there and a subsequent government clampdown. Muslims were in particular danger; they were being attacked at mosques. The government agreed to protect Sali and her musicians, who then entered a state of siege. Soldiers and thugs patrolled the streets with guns, demanding of anyone, "Give money or die."

Here stories diverge. Sali told me that the promoter had failed to pay her for the Gabon concert. She had no money and her personal possessions had been stolen. She couldn't help herself, let alone her musicians. Some of the musicians on that tour remain convinced that Sali kept the money and abandoned them in the Congo. Knowing that I had heard the stories, Sali made a point of denying this. "Among us, musicians are not always literate," she said. "They have not all been to school. There were certain musicians who understood the situation, who understood that it was not the star's fault, that the star herself had a serious problem. But there were others who did not understand. Some people in the group started to talk. They knew the truth, but they preferred to look on the bad side. They said I took all the money. But I didn't have the money. It was *I* who had been betrayed."

Sali escaped siege in the Congo through yet another intervention, this time by a California rock singer named Toni Childs. Childs had heard Sali's voice on Lucy Durán's *Women of Mali* CD and had fallen in love. She simply *had* to have Sali on her next record, which she had traveled to Peter Gabriel's Real World Studios in Box, England, to record. The staff at Real World managed to locate Sali in the Congo, and in January 1993, just as I was making my first visit to Bamako, Real World flew Sali, but only Sali, out of hot water in Congo to rainy England to do the session with Toni Childs. Without her husband to translate for her, Sali was inaccessible to her collaborators and quite disoriented. The recording went ahead, but through a series of misunderstandings the music was never released. By the time Sali returned to Bamako, after nearly two years away, members of her band were trickling back from the Congo with harrowing tales of their abandonment.

The last of Sali's musicians to escape the Congo was Sayan Sissoko, the Manding *ngoni* player, who had been Sali's guitarist for the ill-fated tour. By the time I learned all this, Sayan was my friend. I had first met him when we played with Fodé Kouyaté and the Rail Band in the Tabalé concerts. Sayan had come along on our excursion to Kita with Manian Damba, and he was about the only *ngoni* player who had learned to play old-time West Virginia tunes as banjo-*ngoni* duets with Dirck. I asked Sayan for his version of the Congo story.

"I was there for three years and eight days," he said. "I knew no one there, and we in the band had no money."

"How did you survive?" I asked.

"We played marriages and baptisms. When we made enough to buy a ticket, we sent one person. Even when Sali got back to Mali, she did not try to contact us. Finally, someone went and saw Babani Sissoko in Lagos."

"Babani!" I exclaimed. "Of course." But there was a problem with the story. In 1994 the millionaire was presumably missing in action himself, having overspent on the project in Dabia a few years earlier.

Sayan explained, "Babani had gone from Dakar to Banjul, then to Cotonu, then to Lomé, and finally to Lagos. There was a woman with him there, and one night they saw me on the television. I was playing in a video clip, and this woman said, 'Ah, Baba, I know this guy.' Babani said, 'You know him?' 'Yes,' she said, 'Salimata Sidibé has left him in the Congo.' Babani said, 'Ah, good. He is my brother. It's been three years I've been looking for him. I didn't know where he was.' So Babani gave her money to bring to me to Lagos."

Sayan arrived in Lagos and told Babani of Sali's betrayal. "Babani just said, 'I have told you, Sayan. *Never* travel with a singer. They are not serious.'"

It was hard to connect the jolly woman presiding over our rehearsals with the manipulator Sayan described. The musicians never discussed the Congo adventure. They concentrated on the present work and said little about the past. I kept my ears open but followed the musicians' lead.

Young Harouna easily lived up to Djelimady's high praise. In Harouna's hands, the *kamalé ngoni* became more than an ethnic folk instrument. He could play whatever came into his head: griot standards, Salif Keita, South African pop songs. Harouna built his own instruments, including a twelve-string version that let him play diatonic music, using notes not normally found on the *kamalé ngoni*. I imagined what he might do with musical training and real opportunity. Barou told me I was lucky that Sali allowed me and Harouna to play together informally when the group was not rehearsing. "That is unusual," he warned me. "She is very protective of him."

I asked Barou about Sali's praise song to Babani. It seemed nervy, considering the millionaire's role in the Congo fiasco. Barou laughed. "This whole cassette is praise songs," he said, explaining that the theme of the tape we were preparing was gold and diamond merchants. Every song praised a different fabulously wealthy dealer. "Sali has become a griot," joked Barou.

Then, two weeks into the rehearsals, everything changed. On Monday and Tuesday, we couldn't work because Dounanke and his musicians had other commitments. Then on Wednesday, there was a baptism for one of Dounanke's nephews. Dounanke said it would be over in time for Sali's 3:00 rehearsal, but when it got to be 2:30 and the musicians were still setting up in Dounanake's family compound, Barou and I decided we had better go and let Sali know what was happening. We climbed onto his lavender mobilette and rode over the rough dirt roads along the edge of the rocky mesa. When we reached Sali's compound, Barou told Sali the baptism was running late and suggested that we postpone the rehearsal.

Nothing I had seen or heard from Sali up to that point prepared me for her reaction. She burst into a rage. The gravity that sometimes came into her singing voice bloomed forth as she castigated Barou in a battering of Bambara. The spark in her eye turned to flame. She came at him like a mad woman, shouting and pointing. I kept hearing my name sprinkled through Sali's diatribe. Modibo tried to restrain her. "No, no, Sali," he said feebly. "It's not that. Listen to me." She would not.

This went on for half an hour. Now and then, Sali would turn her ire on Modibo, giving Barou a brief chance to fill me in. "She's gone crazy," he said. "She thinks that you and I are plotting to bring Dounanke's group to America instead of hers."

Instead of hers? I thought. Did Sali too consider me her agent and promoter? Such delusions seemed an inescapable consequence of my work, and this always made me uncomfortable. But this time, no calm explanation of the reality was going to help. With paranoid fantasy running deep, Sali cast Dounanke as the spoiler. "Dounanke is a *faux frère*," she ranted. "I knew all along he was a *bandit!* I will *never* play with him again."

In the confused hours that followed, Barou and I shuttled between Sali's compound, Dounanke's compound, and Saky's studio. "She can't do this," said Saky. "I'm the producer. I'm the one who says who will play on the cassette. It's not *her* money down the drain if this thing falls apart."

We met on Sali's verandah that evening. By then she had recovered herself and was ready to make her case in civil terms. Sali wore a blue skirt and a covering robe with red and white diamonds embroidered on it. Behind her, a leaf-patterned curtain swung gently in the doorway to her bedroom. Before her, Adèze, Barou, Kondé, Harouna, Saky, Modibo, Sanata, Samakou Tounkara, myself, and a few others sat in a circle. Sali spoke at length in Bambara, with Adèze interjecting occasional "Uh huhs." She castigated the musicians for their lack of seriousness, but she did not mention my plot to take Dounanke's group to America. Next it was Saky's turn. He too spoke calmly, but with an accusatory note in his voice. I could feel things heating up, but the meeting ended peacefully. Barou returned to the baptism to play with Dounanke, and the rest of us rehearsed. As Sali sang her praise song to Babani Sissoko, the wind whipped the far branches of the tree in her courtyard. The green leaves waved like frantic paint brushes reworking the canvas of a fading blue sky.

After the rehearsal, Sali's daughter Sanata served a meal of goat in a dark, spicy sauce. We all ate together and a hint of the old *esprit de corps* reemerged. But things were never the same after that. Barou had been shaken by this incident. Not only had he received the brunt of Sali's anger, but he'd been spooked by her references to sorcery. "Sali practices strong magic," he told me. "Once I came to her house and found her with her hands cupped around a white chicken. She was talking to it, preparing it for death. That goat you ate last night was probably a sacrifice. I'm glad I didn't eat it. When she was shouting at me, she said, 'Barou, if I say you won't play with any other group but mine, that will be it. Remember, I'm from *Wasulu.*'"

Barou said that Modibo was Sali's fifth husband, and he doubted he would be the last. More chillingly, Barou claimed that Sali kept young Harouna in her camp using sorcery. "Maraboutic powers," as he put it. "Once, another singer invited him to play on a recording. When she heard about it, she said that if anyone tried to take Harouna from her, it would be the last thing they did." So much for the *kamalé ngoni* prodigy's opportunities.

Around this time, Djelimady returned from Dabia. He expected to depart on his Cuba excursion as soon as his passport arrived. Leaving Dabia had been a sacrifice, but sweet as life was with Babani, Djelimady had a career to consider.

"So Banning," he asked, "you've gone pentatonic, eh?" The phrase "going pentatonic" was one of our jokes, something like "not playing with a full deck." It was good to see Djelimady, and despite his jabs I sensed he was glad I'd found something to do, not jealous at all as Modibo had suggested. I said nothing to him about Sali's blowup. He apologized for abandoning me, and he assured me that the Rail Band would start working again as soon as he returned from Cuba.

I continued rehearsing with Sali for a short time longer. Then one day I came to Sali's compound and Modibo told me there would be no more rehearsals. It was time to record. Saky Kouyaté's studio was disappointing, a small Tascam eight-track cassette recorder on a wooden table. I had not even known it was possible to record eight tracks on a cassette. Surely cramming so much information onto such a small tape would compromise quality. Even with the best engineer, a good result seemed out of reach.

The engineer was Bainy Koita, introduced to me by Modibo as "the best Wassoulou guitarist in Mali." With Dounanke banished, Bainy would take the guitar solos on the cassette. "That's too bad," said Barou. "With Dounanke and you, Sali had the chance to do something different. If she lets Bainy take all the solos, her tape will sound just like all the other Wassoulou tapes." It was true. My advice about using live percussion and varying the instrumentation was ignored. Sali was being handled by her producers. She was in charge of nothing beyond her own performance.

"I don't think Sali's out to make history," I told Barou. "She just wants to get her career going again."

"But she could do better," he said. Barou may have feared Sali, but he also admired her. "Sali could be great, if she just *tried* to be."

I knew what he meant. The idea of an artist with Sali's talent recording in such an amateur studio, setting her powerful songs to silly, fake rhythm tracks, made no sense. I too felt an urge to protest. But what could I offer? I didn't have money for a real studio. And what if I *had* been the producer? What if Sali listened to my ideas? Maybe the music would be more palatable to foreign ears, but would the Malians like it? I lacked the means and conviction to take on these battles. Having made my case at the outset, I now kept quiet.

The recording sessions dragged on, and spirits slumped. One morning I sat half asleep, watching Modibo's brother make up the day's first batch of gunpowder tea. A transistor radio by his side played 1940s swing jazz. Sour as always, Kondé the bassist stood at the street surveying a selection of Chinese watches for sale by a roving street vendor. "The Taiwanese are the biggest thieves in the world," sniped Kondé as he inspected the watches on the vendor's display board. "There's nothing but Mafia there." Kondé bought one anyway, cursing the vendor, the watch, and the Taiwanese as he did it. Then he unleashed his

bile on the project at hand, and soon on the overall pointlessness of playing music in Bamako. "I'm getting my papers and going to France," he
said. "I've got a brother in Paris. It's hard there too, but at least you're
dealing with professionals. It can't be worse than this."

Though we didn't yet know it, our project had ground to a halt. The
producer, Saky, had discovered that Sali was quietly negotiating a deal
to record with a rival producer in France. Saky had chanced upon the
paperwork during one of his visits to the Bureau of Authors' Rights in
Bamako. A showdown between Modibo and Saky ensued, and Saky
called off the recording. With that, the return of Sali Sidibé went on
hold, and I returned to Djelimady's world.

11

Interview with the Millionaire

To be a *griot* is to lower oneself in order to make others greater, even when you know you are richer, more knowledgeable, more powerful.

Barbara Hoffman paraphrasing a griot from Kela in "Power, Structure, and Mande *jeliw*"

Bambara proverb says, "One finger alone cannot pick up a stone." But in the century's final decades, a cult of individuality has emerged in Mali, perhaps bolstered by modern *jeliya*, and it has eroded the Independence Era band culture. Singing stars backed by computer-driven keyboards, drum machines, and freelance instrumentalists have replaced the old regional orchestras. During my stay, the Super Rail Band was all that remained, and it too was now threatened. The public had lost interest. Low attendance at Rail Band shows had the Buffet Hotel de la Gare negotiating an endgame with the band, and though the Rail Band was still recording in Europe, Malian distributors hesitated to release the music. The Rail Band's plight fit a larger pattern of change, but the band's boosters needed someone to blame, and Babani Sissoko, whose pull on Djelimady had brought the band to a near standstill, was the obvious scapegoat.

In Dabia, Babani's musicians had entertained him every night. Ami Koita, Kandia Kouyaté, and Yayi Kanouté had sung round robin high masses of nostalgia and praise that had stretched to the first light of morning. They had performed in the public amphitheater Babani built for such occasions, and each musician had been rewarded with millions of CFA. Back in Bamako, the Rail Band had extended its Ramadan break, leaving the players without pay and the fans without music.

Meanwhile, in the Tounkara compound, everyone waited expectantly for their musicians to return from Dabia. On the homecoming day, Solo Tounkara announced his new wealth by buying a car—a red Mitsubishi four-door with a Turbo engine—and Yayi and Adama each bought a Yamaha mobilette. The *jelimuso* and her *ngoni* player rolled up to the front door together, engines purring, to applause from the entire family.

"Soooolu kili!" bellowed Djelimady's wife. Her song, known as "calling the horses," once summoned Sunjata's mighty steeds, but now *jelis* use it to mark great events. The person being sung *must* reward the singer, and Adama Tounkara dutifully handed his aunt a bill. Adama had bought himself a fine earth-tone *boubou*, and for the first time he looked like a man of means and purpose.

Madou Tounkara greeted me urgently on his return from Dabia and requested a private conference. When we were alone, he produced a crisp 10,000 CFA note, repayment for the money I had lent him back in November. He had not forgotten!

The next day, bicycles arrived for all the boys in the compound—gifts from Douga Sissoko. The doorway was blocked with crudely lettered cartons: "Arabian youth bicycle. Made in China." "It's Douga who has done this to me," said Djelimady. "In two days, they'll all be broken."

The compound buzzed with activity as never before. Adama Kouyaté grilled slabs of beef, Djeneba pounded grain, and girls tended cooking pots while children clamored and rode up the stoop on their new bicycles. Djelimady had bought a refrigerator for his wife, and women sat for hours producing tied-off baggies of cold water and plastic bottles of cold *gimbré*—a sweet ginger drink—to sell to passersby. At the far end of the compound, Yayi Kanouté sat in a state of radical deconstruction, preparing for a wedding two days off. She teased her dyed-red hair until it stuck up like a fright wig. She worked a long *nime* stick—the local version of a toothbrush—around her mouth. Her elongated breasts sagged off to either side of her rolling belly, but she greeted me without a hint of self-consciousness.

It was Friday, the last day Djelimady could have arranged for the Rail Band to play at the Buffet that weekend, but he had not sent word of his return. On Saturday night, we went through the usual motions, but when we reached the Buffet we found it deserted. Having heard nothing from Djelimady, the management had canceled the show. Whether or not this was deliberate on Djelimady's part, it reflected his unsettled mood. Djelimady took no visible pleasure in his family's good fortune. While everyone else celebrated, he lingered in a state of distraction.

Before the end of the visit to Dabia, Babani had announced one further gift to the Tounkaras: a new house in Hippodrome. But Djelimady seemed vexed by the news. "I don't *want* to live in Hippodrome," he confided. "Babani wants me to go there, but I like Lafiabougou. I like to be surrounded with people, children, life in the street. In Hippodrome, you're locked in behind walls."

Babani's generosity had undermined Djelimady's self-determination. Once he had seen his way. He had known where he would move his family. He had had plans for the Rail Band. Now things seemed out of his hands. He felt unsure about his upcoming Cuban excursion; the Rail Band was angry with him for neglecting them; acquaintances and friends constantly approached him for handouts. But while others embarked on spending sprees, Djelimady remained as cheap as ever, and few of those supplicant friends were ever rewarded.

"You must buy a new car," Solo encouraged his brother.

"Why?" protested Djelimady. "The Nissan is fine. They're just waiting for parts." But weeks went by and the old white car never reappeared, and Djelimady grumbled each time he had to hire a taxi.

March 22 was the Day of the Martyrs, a holiday honoring the 150 students and trade unionists that Moussa Traoré's troops had killed on the streets of Bamako during the protests of 1991. These protests had resulted in a new government and, more important, in the country's democratic system. Martyr's Day carried the weight of America's Independence Day, even though it commemorated events that had occurred scarcely five years earlier.

The Martyr's Day celebration would include a mega-concert at the Palais de la Culture, and all over Bamako musicians were scrambling to pull groups together. Barou had been recruited to play with Askia Modibo, a Wassoulou reggae singer. Most of the Rail Band had been tapped by one performer or another. Djelimady and Solo would accompany the *jelimuso* Backo Dagnon.

That evening at the compound, a circus atmosphere prevailed. By now everyone had new clothes, and more bicycles had appeared for the smaller children. The boys' bikes that Douga had given were already starting to break, just as Djelimady had predicted. Both of the twins had injured themselves learning to ride. A jumble of cheaply built bikes cluttered the compound doorway. "It's Douga who has done this to me," Djelimady droned as he passed them.

Out on the stoop, Djelimady immersed himself in hushed conversation with a man I did not know, another old friend asking for money, I presumed. When the man left unhappily, Djelimady stormed into the courtyard. "Adama," he scolded his wife, "where's dinner? We're going to be late!" A bright wah-wah guitar note—distinctly Djelimady—burst from the TV speaker, part of an old Rail Band song used in a car dealer's ad. The note shivered in the air, a reminder of simpler days.

At the back gate of the Palais, Djelimady left the cajoling of guards to Solo, who, lacking his brother's stature, resorted to angry complaining. "This is my artist's card," Solo sputtered at the complacent official barring our entry. "This card admits me to *any* performance in Mali. Can't you see that we're artists? We have amplifiers for the performance."

"Nothing is organized in this country," muttered Djelimady. "Everything is improvised." Traffic piled up behind us. A bus full of artists staying at the Hotel Amitié sounded its horn. Just as Djelimady and Solo were about to abandon the effort and go home, Solo tried one last feint. "I'm the band leader," he lied. "If my musicians show up and they don't find me or this equipment, Backo Dagnon will not perform tonight. And whose fault will *that* be?" More worn down than won over, the guard let us pass.

As the acts began to parade across the Palais stage beneath the looming portrait of Banzumana Sissoko, Djelimady explained to me that Babani had wanted to fly from Dabia for this show. His people had begged him not to venture into such a mob. So Babani had dispatched one of his brothers, Balla, to represent him and give money to the artists. *Jelimuso* Hadja Soumano was the first to pander. Cordless microphone in hand, she leapt off the stage and made her way along the aisles of the sold-out house, exhaling *jeliya* all the way. She climbed over two rows of seats to station herself directly in front of the VIP seating area, where Balla sat dressed in a business suit, smiling coyly, the commando in a *boubou* beside him. On Balla's cue, the commando produced a packet of bills from his satchel and handed it to Hadja, who snatched it away and thrust it over her head to roaring acclamation. There was blood in the water, and now, one singer after another, the sharks came to feed. Backstage, amid the stench of old urine from the latrines, stars rubbed shoulders in a familiar *bogolon* and embroidery fashion show. Everyone watched for the commando to stroll toward the stage with his satchel.

Guinean vocal star Mory Djeli Kouyaté closed the show, just before 2:00 A.M. He had a flashy band, flown in from Conakry, more forceful but also more pretentious than the Bamako acts. Mory Djeli was a giant who strode across the stage grandly in a white robe and red fez and howled in a blustery, vibrato-rich voice. I heard Babani's name and saw Balla and the commando making their move. But this time, instead of rewarding the singer, they pointedly walked past the stage, the commando's satchel remaining clenched under his arm as they exited the hall.

"*C'est la vie, eh?*" Mory Djeli said bravely into the microphone. He managed to soldier on, but the crowd thinned fast. I thought of that old Reverend Gary Davis song, "*Candyman been here and gone!*"

"The public was not happy with Mory Djeli," said Djelimady afterwards. "He didn't sing his songs. People wanted to hear the songs they know. Instead, it was all Babani, Babani. He was just grabbing for money." Djelimady told me that the people had deliberately left while Mory Djeli was singing so that he would know they were dissatisfied. Djelimady also told me that before the show Mory Djeli had received 1 million CFA from Babani. Djelimady laughed for the first time in days. "Mory Djeli got lucky."

Sensing an opening, I decided to risk the question I had most wanted to ask. "Djelimady," I said, "do you suppose you could arrange for me to interview Babani?"

"You want to meet him," he said knowingly. I explained that Babani was the greatest patron of Malian musicians and that I wanted to ask him why he valued them so much. Djelimady smiled again and said, "It's possible."

For almost a week, Djelimady was a prisoner in his compound. Arrangements for the Cuba trip had been left to Bamba Dembele, the Rail Band's manager. Bamba had sent Djelimady's passport to the Cuban embassy in Burkina Faso for a visa. But on Tuesday, the planned day of departure, Bamba was nowhere to be found and no passports or tickets had arrived. So Djelimady waited.

Since Babani's arrival, Djelimady had spent his new wealth in only one visible way. He had dramatically increased the pace of construction at the new house. Every day men worked there, making concrete, molding it into cinder blocks, mortaring them together to complete the first floor in the far section of the house, building a staircase to the roof, and digging holes for the septic tank and its overflow. One morning, during Djelimady's Cuba vigil, he and I taxied from the family compound to the new house to supervise the installation of heavy metal doors.

We sat on my verandah with our guitars. Djelimady's captivity had allowed us to play together again, and though he'd been ornery and half-hearted about it, he had given me a lot of material that week. I remembered what had lured me to Bamako in the first place. As much and as hard as I had worked, I still couldn't get close to Djelimady's sterling guitar tone. Though I now knew basic parts to most of the standard songs in the Manding canon, a mountain of variations stood before me. I was reciting limericks while Djelimady improvised sonnets.

Suddenly Djelimady stopped playing. "Banning," he said out of the blue, "it's now four weeks you haven't paid your food money."

He was right. Ever since Babani had arrived and Djelimady had hesitated to accept my weekly payment, I had stopped offering it, assuming he no longer cared. He did not seem angry with me, but his message was clear: We had an arrangement and, Babani or no Babani, we were going to stick to it. I paid him for the missed weeks.

"By the way," said Djelimady, tucking the money into the front pocket of his *boubou*, "I spoke to Douga about your interview with Babani. I think we can arrange something."

The next day, Babani returned to Bamako from Dabia and Djelimady abandoned his vigil. "It's too late now," he said. "The recording has already gone ahead in Cuba." It was Friday again, and as Djelimady hopped into a taxi—no telling when he would return—I rushed up and asked, "What about the Rail Band? Will we play tomorrow?"

He furrowed his brow and glared at me through the open window. "No," he said, as though stating the obvious. "The Rail Band is finished."

Within hours, Fotigui Kouyaté, the Rail Band bassist, came by the compound to confirm the news. The break with the hotel was official. There would be no more rehearsals and no more gigs at the Buffet Hotel de la Gare. A twenty-six-year institution and a whole era of Malian music had apparently ended before my eyes.

"I don't understand Djelimady," the Colonel fumed. "Look where he is building the staircase. Right in the middle of the courtyard. If he had thought ahead, he would have made the other section of the house two stories high. But he was too cheap for that. He is going to end up with a house that is smaller than the one he has now. And did you see the refrigerator he bought for his wife? It's not a new model. It can't even freeze ice. I don't understand how a man with so much money can be so *cheap.*"

Djelimady had failed to bring Babani to visit our compound, and the Colonel was not taking it well. "It's *Djelimady* who is Babondo's friend now," he insisted. "He must arrange a visit, to show his friend the new house. This is not for money, just to sit down and discuss. We will close the door, and we will understand one another. When he leaves, he will give everyone a packet of new bills. *Oui.*"

More than a week passed before Bamba Dambélé appeared to explain the Cuba fiasco. Bamba said that an official at the Cuban embassy had made a mistake and misplaced Djelimady's passport. It was unfortunate, he said, but quite innocent. Meanwhile, everyone had a theory about what had *really* gone wrong. Djelimady was convinced that the Cubans had blocked his entry. "Now that Mali is democratic," he said, "Castro doesn't like us anymore. He thinks we're with the Americans."

Most people felt that Djelimady had purposely scuttled the trip so he could remain with Babani. "That's what everyone in London thinks," said Lucy Durán, fresh from England. "Djelimady's millionaire has come and now he's letting his career go down the toilet."

It was my first meeting with Lucy. She had gotten word of my being in Bamako and had contacted me by e-mail to let me know she would be visiting for a few weeks. We met for a beer. "Nick Gold is crushed," said Lucy, lighting a cigarette. Nick was the producer who had set up the Cuba sessions. "Do you know who recorded down there in Cuba? *Ry Cooder.* Oh, it just breaks your heart! This was Djelimady's chance. It would have *made* him." Very possibly so. Lacking Djelimady and Basekou Kouyaté, the young *ngoni* master who was also to have played in Cuba, Nick had scrambled to find Cuban musicians to fill out the sessions. In the process, he had created the Buena Vista Social Club, destined to win a Grammy award the following year and to outsell every record release that had ever borne the words "world music."

I told Lucy that as far as I was concerned, it wasn't Djelimady's fault. "He sat there waiting for four days," I protested. "He came back from Dabia just for that."

"Banning," said Lucy firmly, "I'm sorry, but Djelimady is not telling you the truth. They could even have gone without visas. And I promise you, the Cubans did not block anything. They are desperate for things like this. They don't refuse visas for anyone."

Over two beers that afternoon, I got an education from Lucy. She explained to me basic principles of Manding society. She talked about *fadenya*, the troublesome spirit of rivalry between children by the same father and different mothers. I thought about Samakou, forever an outsider in his father's compound. Among the Manding, said Lucy, your father is your first *fadenya* rival. Lucy also talked about *badenya*, the corollary bond of complicity among same-father–same-mother siblings, the force that bound Djelimady, Solo, and Madou Djan so closely. Lucy's current research dealt with female singers and also with cults. There were *komow*, pre-Islamic secret societies that griots can never join and so will never tell you about. And then there was *kono*, the cult of the bird in Kirina, where Sunjata won his great battle against the sorcerer king Soumaoro. That famous battle hinged on a cock's spur, which Sunjata placed on the arrow that killed his foe. The cock's spur was Soumaoro's Achilles' heel, since it came from his totemic animal. To touch it violated his pact with the ancestor spirits, the source of his supernatural powers. Lucy pointed out that Sunjata learned this crucial secret because one of Soumaoro's wives had betrayed him.

"The bottom line," Lucy concluded, "is that nobody in Mali likes to tell the truth. Because to tell the truth leaves you vulnerable to your enemies. Any fact about you—your real age or birth date, your mother's name, your exact weight—can be worked by the fetishists. So to protect themselves, nobody divulges real information. That's what makes doing research here so damned maddening."

That evening I prepared my questions for Babani Sissoko, but the list felt incomplete. It was hard to admit, but aside from my desire to coax some truth from the millionaire, I couldn't help but wonder if he might not also pass *me* one of those packets of bills. The Malians I knew had no qualms about this. They assumed that I would return wealthy. But such thoughts embarrassed me. What business did I have taking money from a Malian stranger, a man I knew little about? Yet I couldn't help myself. *Toubab*s like me got the best of everything in Bamako, I reasoned. The most comfortable chair. The coolest drink. The choicest morsels of meat. The front seat in the car. We were spoiled every step of the way in Africa. So why not a little good fortune from the magnanimous millionaire? There was no escaping it. I too had succumbed to my own awkward strain of Babani Fever.

At Madou's suggestion, I had learned to play a *jeli* song called "Bambougou N'chi." It told the story of a Bambara king who ordered miles and miles of canals dug through the desert to connect his palace grounds to the Niger River. He wanted to look out his window and see hippopotami. "Babani likes to think he resembles that king," Madou Djan had told me. "If you play this for him and you play it well—very slowly, he likes his music slow—Babani will give you money. Maybe even a car."

On the allotted day, I sat before the television in the Tounkara compound for three hours. When Djelimady still hadn't arrived to take me to the interview, I went home to bed, unnerved and exhausted. "Why didn't you wait for me?" blurted Djelimady from the back window of a car as it lurched to a halt beside me the following morning.

My heart sank. "I *did* wait," I said feebly, "right up until 9:00."

"Banning, I've told you. Babani's schedule is always improvised. I came for you at 10:00 and they told me you had gone home to sleep. You have to *wait* for me. Now, listen. I'm going to the presidential palace with Douga and Babani today. But tonight," he declared as the car began to roll, "come at 6:00 and *wait* for me."

"He's lying," said Djelimady's wife matter-of-factly when I reached the compound and reported this conversation. "He came home and went to bed. He was so tired he could barely talk."

I walked all over Bamako that day in 100-degree heat. The city was so jammed up with traffic that taxis made no sense. Exerting energy in that kind of heat put me in a drugged frame of mind. Images leapt out at me—a cart loaded high with yellow and brown bananas; twisted twigs trampled into the dirt; the shimmering, baking drive leading up to the train station; arms and legs tangling in crowded *bashées*; a man holding a dead chicken over a burning newspaper to singe its last feathers off. I stared at that chicken as the feathers blackened and the pink skin sprouted beads of oil. A woman washing clothes in her compound wore her hair tied into long black spikes, like malnourished carrots groping into the soupy air. Skinny-legged boys in baggy trousers played soccer in the dust. Cooking and rotting in the blaze, everything smelled. On one of the crammed market streets near the Boutique Informatique where I got my e-mail, the smell of burning hair assaulted me, triggering instinctual alarms—flight or fight.

Moving from destination to destination, I fended off peddlers. In the big traffic circle near the Maison des Jeunes, I had just ditched a Liberian refugee selling diamonds when a boy from Kayes tried to sell me hunks of what he said was gold.

"If I don't sell this gold, my boss won't take me home," he pleaded. "You name the price. Anything." I looked at the bubbly black and gold nuggets in the boy's hand and told him to go away. How had this city of desperadoes and hustlers produced such a smooth operator as Babani?

In the end, Solo drove me to Babani's compound in Hippodrome. "We'll find Djelimady and Douga there," he assured me. He had dressed himself in a green and brown tweed suit with double-breasted jacket; white pinstripe shirt; a wide, dark green necktie that set off the green filaments in his jacket; black dancing pumps that shone like polished silver and sported small gold bows; and—the *coup de grace*—a brown felt-brim hat, cocked slightly to add a note of unscrupulousness and danger. With his short hair and small, almost painted-on mustache, Solo looked like a Cotton Club gangster. About then, I noticed that I had forgotten to put on a belt. What did it matter? Next to Solo, I could look only like the threadbare American journalist I was.

"You don't plan to bring your guitar, do you?" Solo asked.

"Well, I was considering it," I said.

"Leave it here," he said. "Everybody in the world will be at Babani's. Don't bring anything you don't need for your interview." So much for my slow reading of "Bambougou N'chi."

Along the drive, we listened to a tape the Tounkaras had recorded in Dabia. Kandia Kouyaté sang "Sunjata" and sounded fabulous. "You haven't been working on your Bambara since Dirck left," Solo said, shaking his hatted head as we neared town. A grand squall from Kandia had elicited deep sighs of satisfaction, and Solo's reproach lamented my inability to appreciate the *jelimuso's* exalted meaning. "So much of the griot's art is in the words. You really need to *work* on the Bambara to appreciate that."

Later, back in America, I would hear this recording again on a tape that Kassim Kone purchased in a Malian market. The anthropologist would shed some light on Kandia's praise. "*Baba,*" she sings, "*between Dubai and Bamako, people have said a lot. But your story lies in darkness, a darkness no one has yet shed light on. Golden trumpets have been played for Alexander the Great. Silver horns were played for Alexander. But he failed to live his life to the fullest before he died.*"

"She is telling Baba to live life fully," Kassim told me then. "Alexander was so powerful, but now he is gone." Kandia sings the names of Babani's ancestors, saying that each is "*lying down with bullets and gunpowder in Kemuna.*" This was a way of saying that Babani's ancestors were warriors. "Kemuna is a ritual stone in Dabia," Kassim explained, "a place where bulls are killed each year."

Kandia's rhetorical art was lost on me as I drove toward Hippodrome with Solo that evening. His condescending attitude might have annoyed me, but another demon was nagging at my gut. What was it? Fear? Perhaps. I realized that I longed for this interview to be over. I had played out so many scenarios in my mind. In one, Babani would celebrate my work for African music and my friendship with Djelimady and plop a stack of fresh notes before me. In another, he would toy with me, be obtuse, build my expectations and then give me neither information nor money. If I asked hard questions, I might anger him or embarrass Djelimady. If I fawned, I might get nothing of any use. Was I a journalist or a supplicant? The closer I got, the less certain I felt. More than anything, I feared botching the opportunity and being left with self-recrimination over something I had done or failed to do. In my confusion, I didn't even know how I would measure success or failure.

We turned off Route de Koulikoro and approached the gate outside Babani's mansion. A street wedding was in progress at the corner, and barricades erected at either side of the mansion fended off celebrants and oglers. The public siege of the mansion had become routine, and the scene had the feel of a recently ended rock concert, with stragglers leaning against police barricades and logy security men lurking. I followed Solo and we made our way past a few gentlemen in *boubou*s. Solo's hushed greetings were met with skeptical responses. My suspicion that his gangster outfit might be the problem was confirmed when an old man in a fez muttered, *"bandit,"* as Solo passed.

At the gate, I noticed the uniforms of the security men—policeman-blue with badges that read, *"Chef Syndicat Babani Sissoko."* We had not yet presented ourselves to the guard when a new gray-blue Chevrolet minivan with smoked windows pulled up, and from it emerged Babani's tall, goateed commando bodyguard. The *boubou* he had worn at the Palais a week earlier had given way to golf attire: a white polo shirt, slacks, and track shoes, soiled, of course, with red Bamako mud.

I had watched Djelimady greet this man at the Palais. They had embraced and slapped each other on the back like old friends. "The big guy," Djelimady had told me, in reference to the second bodyguard, who was actually shorter but built more like a sumo wrestler, "he is for throwing people out. Crowd control. This one," he said, referring to the statuesque commando, "his specialty is hitting." Djelimady's French phrase, *"uniquement pour frapper,"* had stuck in my mind. Djelimady claimed that these guards were paid $1,000 a day.

After the Dabia excursion, I had the impression that the Tounkaras and Babani's elite guard chummed together like insiders in a political campaign road show. So it came as a shock when the commando eyed Solo like so much roughage and said, "Who are you?"

"Solo Tounkara," he replied mildly. Then Solo spoke quickly, using the words *"artiste"* and "Dabia," hoping vainly for the commando to soften his stance.

"And who's he?" he said referring to me.

"A journalist," Solo replied. "He's come to interview Babani." Solo used the French word *interoger,* rather than the usual *entrevuer.* It sounded harsh. "We'll just go in and wait," he concluded.

"No you won't," said the commando. "Not until I get confirmation. No journalists come in here without confirmation. Does he have a card?"

I fumbled in my back pocket and produced a calling card, soggy with sweat. "Speak French?" the commando snapped as he took my card. I assured him I did.

Solo broke in with a fatal note of irritation and said, "All you have to say is Solo Tounkara. I'm in the family."

"The family is four brothers and one sister," retorted the commando. "Is your name Sissoko?" Solo's eyes hit the dust. The commando's tone was ugly, suggesting a colonial authority. "This is *not* your family." Solo paced lightly, struggling to preserve some shred of dignity. Soon the commando returned and admitted us. "He's washing and praying now," he said. "You'll have to be patient."

As during my previous visit, the house was lined on both sides with new vehicles. The facing rows of chairs that formed an L along the front of the house and down one side of the garden fence were mostly full of men in *boubou*s or business suits and just a few women in gowns. The lines of chairs had been pressed forward and a ten-foot extension to the house's front salon was under construction. A forest of dried, thin, denuded tree trunks were jammed in at odd angles to support the new roof as the concrete dried. Inside the construction zone, tools mingled with hay upon which sheep slept, awaiting slaughter.

We had been sitting for almost two hours without eating when I spotted Douga and Djelimady at the gate. My mentor swept down the aisle of seated supplicants, his purple *boubou* catching the breeze. He smiled and greeted friends, and when he came to me he said with satisfaction, "Ah, Banning. You are there." I had not waited for him as instructed, but now we had moved on to a new improvisation. "I'm tired," said Djelimady. "This morning, we were at the presidential palace. Babani was received by the prime minister. He spoke on television. This afternoon, we were across the river. Babani bought two houses there today, bigger than this one."

We sat for an hour or so, my thirst and hunger gradually overpowering my desire for Babani's story or even his money. Then Babani arrived, dressed in a dark blue suit. He looked harried and entered the house greeting almost no one. Djelimady fussed. "If only you had been here this morning," he said. "He was relaxed, talking. You would have had a good interview." I steeled myself for a washout. Soon, without warning, Djelimady stood up and said, "Let's go." We headed for the door, where Douga was entering the house.

We passed through the unfurnished foyer and took the wide, broken-tile stairway up to the second floor, where Babani held court. Looking down the hallway upstairs, I saw at its end a pair of frosted glass doors with bright light behind them. It looked like the entrance to a dentist's office. Just before that, a door on the left led to Douga's room, a simple affair furnished only with four of Bamako's ubiquitous lawn chairs and one mattress on the floor, made up with pink sheets and a lacy spread. A TV on a rolling table was nearly halfway through playing a videotape of the James Bond film *Octopussy* in English.

Immediately the film's images hit home as a big money payoff turned into a chase scene through a crowded city in India. This involved motorized rickshaws, bladed weapons, and fat wads of money. When two of these cash bundles got away and flew from a rickshaw into a beggar's coin basket, everyone laughed with gusto. As the film progressed, a bowl of rice and meat sauce arrived, and we all ate together.

At almost 1:00 in the morning, we entered Babani's salon, an air-conditioned, fluorescent-lit, rectangular room about twenty-five by fifteen feet. Once again, there was little furniture. One of the puffy chairs used at the outdoor soirée I'd attended now swallowed Babani, still in his dark blue suit. Two men seated to his right were hunched over a brown briefcase. Around the room stood six almost life-size blowup photographs of Babani Sissoko. Each was encased in a deep wooden frame that left room for a neon light all the way down one side. The best one showed Babani in a fancy parlor chair, surrounded by the normal furnishings of the Western wealthy—paintings, china on a fancy table, a Persian carpet. "In America," said Djelimady.

Babani shook my hand but then returned to other matters. "Get ready," Djelimady coached. "Just start asking your questions. He has many people waiting. You may get only five minutes."

I knelt on the carpet before Babani. I noticed that his briefcase contained stacks of packeted 10,000 CFA notes, about $20,000 by my estimate, surely enough for an evening's amusement. Babani removed the packets and arranged them in a pile more than a foot deep. He pulled the pile toward him until it stood against the base of his chair. Then, in an odd touch of modesty, he covered the top of the pile with a sheet of cardboard. I began to ask questions in my best French. "Mr. Sissoko, how did you become the greatest patron of Malian musicians?"

Babani peered down at me with catlike eyes. "That astonishes you," he said. For all the activity in the room, his attention, once focused on me, seemed complete.

"Yes it does," I allowed.

"You know the fruit, the mango?" he asked. "When it starts, it's very small. People don't even see it. But when it becomes big, everyone notices it. We have a proverb among us. If a snake stays hidden, it will live a long time. But every day, if people see snakes, snakes, they will kill them. Now, people have discovered that Baba has money. But Baba was a billionaire for twelve years before anyone knew."

Babani smiled at me, a disarming, friendly smile that made crow's-feet play at the corners of his eyes and veer downwards across his temples. "When did they find out?" I asked.

"In 1984," he said, "I left Gabon. I returned to my village. I looked at it. It is a village that used to be big. But by then, to get water to drink in the village, people had to go eight to fifteen kilometers. Many marriages were ruined because of water. Many people refused to live in Dabia or to let their children marry there because they would suffer with no water. So in '84, I arrived at 7:00 in the evening. I saw how things were. And I cried."

I struggled to follow Babani's French. Sometimes his narrative trailed into mumbles. Sometimes he inserted confounding phrases of Bambara that left me unsure as to his meaning. The transcription I now report owes much to the help I later received from Kassim Kone. But even at the time, I understood that Babani was not simply answering my question about how he became a patron of Malian musicians. He was describing his greatest achievement in life. Kankan Musa, the fourteenth-century Malian king, brought African gold to Mecca and gave so much away in Cairo that he devalued gold prices there for a decade and drew the eyes of the whole Arab world to his kingdom. Bambougou

N'chi dug his canals through the savanna so that hippos could graze below his windows. Babani Sissoko rebuilt Dabia.

"Dabia, from the month of March until late August, is dangerous," he said, "because there is a lot of wind. When the women prepare food, they must close all the doors so that the fire does not spread. I was born at 9:00 in the morning on the seventeenth of August 1945. In these years, there wasn't much rain. My father had gone to the army. After my birth, they asked for fire to light my mother's room. Everyone went to the fields. One person stayed with the fire. And after a half-hour, the wind came. It came into the room and the room caught on fire. The fire burned the whole house, except the room where I was sleeping. So I had to rebuild the village because my birth had brought misfortune to my mother, the woman who made me, and to the whole village."

"People said to my brothers, 'Your brother. He's an imbecile. He's an idiot. Why doesn't he build factories?' But I said, 'God is great. My heart is clear. I am Muslim. I am Protestant. I am Catholic. Our God has said once you've gained your own good fortune, you must help the next one. You must pass the bread to everyone.' People asked, 'Where does Baba still have money?' Well, it's simple. No one reveals the door to his happiness. You never tell your secrets."

Then Babani focused his attention on me. "There is a reason that moved you to be interested in Africa," he said. "You are planting seeds, and in the future there will be fruit. People will not know that you have suffered—sickness, heat, the water, all that you have accepted." He was flattering me, playing the griot!

"Mr. Sissoko," I said, "tell me about your love of music."

"You go to Africa," said Babani, "and you find there is no museum. The museum of Africa is music. It is the griot. Africa organizes itself around dignity. But what shows dignity? It is music. Today, you have the Sissokos. They are proud. The Keitas. They are proud. Traoré, Diarra. But why are these families still proud? It's because of the music and griot tradition that tells them their history. All the African presidents who love their music are powerful. All that's left in Africa now is music."

Babani returned to his own story. "My father played music," he said, "very, very well. One day, he was in the room where we slept. He played music, music, music. And I listened. But as I wasn't saying anything, he suddenly said to me, 'Imbecile! You are mocking me.'

"'What did I do?' I asked.

"'You don't feel the music.'

"I said, 'Sure I do.'

"He said, 'I've played all this music. And you do nothing. You just lie there.'

"I said, 'Yes. I'm listening.'

"He said, 'What do you want to do? What's in your head? Don't you follow your tradition?'

"I said, 'Yes.'

"'But how? If you follow your tradition, then pick up the guitar and play it.'

"'I don't know how to play.'

"He said, 'Well, then I will kill you.'

"I said, 'All right. You brought me into this life. If you want to kill me, fine. There's nothing I can do about it.'

"He said, 'You are going to tell me. Why do you refuse to play music?'

"So I said, 'Think of your father. He is dead now. He didn't leave anything, no money, no gold, no clothing. Nothing.'

"'Yes,' he said, 'and afterwards, I told you your grandfather is dead. He was a warrior, who killed with guns, a sort of dictator or king. He was good.'

"'But your father died without leaving me anything.'

"He said to me, 'You also risk dying without leaving anything. Because you refuse to follow your tradition.'

"I said, 'This music is very important. You are right. But people don't understand its value today. When the time comes, and if I can, I will show the true value of this music.'

"He was annoyed and began to cry. He said, 'What are you going to do? You didn't finish school. Your grandfather wouldn't allow it. You didn't go into the army. Your grandfather wouldn't allow it. Are you going to become a thief to defend African music?'

"I said, 'No.'

"'Then what are you going to do?'

"'Follow my destiny. My destiny is there.'"

Babani told the story of how he became a patron of griots in Dakar in the early 1970s and how his father, hearing of this new patron, went to visit with his *ngoni* and was shocked to find his own son. Babani drew the tale out, dwelling on his father's amazement that his son had become friends with Leopold Senghor, then president of Senegal and one of Africa's great writers and intellectuals. I sensed growing restlessness in the room as Babani danced around the issue of how he had become so rich. They had heard it before. I jumped in with one final question. "Mr. Sissoko, every musician in this city is writing a praise song for you now. Do you ever feel they are trying to manipulate you in order to receive favors?"

"No," he said. "You see, the griots come from the most dignified society. Very, very dignified. There are people who have billions, but they don't care. We have many billionaires here. But you can't play music for an idiot who doesn't understand it. The griots want to give to someone who understands their value because they have this dignity. People who spend on griots buy their dignity."

In those words, I felt I had gotten an answer that meant something: Babani gave to musicians to buy grace and to feed his own story into the river of griot lore that will flow on through the coming centuries. But this night he was talking not to a griot but to a writer. Did he know the difference? Did I?

The interview ended abruptly. The *funé* I had met in Kita, Ishaka Kouyaté, leapt to his feet and praised Babani, who turned over a stack of bills, stood, and swept out of the room. Djelimady, Solo, and I descended the stairs and went out to the front of the house. It was almost two o'clock in the morning, but the crowd seated in chairs there had not dwindled. Sayan Sissoko was there, tickling his *ngoni* while beaming Ishaka played along on a beat up twelve-string guitar.

A skirmish broke out at the gate. Apparently a woman who made clothes for people in Babani's entourage had left the compound earlier, and when she returned the guard didn't recognize her and refused to readmit her. Outraged, the woman tried to force her way in, occasioning a scuffle and then the hailing of the commando who, true to his specialty, hit the woman. Babani appeared in the yard during the noisy aftermath and went to the door to sort things out. In the confusion, the old guitar was left unmanned. I picked it up and began to find the notes of "Bambougou N'chi." "Not now," said Tiekoro Sissoko, seated beside me. "This is not a time for music." Djelimady signaled that it was time to go, and Solo drove us home through the deserted city.

"You should have *asked* him for some of that money," said Barou the next morning. He was aghast. "If it had been me, I would have left with money."

"How?" I asked, annoyed by this cockiness.

"Can't say," he shrugged. "I would have listened and watched, found out what pleased him and figured out a strategy. But I would have *succeeded.*"

Everyone I told about the interview reacted as Barou had. By the only measure that counted for them, I had failed. The Colonel was speechless. Toumani Diabaté and Sali Sidibé acted as though I had lost a close relative. Only Djelimady approved of my conduct at the interview, assuring me that it would have been unwise to ask Babani for money. "That's not your personality," he told me. "Babani liked you. He told me this morning: 'Your American is good. You must work with him.' What you have to do, Banning, is go home, make your radio program, write your articles, and then send him copies. You'll find that the next time he is in the United States, he will find you. If you had asked him for money, he would not have given it to you. I've never seen him give money to someone who asked for it."

Djelimady's words reassured me. Still, I was left with puzzles. The man who had fallen in love with the Rail Band all those years ago and had risen to such heights to defend griot culture was now creating havoc through his generosity. The Rail Band was finished. And for all their new wealth, the Tounkara family and all the griots of Bamako seemed awash in a craving for more.

12

Sacrifices

We are traditionalists. It's an attitude I disapprove of. It's we who make the history, and if we refer only to what has passed, there will be no history. I belong to a century that has little in common with the time of my ancestors. I want society to move.

Salif Keita

On April 1, I had spent five months in Mali. In a few weeks, Muslims all over West Africa would celebrate Tabaski, *la fête de mouton*. Tabaski commemorates Abraham's sacrifice of his son Isaac, and it is observed throughout the Muslim world. The names and particulars vary, but the common denominator is sacrifice. Early in the morning, every male head of family must slaughter a *mouton*, or sheep, as a religious offering and a sign of renewal for the start of a new year. Tabaski's emphasis on feasting and socializing made the occasion more accessible to a visitor like me than the austere observations of Ramadan had been. Gnawing on grilled ribs is a communal pleasure as easy to share in as any holiday feast, except for the sacrifice itself. Before the party begins, Tabaski calls for an intimate act of killing, to take place in the street for all to see.

"Quite gruesome really," said Lucy Durán, the British musicologist. "Be sure you have lots of coins and small bills on hand. Everybody expects a handout."

The sacrifice itself is one of those strands of ancient pagan ritual that sometimes emerge from the wound cord of African Islam. People told me that in richer times, the dead sheep were actually left to rot, or that their lean corpses were given to the poor. For as long as the Malians I knew could remember, families have eaten their *mouton* and shared it with visitors during the three-day celebration. A man who fails to buy at least one *mouton* for his family suffers in the eyes of his neighbors and relatives. So even before the end of Ramadan, the doomed beasts begin to appear everywhere, tied up by doorways in twos and threes, gathered into makeshift corrals, and herded off to market.

In the big *mouton* market between Lafiabougou and Djikoroni, I had noticed the growing population. Fulani herders in blue and white turbans kept their animals under shabby roofs to protect them from the sun. The creatures lay on beds of straw, which they gradually ate away. At first they far outnumbered the customers, but as Tabaski neared the price crept a little higher each day, ratcheting up the pressure to buy. One night on Rue Kasse Keita, I encountered an enormous herd being moved across the road in the cool of night. There must have been a thousand *mouton*, ghostly white cargo tramping up clouds of dust.

"Tabaski. *Ce n'est pas bon pour les moutons,*" Djelimady joked as we passed sheep along the roadways.

A Malian *mouton* has coarse, straight fur and droopy ears. Some translate *mouton* as "ram," but that word suggests robust power rarely seen in these scrawny creatures of the savanna. To me, they were sheep, hapless and forlorn. Most are white, though they can have brown or black markings. Some have white front ends and black or brown back ends, as if the rear half of their bodies had been dipped into a vat of paint. The larger ones sprout horns and have a more dignified appearance, but *mouton* behavior is rarely dignified. They stick together, as if numbers provided safety. Each morning as I walked to the paved road, I would see them huddling by the shaded walls of buildings, wallowing in horrid mud or their own excrement. They uttered amazing sounds, croaking and bleating in scratchy, almost human voices. Hearing one from my bed, I imagined the thin cry of an old man calling for his bedpan, at once urgent, ornery, and pathetic.

One hot April night, I got back to my house late and came upon Samakou Tounkara standing by the gate with another young man, the two of them shirtless and holding hands. I asked Samakou about his plans for Tabaski. Would he be "gorging a *mouton*," as the phrase went?

"No," he said with evident relief. That was only for heads of households. "I'm still young," Djelimady's son protested. "What's the hurry?"

Djelimady had disappeared again with Babani, this time to Lomé, the capital of Togo. I was resolved to stay in Mali for as long as I could stand the heat. But already my back and arms had broken out in a stinging red heat rash I could not quell. I knew that the end was coming, and I resolved to concentrate on interviews. For me, the month leading up to Tabaski would be a time for visiting musicians outside my familiar circles. I left my guitar at home. I had plenty of music to work on; I needed to talk with people.

The *jelimuso* Kaneba Oulen Kouyaté proved a disappointment. She had recorded a song about democracy that had touched a nerve nationally, but she didn't seem to understand why. I couldn't tell whether people were reading more into the song than was there or whether Kaneba's limited French was betraying her. When I asked her to flesh out her critique of Mali's new political reality, nothing emerged. The singer had sparked a debate about the meaning of democracy in Africa, but she herself seemed unprepared to join it.

Kaneba's song interested me because it was a rare example of a griot tackling a modern social issue. Most of the criticism I had heard of griots centered around their greed and their willingness to manipulate people. But I was also beginning to sense that some saw griots as a regressive force in a society that needed to advance. Guinean film professor Manthia Diawara addresses this matter in a fascinating book called *In Search of Africa*. Diawara spurns the griots' seductive "narrative of return" and its "power to keep West Africa in a retrograde position." Diawara writes, "Not only have griots fixed for eternity the meaning of the hero, the leader, and identity in Mande societies; their narratives have also constituted an insurmountable obstacle toward modernity for men like Sekou Touré [the Guinean dictator]."

In Touré's Guinea and Modibo Keita's Mali, griots actually consolidated power for the post-independence era. Sidiki Diabaté—Toumani's father—began a movement in support of griot culture during the dying years of French rule. Sidiki called it the Kaira Movement, after the modern griot classic "Kaira," which means "happiness."

"The Kaira Movement was going from village to village and staying for a week at a time," Toumani told me. "The whole village would stop. There was lots of spirit and ambiance, but no work. People just wanted to keep their tradition, but the French didn't understand. They thought it was an attempt to destabilize colonialism." Sidiki actually went to prison over this, but after independence he became an influential figure throughout the region for his work in shaping the Instrumental Ensemble of Mali, a mainstay of Modibo Keita's cultural legacy and of modern griotism.

Interestingly, people of Sidiki's generation tend to be the harshest critics of today's pop griots. One night in the prelude to Tabaski, I met Lucy Durán at the Miss ORTM beauty pageant at the Palais de la Culture. This was a borrowed ritual, inexpertly rendered, occasionally comical, surprisingly popular. Lucy and I were marveling at the oddity of girl contestants prancing the stage to Salif Keita's "Mandjou"—praise song to the murderous Sekou Touré—and of griots singing beneath banners for Claremont cigarettes big enough to rival the Palais's ubiquitous portrait of stern old Banzumana.

Lucy had interviewed a legend of *jeliya* that day, singer Fanta Damba. During the 1960s, Fanta Damba of Segu and Fanta Sacko of Kita became the first *jelimusow* recording artists. Sacko, who happens to be Yayi Kanouté's mother, wrote Mali's most famous love song, "Jarabi" ("My Love"), and paved the way for a new generation of women singers who would probe the dynamics of love and marriage. Damba, on the other hand, sang the great historical epics. Her stage career had ended some years earlier, and Lucy had discovered a recluse who rarely left her compound. But Damba watched what was happening on television; she listened to the radio and she did not like what she saw and heard. "*Jeliya* is dead," Damba had told Lucy. "It's a dead horse. You can kick it, but it won't get up."

For Fanta Damba, spectacles like the one we were watching—girls hawking foreign fashion to the tune of bastardized Manding pop—and even the street parties with their cycles of easy praise, debased the *jeli*s' ancestral art. There was no saving grace or silver lining for Damba. *Jeliya* was *dead*, and Bamako's groping attempts at creating a pop culture were a sorry replacement.

Sadio Kouyaté, a younger *jelimuso* from Segu, saw things differently. For her, this was a good time to be a *jeli*. Sadio told me how the arrival of amplifiers in the 1960s had made it possible for griots to make real money in modern times. "People give us lots of money now," said Sadio. "Before, they didn't give much. We sang, but sometimes people couldn't even hear us."

Sadio had recently returned to Mali after ten years in Paris and, unlike Kaneba Oulen, she had no trouble criticizing Mali's new democracy.

"People run traffic lights," she told me. "They steal from stores. That is not *democracy*. Democracy is respect; it is peace. I'm afraid that we in Mali are not yet civilized enough for democracy." But when I asked Sadio if she ever used her music to challenge the nation's political conscience about such matters, she replied with an emphatic no. "I keep my mouth out of all that," she said. "These are not interesting subjects for a griot. At one time we sang about politics, but now we've left that aside. Because here in Africa, there are always changes. Coup d'états. We don't want to sing governments. Because when the government changes, people don't see us as griots but as politicians."

When Modibo Keita took the helm of the new Republic of Mali in 1959, griots inspired by the Kaira Movement sang his praises. But when he was ousted and executed by Moussa Traoré in 1968, those griots faced problems. Sadio's reluctance to sing about political realities revealed a caution that ran deeper than the running of red lights. Politics, including the new democratic variety, was for her still a matter of personalities, not ideas.

I spoke with Sadio in the air-conditioned offices of a private radio station called Radio Kledu. Back in 1992, Mali became the first West African nation to allow private radio broadcasts, and the change opened the door to all sorts of modernity. In the past, citizens had been forced to listen to a single government broadcast, which interspersed political speeches with music from around the new nation. The late griot icon Banzumana became a national figure through his radio performances. But since 1992, anyone with a cassette deck, a microphone, and a transmitter has been allowed to go on the air and broadcast at will. If there were twenty stations in Bamako when I was there, half of them were as rudimentary as that, some powerful enough to be heard in only a few neighborhoods.

Radio Liberté, one of the original private stations, was far better equipped. My guide there showed me bullet holes in the station's exterior wall. He told me that the station had once run a talk show in which women called in complaining about the rudeness of the men who worked the *bashée*s. Within hours, a band of incensed *bashée* drivers had attacked the station, nearly destroying it. Radio Kledu, where I met Sadio, was by far the best-financed station. It had plush broadcast studios, editing rooms, and a sweet deal with Voice of America, all financed by a mysterious benefactor. Radio Kayira fell somewhere in the middle, shabby and thrown together, but high powered enough to be heard beyond city limits. Kayira was perched atop a three-story building and its antenna rose high above Djelibougou, the neighborhood where most of Mali's top musicians live. The station had bolts of *bogolon* cloth deadening the sound in the broadcast booth, and a big collection of West and Central African cassettes.

Kayira was the station most critical of the new government. Some thought of it as "the opposition," but the man who showed me around, technical director Mamadou Sylla, denied that. "We are often *in* opposition," he told me, "but we do not back any political party. We critique everybody."

Mr. Sylla told me that the government had tried to close Kayira down in 1994. "They sent police to break up our studio," he said. "Then they tried to change Article 7 of the constitution, the one that guarantees a free press. The government thought there was too much liberty. It had gone too far and they wanted to limit it." Mr. Sylla said that all the stations in Bamako had threatened to stop broadcasting if the planned change went ahead. The government had backed down.

Mr. Sylla took me out to an open verandah on the roof of the building. There he unlocked what looked like a closet, inside which sat a large, slab-like transmitter, coated with dust. "We use this one for double-frequency broadcasting," said Sylla. He told me that the government occasionally jammed a frequency in order to block out a program that criticized the state too harshly. Apparently listeners knew to scan the dial if a show was interrupted, since a station with two transmitters would put out the signal on a different band. If a show was successfully jammed, the station could even send a tape to another station, which would then broadcast it. "There is no serious rivalry among the stations," said Mr. Sylla. "We all work together." That will change, of course, the day real advertising money begins to flow their way.

Private radio has provided opportunities for musicians and aided the rise of new genres, notably Wassoulou music. Musicians and producers had still to work out the rules of engagement with radio stations. They feared that the new richness of radio might dissuade the public from buying cassettes. But most seemed to understand that the true enemy of commercial music was not radio but cassette piracy, which skims away as much as 80 percent of an artist's potential earnings on a recording.

The moment a new cassette goes public, its producer enters a race with time. He must hustle to sell as many legal cassettes as possible before cheaper pirate copies flood the market. The difference between a two-week and a three-week delay can mean thousands of legitimate sales, maybe tens of thousands in the case of a major artist. The French cassette producer Philippe Berthier came up with the idea of feeding radio stations one or two songs in advance to prime the market. Oumou Sangaré's manager-husband played me an advance copy of her new cassette, but he steadfastly refused to let me make my own copy for fear that the music might fall into the hands of pirates. "We're waiting until the rains start to release it," he told me. "Most of the pirate copies come up from Guinea, and when the rains start, some of the main roads close. That might delay the arrival of pirate copies a week or more."

In the bustle of the downtown market, I ran into Madou Bah Traoré, the Wassoulou guitarist I had abandoned in order to work with Sali Sidibé. He seemed to bear no grudge and began telling me about his own battles against the pirates. I said I was interested and he invited me out to his house to discuss it. There Madou Bah told me he was planning a trip to Sierra Leone, where he hoped to meet a man called Kalwani, the greatest cassette pirate in West Africa.

"He's a Pakistani who was based in Liberia for years," Philippe Berthier had told me. "He started out making match boxes. All the match boxes that you see here, if they weren't made in Mali, they were made by Kalwani. Then he moved into cassettes. He made his cassettes in Asia, Singapore and countries like that. He imported them to Liberia in containers and distributed them throughout West Africa. When there were problems in Liberia, he moved to Sierra Leone. He has a factory there."

Madou Bah believed that no operation of this scale could go on without the complicity of the Malian government, and he had a plan to foil Kalwani's trade. "I'm going there to better understand how he works," said Madou Bah. "It's for research." Madou Bah said that major artists and producers were dealing directly with Kalwani and cutting the smaller artists out. "He buys whole catalogues," Madou Bah told me. "If there are five or six artists coming out under a single producer, he buys them all for 10 or 20 million CFA, and he tells the Bureau of Authors' Rights. Kalwani does not release a product without informing them. So they are complicit in this too."

Madou Bah planned to go to Kalwani as a producer, to learn what he could and then use the information to expose the whole operation. "In 1948, there was a conference in Belgrade," he told me, directing my attention to a large official document. "UNESCO guaranteed the protection of artists in all member countries. Mali was there. I'm going to implicate our own government in this piracy, and then confront them with the evidence." I had to admire Madou Bah. While others complained about the running of traffic lights or sat out contemporary debates altogether, he was taking action, however quixotic, on an issue that affected the lives of musicians like no other.

During this period of visits, I was lucky to spend time with two of Mali's most colorful and best-known musicians, the Songhoi guitarist from Niafunké, Ali Farka Touré, and the top songbird of Wassoulou music, Oumou Sangaré. Thirty years Oumou's senior and a product of the colonial era, Farka is by turns a charmer and a curmudgeon, a man concerned with living out his years in peace and looking after his family, not with molding attitudes in the new Mali. Oumou, by contrast, is a woman of causes and a powerful role model for the present generation of female singers. The old man of the north and the princess of Wassoulou have something important in common: Neither is a griot, and their successes have undermined the *jelis*' traditional supremacy in music.

Oumou sings with the understatement and nuance of a jazz great. Her recordings studiously avoid the electronic sounds that cheapen the work of most of her Wassoulou followers. Malians love Oumou's music—proving that they don't need drum machines to find pop music entertaining—but they revere her most for her polemics, especially her broadsides against polygamy and arranged marriage.

The Oumou Sangaré I had met during her two tours in the United States was reserved when not performing, even a little intimidating. In Bamako, I saw her more playful side. Once I came upon her in a hallway during an event at the Amitié Hotel and was startled by her beauty. She wore a black dress, pleated and glittering, and shields of feathery gold jewelry that covered her wrists and hands. "I should have brought my camera," I sputtered.

"Really, Banning," she replied, looking away, "you *mustn't* neglect these things."

Oumou preserved a girlish demeanor at age twenty-seven, despite being over six feet tall. She had married a Malian of means named Ousmane Cherif-Haidara, and they had a son. I first went to their house in Djelibougou to interview Oumou near the end of Ramadan. It impressed me that the presumed assailant of traditions was observing the holy fast. She told me to come after dark so we could eat together, and when I arrived she cooked ribs on her backyard grill.

After dinner, I asked Oumou about the pros and cons of tradition. "When you see me perform," she said, "you can feel that I defend traditions. I dress as a Malian woman. My musicians dress traditionally. The instruments we use are typical traditional instruments. I want to hold on to our traditions. In the traditions, women are respected. The trouble is that men today take just what they want from the tradition, and the rest they reject."

Oumou made a point of telling me that she was not educated, but her attack on polygamy was based on an astute reading of the Koran. "My religion does not *force* a man to marry four wives," she told me. "It says to a man, if you are afraid you may be unfaithful to your wife, go and find another, but on the condition that you must treat both of them the same way. Already, that is difficult. It's hard to love two wives the same way. And it's expensive. But even sexually—please excuse me—you must not favor one. That is *very* difficult. Imagine with four wives, and you must love them all exactly the same way."

Oumou loved to confront men during her shows. "How would you like it if we women took four husbands?" she would taunt. If they shouted back, she beamed with delight. "And I suppose *we* don't get jealous? Is that what you think?" Oumou's act was unlike anything on the Malian stage. But her pique was more than good theater and more than vengeance, though Oumou spoke movingly about the ways she had suffered as a daughter in a polygamous family. The *jelis* were forever reminding families of their roles in history, boosting the family as a pillar of society. But Oumou was there to point out that polygamy weakens families. It forces men to spread their limited wealth thinly. It creates rivalries between half-siblings that can infect and destroy family enterprises like a trade or business. *Fadenya*, the persistent jealousy between children of the same father and different mothers, has been foiling transgenerational aspirations throughout West Africa for centuries.

Ali Farka Touré was another matter altogether, perhaps the most enigmatic figure in Malian music. His successes abroad dwarf those of other Malian musicians. Salif Keita may have sold more records, but while he was nominated for a Grammy award, Farka *won* one—not by turning his music into dance pop but simply by playing the traditions he's loved all his life (albeit with rock legend Ry Cooder on the record that won the Grammy). Normally Farka performs with just his guitar, his voice, and two percussionists who wear metal rings and tap out sultry rhythms on dried, halved calabashes.

Farka is renowned for the mysterious connections between his music and American blues. The banjo's African roots interest musicologists, but the evidence for this link lies in the physical instrument, not so much in its music. With Farka, the music itself persuades listeners that they are actually *hearing* the roots of John Lee Hooker and his peers, roots that branch out from the fingers of the Mississippi Delta all the way to the lonely meanders of the northern Niger.

Behind this romantic notion lie paradoxes. For one thing, Farka had heard John Lee Hooker before he became a sensation in Europe during the 1970s, leading some to question who influenced whom. A survey of other musicians in the Timbuktu area would put some of those doubts to rest; they *all* sound bluesy. But for whatever reasons, the "roots of the blues" excitement has mostly focused on Farka. Fifty-eight when I knew him in Mali, Farka had lost interest in touring internationally. He said he did it only as a favor to his manager, Nick Gold, the same man who wanted to send Djelimady to Cuba. With four wives and eleven children to support, Farka had to like the money he earned on the road, and when touring he dutifully played the African bluesman, donning a porkpie hat, nursing a flask of whiskey, and hypnotizing audiences with his elliptical songs from the edge of the Sahara. But foreign journalists annoyed him, especially when they asked about the blues.

"John Lee Hooker plays tunes whose roots he does not understand," Farka told me in Boston in 1993. "He understands the spirit, but it is never Western. *Never.* It comes from Africa and particularly from Mali. [Hooker] talks about things coming from alcohol, but that's not it. It's the land, nature, animals. The music comes from history. How did it get here? It was stolen from Africans. And Clarence [Gatemouth Brown]. I can teach him things, but he cannot teach me. For ten years I can teach him African tunes without repeating a note."

Americans tend to think of the blues as the Rosetta Stone of our popular music and to see Farka as a quaint African playing a primitive rendition of our national music. Meanwhile, Farka sees the blues as a dilapidated, half-remembered remnant rescued from Mali's bottomless musical treasure chest. If there is a historical connection, Farka asks the right question. How did it get there? In the answer, more paradoxes.

The northern peoples from whom Farka descends had their heyday during the Songhai Empire, which followed the decline of Sunjata Keita's Malian Empire in the fifteenth century. Ruling from the city of Gao, just east of the Niger River's northern bend, Songhai was built on the strengths of two earlier empires, Mali and, before that, Ghana. Songhai's leaders created institutions—the region's first professional army, a system of local governments, and, in the flourishing market cities of Djenne and Timbuktu, renowned Muslim universities capable of training world-class Islamic scholars as well as doctors and judges. Songhai proved the most powerful of the three Sudanese empires but also the shortest lived, and by the end of the sixteenth century, European seafarers along the West African coast had badly undermined the trans-Saharan trade routes. Wounded economically, the last giant of the western Sudan fell to the belligerent Berbers in the north, paving the way for colonial invaders.

Long before the fall of Songhai, slave hunters worked war-torn regions of West Africa, gathering victims they would sell to European buyers on the coast. Some of these northern peoples must have found their way to the Americas as slaves, and modern music surely bears some imprint of this history. But the percentage of northern Malian people among the American slaves has to be small, probably smaller than the percentage of Bambara people, who also play music with marked similarities to the blues, and certainly smaller than the percentages of Mande, Yoruba, Congo, and Angolan peoples. Farka claims he can tell you the town and ethnic group responsible for the Delta blues sound. But how could any one group be credited for such a dominant music style emerging from the American South?

Rather than debate that sort of question with journalists, Farka prefers to stay home with his family and his rice paddies on the banks of the Niger in the town of Niafunké, well on the way to Timbuktu. Even a trip south to Bamako seems like a visit to a foreign land for Farka. Ever since the '60s and '70s, when he first established himself as a musician in Mali, Farka has battled the cultural dominance of the Manding and Bambara peoples. His impatience with the griots' exploitative flattery is legendary, and he remains something of an outsider in the Malian capital. When Farka does play there, it is mostly for foreigners at the French Cultural Center.

"We are all proud of Ali," Madou Djan Tounkara once told me, "but we don't understand why you Americans like his music so much." Anyone who visits the Bureau of Authors' Rights can see figures that testify to Farka's success. "My God, Ali's done well," I once heard Djelimady say after a such a visit. "He's ahead of us all overseas. *Way* ahead."

Shortly before I arrived in Bamako, Farka made an investment in the Malian music business. He bought into the French producer Philippe Berthier's cassette duplication facility, which now goes by the name Ali

Farka Touré Associé. The musicians of Bamako balked. "Why did he buy that old equipment?" Djelimady asked bitterly. "He had a lot of money. He could have bought something new. He could have *added* something to this place."

Nick Gold once managed to coax Farka and Oumou into a London recording studio to do a song together. Farka took pleasure in forcing Oumou to sing in Peul, her ancestral language, which he speaks and she does not. Oumou came away parodying Farka's assertion that everything is better in Niafunké. "To hear him talk about it," she would say, "you might think Niafunké was paradise on earth. The food is better. The climate is better. The people are better. Even the air you breathe is better."

I would have to take Farka at his word about Niafunké's pastoral pleasures, magical cures, and *jinns*—invisible spirits that can bewitch or enchant. With the hot season raging, travel north was out of the question for me. Luckily, when Farka came to Bamako, he stayed with his sister, only a few blocks from my home in Lafiabougou. I used to peer down that road as I passed, hoping to spot Farka's white land cruiser. Joyce Miller, the American schoolteacher, was with me the night I finally found him. He was delighted to see us. He showed us to his room, small and crowded and equipped with a television and a cassette player. He immediately put on a cassette of poorly recorded Songhai *takamba* music. "This is music purely for the spirits," said Farka, and he began to shiver and sway to the scratchy wail of a bowed string instrument.

Farka sent one boy out for soft drinks and told another to bring tea. When the tea came, the boy tried to serve Farka first and was scolded for not starting with Joyce. The deep green shot of tea with its head of yellowish foam refreshed and revived in the heat of night. Farka took his glass of the murky elixir. He held it between his thumb and index finger and made a two-part swooping motion with his arm—back and forth through the air—so that the glass hung briefly upside down on each pass. He then sucked loudly at the foam—*ffffttftftft*. For an hour or so, Farka savored the mysteries of the northern tribes, the Songhai, Tamasheck, Dogon, and Peul. One small northern tribe were the "Jews of Africa," he said, without explaining. Farka talked about a man who could heal broken bones by applying herbal packs to them. He talked about a place where the Niger and Bani Rivers meet, and if you drank the water from one and then the other, you would die instantly. He said that all the rivers in the world meet in the Pacific Ocean. Mysteries and more mysteries.

At one point, Farka recalled his first visit to Bamako in 1954. "There were just three markets then," he said, "and only two paved roads. There was nothing but a drawbridge going across the river. And where the television station sits now, there was only water. There were no bands. The only place they recorded music was at Radio Sudan."

Farka used to work as a chauffeur for Radio Sudan, and it was there that he made his first recordings in the 1960s. Nick Gold had asked Farka to go there and get those old tapes because he wanted to release the best of them on a retrospective CD. Oumou's husband had told me the story. "Farka didn't want to go," he said, "and he didn't want to tell Nick why. There are people at ORTM who still remember Farka as their driver. He didn't want to see them. Farka is a very proud man."

Farka had come to Bamako to compose and record music for a film about life on the Niger. He was finding the work tough going. Sitting in front of a television monitor, he had to observe the footage and create music on the spot. "The camels sit down," he told Joyce and me. "The camels stand up. Now, the camels are walking. And you have to *play* for them."

A few days later, I dropped by Farka's house just as Oumou was pulling up in her white Mercedes. Lucy Durán, who was staying at Oumou's house, also emerged from the car.

"I'm hungry," said Oumou.

"Ugh," gasped Farka, "not me. I'm too tired to eat." Farka had spent another trying day in the studio with the camels. He invited us all to come and dine with him and his sister the following night, when the film project would be complete. He pulled out 50,000 CFA and handed it to a boy, instructing him to take it to his sister and tell her to be ready. Before we left, Farka took Oumou and Lucy each aside for a private conference.

"He wanted to show off his weapons," Lucy deadpanned as we climbed into Oumou's car. Oumou announced that she too had been shown Farka's collection of vintage muskets. The two women commiserated about Farka's Old World ways.

Oumou's Mercedes had a problem. It squealed as though something sharp and metallic was scraping against the brake plate. The sound was so loud and unsettling that most car owners in America would have pulled over immediately and called their mechanic. Oumou just turned up the stereo.

We settled on a restaurant called Pizzeria for dinner and, for once, as the sign outside always advertised, Toumani, Keletigui, and Basekou—

the Manding *jeli* super-trio—were actually there playing music. Keletigui spotted Oumou and announced that "the greatest singer in Mali" had just arrived. Oumou was flattered but embarrassed. In only a sweater and slacks, she felt underdressed. She had wanted to sit in the car, but we had insisted she come in and eat. Oumou had never tasted pizza and found it a revelation. As we ate, she became animated and chided me over my failure to get money from Babani or to learn his true profession during our interview.

Oumou insisted on driving me home to Lafiabougou, even though it was out of her way. She swooned upon seeing Djelimady's house, with all its evidence of construction. "It is rare to see a Malian musician who spends his money wisely," Oumou gushed. "Most of them drink and smoke and waste everything on women. It takes *discipline* for a musician to build a house. I admire that man."

The day we were to dine with Farka and his sister was as hot as any day I had ever experienced, and I had chores to do in Bamako. At one point I had to cross the Niger River, but seeing that traffic was jammed leading to the old Bridge of the Martyrs, I decided to walk rather than struggle with a taxi. At a certain point, heat no longer oppresses you. You just float through it, semiconscious but no longer suffering. I noticed that pedestrian and bicycle traffic on the bridge was unusually dense that day. Strangely, there were no cars at all. Up ahead, I saw a concentration of bodies, all moving together, and a shot of adrenaline jolted me from my daze.

I had been reading for weeks about student unrest in the city. The state-owned television had said nothing about it, but the press had been full of stories, including reports of violence and shootings by the police. The same young Turks who had felled a dictator in 1991 were now impatient with the democracy that had followed. The government wanted to cut grants to students. The students wanted the government to build a real university. A fight was building. Alone, facing that crowd, I felt afraid for the first time in Bamako.

I turned back toward the sweltering city. Just behind me was the spot where a semitrailer truck had driven off the bridge ten days earlier, killing the driver and leaving the guard rail bent over a twenty-foot stretch. Now the rail was bent in the opposite direction, back toward the road. All at once I understood, and relief washed over me, leaving me hot and weary. The people in my path were not protesting students; they were laborers gathered around the hulking, rusted cab of the semi.

They had dragged the massive cab out of the water and were now inching it slowly off the bridge using brute manual force.

"Do you think he drove off that bridge on purpose?" asked Lucy that night as we sat down to a chicken feast at Farka's sister's house in Lafiabougou.

"No," insisted Ousmane. "He just went out of control." I didn't get the impression that Ousmane knew this for a fact. Such a showy suicide, perhaps any suicide at all, just seemed unbelievable to him.

Farka's niece had prepared an enormous platter of chicken, rice, and vegetables. Farka, due to leave for Niafunké the next morning, could not sit still, he was so happy. When the music began, I turned out to have the only guitar, which meant that I would not get to play it. Mali's most renowned guitarist didn't play much either, but his accompanist, Afel Bocoum, was there, which put me third in line and effectively out of competition. Farka sprawled on the carpet and rapped his fingers on a dry calabash. He sang, danced, and bullied Oumou until at last she sang in Peul. "It's your language!" he cried.

Lucy entertained me with stories. She told me that one of Oumou's most dedicated fans, a transvestite from Niger, had visited Oumou's house that morning. A fat, wealthy man, he apparently spent most of his time in Dakar, where, in drag, he liked to seduce other men and then "surprise" them in his hotel room. "When they figure it out, he asks for money," said Lucy. "And if the client refuses, he steals their ID card." According to Lucy, the man from Niger boasted a large collection of ID cards.

I looked over at Oumou, who was thumping on a calabash, laughing, sparring with Farka under the watchful eye of her husband. It crossed my mind that for all her candor, Oumou would not have told me about the transvestite from Niger.

Even before she was crowned, Miss ORTM triggered controversy. During the dance competition on the last night of the pageant, the winner-to-be performed her own version of the Songhai *takamba*. The judges either hadn't noticed or hadn't cared about the dance's lack of authenticity, and Songhai people were offended by this fresh evidence of the Bamako elite's insensitivity to the cultures of the north. Now ORTM had to air scenes of protest by local Songhai students.

I watched this televised flap over dinner with the Tounkaras. Babani Sissoko also made news that night. Babani had launched an airline in Lomé, Air Dabia-Togo. In a dramatic maiden voyage, the carrier's first flight had taken a planeload of West African Muslims to Jedda so they could make the holy pilgrimage to Mecca. The Togolese Radio Band, with Djelimady on guitar, had serenaded a gala sendoff for the pilgrims.

Far more than the bungled *takamba* dance, this news riled Bamako. The airline's name—Dabia-Togo—paired Babani's tiny native village in the Malian *sahel* with the West African nation that had made the airline possible. Malians were furious. Why should Babani have to go to *Togo* to put his airplanes into service? The reason involved a contract Mali had signed years earlier with the French-owned carrier Air Afrique. Air Afrique held rights to the Bamako airport and could not be cut out of the equation as Babani had wanted. "You should have heard the radio today," said Barou when we met for a beer. On talk shows, in commentaries, and in the print media, the message had been the same: France had gotten the better of Mali once again.

Barou often had lashings of criticism for President Konaré's administration. He and Moussa Kouyaté, the Tounkara family griot, were among a handful of Konaré contrarians I knew. They had presumably supported the overthrow of Moussa Traoré, but they felt that Konaré had not lived up to the revolution's promise. Their view sparked political debate at the compound. Barou and Djelimady had been arguing about who deserved credit for paving roads, who was more corrupt, and who had a better plan for Mali, ever since I'd arrived. They sounded like Democrats and Republicans arguing back in the United States. These were unlike political discussions I'd heard in other African countries, where, if debate happened at all, it tended to divide along obvious lines: ethnicity, color, social class. But Barou and Djelimady seemed to be having a discussion of ideas.

Most Malians I met liked President Konaré, in part because he had stood up to France. When newly elected French president Jacques Chirac had invited West African heads of state to meet him in Dakar, Konaré had refused to go. If Chirac wanted to talk, he would have to come to Bamako. The stand had been popular, but now even Konaré's supporters were angry about Air Dabia-Togo. "The government hesitated," said Barou. "They should have done something."

On the morning after Djelimady's return from Lomé, the temperature climbed to 115 degrees Fahrenheit. The twins led a brigade of boys on bicycles up and down the street. Two little girls splashed in a filthy puddle. In the courtyard, Samakou sat motionless, drenched with sweat from some great exertion, while girls and women worked busily around him. Djelimady emerged from his room, slit-eyed, mouth full of tooth-paste, his husky frame wrapped only in a towel. He mumbled, *"Ça va?"* and then sat alone and silent, awaiting his turn in the washing area. "He's tired," Djelimady's wife explained. "Didn't sleep all night."

After washing and dressing, Djelimady emerged a new man in an olive drab, military-style business suit, a souvenir from Lomé, and the tales of Togo began. "Babani is more popular than the president in Lomé," boomed Djelimady. "The president put a special mark on Babani's car. All the military people and police saw that mark and let him go anywhere he wanted. Babani didn't even have to stop at traffic lights."

Djelimady said that Air Dabia-Togo's maiden flight to the pilgrim-age at Mecca had been a stroke of genius. "Lomé is now 50 percent Muslim," he reported. "When they watched that plane take off . . . oooh! *Ba, ba, ba, ba.*"

Everything in Lomé sounded enchanting through Djelimady's eyes. It was like Farka talking about Niafunké. The weather was fantastic, not hot like Bamako. The people were friendly and happy. The food was great. The Radio Band of Togo was thriving after five years of privati-zation, a good model for the Rail Band, said Djelimady.

A taxi pulled up on the street, and a well-dressed Malian man about Djelimady's age emerged. "Doumbia!" exclaimed Djelimady, standing to greet his visitor. This was one of Djelimady's boyhood friends. Doumbia lived at the Manantali Dam, which was built by the Germans after World War II. He was in Bamako for the holidays.

"Twenty-eight years in the military, this guy," said Djelimady for my benefit.

"Really?" I exclaimed. "Under Moussa Traoré."

"Yes," said Doumbia. "I was a personal friend of Moussa Traoré."

Djelimady snickered. *"Ce n'est pas bon, ça,"* he said.

Then Doumbia told a remarkable story. In 1991, as Moussa Traoré's regime was about to fall, Doumbia had been stationed in the north, lead-ing government forces against the Tuareg rebels, who were fighting once again to seize control of Timbuktu. This was an old fight. Tuareg nomads have been traditional enemies of the sub-Saharan tribes. "They think they are Arabs, and better than the rest of us," Djelimady often said. Since the fall of the Malian Empire around 1450, the Tuareg had cap-tured Timbuktu several times, only to be driven out later. In the wan-ing days of Moussa Traoré's regime, the Tuareg had launched another assault. Tuareg rebels had kidnapped Doumbia's family during a raid. He had requested permission to rescue them by force, but Moussa Traoré, facing problems of his own, had refused. Doumbia had disobeyed orders and used his soldiers to attack the rebel camp near Timbuktu, killing eighty-three Tuareg. Doumbia had succeeded, but the escapade had ended his military career. After Moussa was deposed and arrested, Doumbia moved his family to Manantali.

The Tuareg conflict simmered on as before. During my stay, the Konaré government brokered a tentative peace, and in a demonstration of good will, Tuareg and government leaders held a ceremony in Timbuktu. They built a mountain of some three thousand guns and set it ablaze in the middle of the desert. The image of those burning weapons made the television news night after night. "Show me one other country in the world where they've done *that*," boasted Djelimady.

That April, a *New York Times* editorial singled out Mali for praise, leading with a description of the fire at Timbuktu. The piece went on to praise President Konaré's condemnation of the one-party state and to laud his humanity in letting his predecessor Moussa Traoré live to see what democracy looks like. A Malian court had sentenced Traoré to hang in 1993, but Konaré had refused to carry out the sentence, citing his moral objection to capital punishment. The *Times* concluded by scolding the Clinton administration for not sending officials to Bamako.

"They should send someone," Djelimady remarked upon hearing this. "We're democrats too, now." But the burning of arms had not impressed Doumbia. "The fighting will go on," he said gravely.

Djelimady shifted the conversation back to Babani. "He is going to Dubai for the holidays," said Djelimady. "He's ordered one hundred *mouton* sent to Dabia for Tabaski. Which reminds me . . . Fulani!" he shouted at the nearest twin. "Get me a taxi. I'm late!"

Djelimady and Doumbia shared a taxi into town and I made my way to Barou's house, where everyone wore long faces. The family had not been able to pay the electricity bill since October. They owed 40,000 CFA, and the power company, eager to collect debts before people spent all their money on the holiday, had cut off power. Without fans, no one, including Barou's baby daughter, could sleep. Barou had one week to pay the bill. If he failed, the power company would come and remove his electric meter. Then, in order to restore power, he would have to apply like any new customer, wait months, and pay a steep installation fee.

"It's making me crazy," Barou complained. "And now Tabaski is coming. I'm supposed to buy gifts, *mouton*. How am I going to do that? Djelimady is my last hope."

Djelimady's new wealth was driving wedges between him and his impoverished friends. He was like the International Monetary Fund, and poor, mismanaged nations were there with outstretched hands. Djelimady was even less inclined to empathize with the self-inflicted misfortunes of others than the famously stern IMF. So I was not surprised to hear later that Djelimady was unwilling to help. In fact, when Barou made his plea, Djelimady became angry and shouted in front of everyone in the compound, making Barou out as just another hustler. "Everyone thinks I have money now," Djelimady reportedly raged. "Well, it's not true. I have problems too. Ask my wife. Ask my brothers. I care more about them more than I do about you, and I haven't given them anything."

Djelimady's wife consoled Barou, conceding that Djelimady had humiliated him unnecessarily. In the end, Djelimady offered his old friend 5,000 CFA, which Barou, more desperate than proud, accepted. "What is this?" he asked.

"That's my contribution," Djelimady replied.

"It would be different if I had asked him for money for myself," Barou told me bitterly. "But it was for my family. He *had* to respect that, but he didn't. There is no friendship left between us."

We were at the home of Sayan Sissoko when Barou told me this. There had been a death in Sayan's family and the mood there was gloomy. For Barou, despair had hardened into a sense of betrayal. He had loved Djelimady. He had called him the best guitarist in Africa and had felt honored to be his friend, and even after Solo and Yayi had cut him from the American tour, Barou had been prepared to forgive and forget. Now there was no going back. "People here are no good," said Sayan in sympathy.

A fresh wind blew in. The sky went gray with dust. It felt as though rain was coming, but it did not rain. Instead, as night fell over Djikoroni—a neighborhood with no electricity—a misted half moon glowed low in the sky and the heat dissipated slightly. Sayan finished restringing his *ngoni*, but he did not play it, not even to test it, as there must be no music in a Malian compound during the days following a death. Sayan set the instrument aside while a young boy brought out the television and hooked it up to a car battery. Darkness enveloped us, but for the flicker of video images and the dim glow of the moon. There was silence but for the gentle sobbing of Sayan's sister-in-law, the occasional bleat of a *mouton*, and the tinny chatter of battery-powered radios and televisions.

Later, back at the Tounkara compound, Djelimady and I sat on the street playing guitars until 2:00 in the morning. After some time, we discussed Barou's problem. "I gave him some money," said Djelimady. "Did he tell you?" I said he had. "But Barou," Djelimady went on, "he should have been paying those bills. It's not good to let things get ahead of you like that." I knew that Djelimady was deflecting blame, as was his habit. I also knew he was right.

As we were finishing our session, Douga Sissoko drove up in his Opel Monterrey. Despite the late hour, he had arrived to dispense pre-Tabaski gifts—new *boubou*s for Djelimady, Solo, and Madou and 50,000 CFA for Djelimady's wife. He reached into his *boubou* and pulled out two fat bundles of American $100 bills. Everyone was speechless. With a wily smile, Douga slipped the money back into his *boubou*. "Twelve airplanes now," he said, "727s for Air Dabia. Just arrived last night."

Douga gave me a ride home, where the Colonel and a few others were still awake. Douga got out and greeted everyone, handing out small notes, 500 and 1,000 CFA to each of the Africans. The Colonel was not impressed.

I had agreed to contribute to the purchase of two Tabaski sheep, one for the Tounkaras and one for the Colonel and the others in my compound. "Shouldn't we buy now while the prices are still low?" I had asked the Colonel weeks earlier.

"No," he had said. "If you buy now, you have to feed that animal. You have to buy a bundle of fresh leaves in the market every day. It takes time and costs money. It's not worth it for just one sheep. Then if it gets sick, you have to treat it. That too will cost you. And what if someone steals it?" The time to buy a sheep was at sunrise on Tabaski morning, when the vendors are desperate. "When they see the sun coming up," said the Colonel, "they become reasonable."

Joyce agreed to help us. She would bring the Jeep at 5:00 on Tabaski morning, and we would go to the *mouton* market. Joyce and the Colonel would buy the animal. I would watch from a distance.

"Joyce," said the Colonel, "you must learn some Bambara now."

"Oh, must I?" she asked, lighting a cigarette.

"*Lahilan saka*," said the Colonel.

"*Lahilan saka*," Joyce repeated. "What did I say?"

"That is the sacrifice of the ram," said the Colonel. "*Lahilan saka. Oui.*" The Colonel gazed at his negotiating partner. Then he asked, "Joyce, what do they sacrifice in *your* religion?"

On the evening before Tabaski, Djelimady led the excursion to buy sheep for the Tounkara household. By the Colonel's calculations, we were going at exactly the wrong moment, but Djelimady showed no interest in crack-of-dawn *mouton* shopping. So in the fading light, Djelimady, Madou, Solo, and I got into the Mitsubishi and made our way over the rough road that leads out onto the garbage-strewn plain dividing Lafiabougou from Djikoroni and the Niger river. Twelve-year-old Moise rode along beside us on his bicycle with Colos straddled over the handlebars as a passenger.

The *mouton* market presented a macabre spectacle. Fulani men in turbans and shepherds' robes, dark blue, gray, or white, were leading sheep among the prospective buyers. Each sheep had a short rope tied around its neck. Once the bargaining for an animal was complete, the seller would tack on an extra 500 CFA for the rope. There was no way to control the animal without it, so the client always gave in. Those who had made their purchases could be seen dragging unwilling beasts away or tying them up for storage in trunks, on roofs, or lashed to the backs of mobilettes like sacks of rice.

As the sales pitches began, Djelimady became sullen. There were few things he hated more than bargaining with his countrymen. "Why can't we just have fixed prices?" he grumbled. "Ever since democracy, everybody is a bandit." Eventually Djelimady closed a deal on a large black and white creature with sizable horns for 55,000 CFA ($110), not including the rope. Solo quietly settled on a smaller white beast for 34,000 CFA. The Tounkara brothers tied up their *mouton* and loaded them into the trunk, and we drove home, Moise and Colos charging gleefully ahead in the stream of light the Mitsubishi cast onto the pitted road. Back at the compound, Djelimady tied the two animals to the tree by the cooking area in the courtyard. The women had been washing and the smell of brown soap clung to the air.

After dinner, Djelimady and I went out to the stoop to play. We played Guinean songs, which have Manding harmonies but a more romantic, Latin feeling to them. Douga dropped by to report that Babani had bought his hundred sheep for Dabia but then had waited too long before sending them on one of his planes. The plane could not land at Dabia after dark. So they had had to telephone Dabia and arrange for trucks to go out and buy another hundred animals for the village feast.

"In a few days," Djelimady speculated when Douga had gone, "there will be *mouton* going cheap at Babani's house."

My alarm radio sounded at 5:00 in the morning with a BBC news anchor droning about events in London, Bosnia, and Sri Lanka. Outside in the first light, the Colonel was making his way down the ladder from the roof where he slept on hot nights. He wore wrinkled trousers and a red and white striped shirt. Joyce arrived exactly on time. As sliver clouds on the horizon went pink in anticipation of sunrise, we rolled along Avenue Sheikh Zayed, past the craggy summits of the Wayanko mesa toward Djikoroni.

We homed in on the same market I had visited with the Tounkaras the evening before, only now from the other side, traversing a long concrete wall that hid us from the vendors' view. Joyce and the Colonel walked into the market while I lingered, observing from afar as the rising sun poured phosphorescent pink and then red-orange light over the parched plain. Soon I saw Joyce and the Colonel leading a medium-size white sheep away from the vendors' stalls. The Colonel's strategy had worked. The bidding had opened at 85,000 CFA, but the Colonel had played a stiff hand and closed at just 26,000, plus 500 for the rope.

Back at the house, the Imam from the local mosque was waiting. Everything happened quickly. Three men laid the sheep down and secured it. Then the Imam placed his old knife blade against the creature's throat and began a rapid sawing motion. As Joyce and I left for the Tounkara compound a short while later, the Colonel and another lodger had dragged the headless corpse into the courtyard and were busily cutting, hacking, breaking, and tearing it into cookable pieces.

Sometime during the night, a third sheep had appeared at the Tounkaras', a contribution from Adama Tounkara's mother, Nene, the number two matriarch of the family. Ina, Djelimady's mother, had gone to Kita for the holiday. When we reached the compound, we found all three beasts tied to the tree outside at the corner of the house. The compound hummed with expectation. The children sported new clothes, frilly dresses for the girls and smart gray suits for the twin boys. Labors over hair at last complete, the women turned to final touches, makeup, and brand new dresses. Djelimady, Solo, and Madou appeared in the grand *boubou*s that Douga had delivered—three shades of blue: sky, azure, and sapphire.

Joyce and I had agreed to accompany the Tounkaras to mosque for the morning prayer, my only participation in religious practice during seven months in Mali. As far as I knew, this was also the only time Djelimady went to mosque during that time. At Lafiabougou's main mosque, a massive gathering was underway. Tradition holds that men and women must pray separately, so Joyce and the old woman headed off one way, leaving five Tounkaras and me to squeeze onto two prayer mats. We waited while a rogue's gallery of cripples, amputees, cragged blind men led by wide-eyed boys rattling tin cans for coins, and other assorted mendicants and almsmen paraded through the rows collecting from the faithful. Islam asks its followers to be generous to life's less fortunate on this of all days. Boys worked the crowd making change for the givers.

At last the *muezzin's* cry rang from the megaphone speaker on the mosque tower, and the gathering of thousands rose to their feet in silent row upon row. Young Fuseini stood close at my side and gave instructions. "Banneeg! Banneeg!" he whispered in anticipation of each move. The prayer cycle involves kneeling, then bending forward, then rising to the kneeling position again before the final, complete prostration. Each move takes place on verbal cue so that everyone acts in unison. After two complete cycles—or *rakats*—a matter of no more than ten or twelve minutes, the ceremony ended and the rows of the faithful dispersed in a colorful, chattering mob. It was like Easter Sunday after church, as folks who hadn't seen one another in a long time smiled, shook hands, and asked after each other's families.

I had rehearsed Bambara blessings for Tabaski, wishing long lives to people and their families as well as for more unlikely things, notably that we should all pray together again on Tabaski a hundred years hence. As we returned to the compound, we were greeted by music. Adama Tounkara had plugged in Solo's electric guitar and Tareta and Yayi were taking turns singing into the cordless microphone, regaling the family with homegrown *jeliya*.

Now the time had come for the central ritual of Tabaski. I knew that Djelimady hated his customary role. He had once told me that he did not like to kill anything and that if he watched an animal being slaughtered, he could not eat the meat. Nevertheless, as head of the family, he was expected to cut the throat of a sheep and spill its fresh blood on the street. And I was expected to film it.

Djelimady, aided by Sambry and Moussa Kouyaté, laid the creatures down one by one and sawed into their throats with a sharp knife. The dying animals gurgled horribly for a few seconds and then continued to kick and twitch for awhile. Solo and Madou stood by in solemn nonparticipation. Djelimady killed the first two animals. Moussa killed the third, proclaiming as always his sacred duty as a griot.

Djelimady was not well that day and quickly retired to his chair in the courtyard while a ghoulish festival of butchery got underway. Sambry and a friend, shirtless and resolute, tied each sheep carcass in turn to the tree and then skinned and disemboweled it. They chopped its torso into racks of ribs, sectioned legs, and hacked out globs of pink stewing meat. Soon they were drenched in sweat and spattered with blood and shreds of gut. Moments earlier, Sambry had looked like a young monk in his white *boubou*. Now he looked like a crazed guerrilla soldier in the midst of mayhem. Little Yayi poked a knife into a bucketful of coiled intestines. Moise charged into the courtyard displaying a plastic bowl containing six mango-sized testicles. The twins had fired up a tea stove and were using it to fry up chopped bits of some internal organ. The joy and general hubbub was like nothing so much as Christmas in a big American household. Only in place of ribbons, wrappings, and colored string were slippery fresh pelts, bug-eyed heads, and buckets of sorted entrails.

I joined Djelimady in the ritual of visiting the neighbors. "This is how I keep a good home for my family," he said as we marched toward the first adjacent doorway. "I greet everyone around here on festival days. All my neighbors. That way, we never have a problem with them during the year."

By the time we returned to the Tounkaras', the first *mouton* ribs were coming off the grill, sizzling and delicious. The meat is a little oily and heavy, but even unadorned it has undeniable grit and flavor. Soon Djelimady announced that it was time to begin his citywide rounds. He popped a couple of Flagils—high-powered antibacterial pills—for his ailing gut, and along with Solo and Madou climbed into the Mitsubishi and headed toward the city.

I stopped by to see Barou and his family. In a Dickensian touch, they had just managed to pull together the electric bill payment so that power could be restored for the holiday. Barou wore a new set of smiles, and he thanked me for my 5,000 CFA contribution to the cause. Brehma, his tailoring brother, had come through with money for a sheep, so celebration was underway. Barou and his mother made me eat more grilled meet, the second of some seven feedings I would manage that day.

My own long day of visits culminated in an evening garden party thrown by the French sound engineer from the French Cultural Center. It seemed, at first, a pleasant manifestation of modern Mali. French people sat at one table drinking beer and wine, while Malians sat at another sipping tea. Everyone ate *mouton* while Toumani Diabaté and a small group entertained. But as the air thickened to produce the first actual rain in months, the mood soured.

I was inside when the shouting began. When I stepped out onto the porch, I saw the sound engineer staggering toward the garden gate and howling out to the street where the skirmish was unfolding. Apparently one of Toumani's cousins had asked one of the engineer's friends to pour him some wine. The swarthy Frenchman had replied, "I'm not a *bartender*," and that was all it had taken. Now everyone moved out to the street, ready to brawl but for the rain. Barou and I hopped a taxi with our instruments. By the time I got home, the rain had stopped—just a tease in the end—and the moon shone through a hazy patch of sky. Inside my room, hot walls steamed the air, and the red heat rash ranging across my back stung each time I rolled over. For once, no *mouton* sounded.

13

Giving and Taking

**When colonials came ashore, they didn't say, "We're here
to steal your land and take your resources and employ
your people to clean our toilets and guard our big houses."
They said, "We're here to help you."**

Michael Maren, "The Road to Hell"

The battered yellow taxi rumbled through the center of
Bamako. I stared from the windows hungrily, trying to see
everything. A shop of hand-painted mirrors. Furniture mak-
ers constructing tall, French-style armoires with hand-carved
doors. Pedestrians, cyclists, mobilettes, pushcarts, and cars,
all moving together through a narrow street. A mountain of
rice sacks. A boy holding a black and white hen by the wings.
Thick, hot, smoky, dusty, redolent air swirling through the
crowd. Even the taxi driver seemed from another era, with
his weathered face, English cap, and heavy tortoiseshell
glasses. He was not happy with me.

"Five hundred CFA," I had insisted before getting in.

"Noooo," the driver had moaned. "That is not right. It's
a thousand."

"Never mind," I had said, stepping back, "I'll find someone else."

"No. Come!" he had snapped, angry but defeated.

"They expect you to bargain," foreigners in Africa like to
say. "If you don't, they won't respect you." So haggling
becomes a habit, a way the outsider learns to deal with

218

anonymous Africans. When the person you're bargaining with grows exasperated or huffy, you know you're getting close to a fair price. A sulking taxi man is a sign that you've done your job well.

Over and over in Bamako, I felt forced to choose between being a sap and having friends or standing firm and remaining at a distance. In the markets and taxis, I bargained and chiseled and took the consequences. Let them see me as another tightfisted white exploiter. After all, you can't erase a century of ill will each time you buy a bolt of cloth or a pair of shoes. In musical settings, though, I hoped for more gracious interactions. I asked to be taught things openly, as if to say, "Trust me. I won't disappoint you." Most of the musicians I played with responded in kind, and our exchanges were like the music itself, a theme expanded through improvisation, more elegant than market bartering, but negotiation just the same. In the end, even the most intangible things have prices. The griot praises; then the praised one names the reward.

Sometimes I thought about the legions of international aid workers in Mali, and how different their assumptions about Africa were from mine. They looked around and saw sickness and suffering, good people held down by backwardness. They came as saviors and offered stern lessons, tough love. I looked around and saw a cultural lodestone, musical diamonds and gold everywhere. I wanted the Malians to give *me* the hard lessons.

This reversal of roles flattered people, and it gave me an early advantage in negotiations. As a white American guitarist, I got to play with the Rail Band and record with Sali Sidibé, even though a host of Malian guitarists half my age could play these styles better than I ever will. In Bamako, I learned music that will be with me forever. What had I given in exchange? Guitar strings, straps, cords, and capos. An amplifier. Microphones. In return for timeless treasures, I was leaving things behind that would do well to survive a few years. Of course, these were things that could not be bought in Bamako, so their value was artificial. Once again, the advantage was mine.

My most generous teachers implicitly believed that I could offer them something beyond musical gadgetry, however dear. They assumed that as a journalist, I could write things about them that would help them to come and perform in America. I could go to New York and Boston and whisper in the ears of the powerful. I could "arrange contracts." The truth was that in 1996, few American promoters were willing to bring African musicians to the United States. A decade earlier, there had been a surge of American interest in African music. Superstars like Salif Keita, Oumou Sangaré, Ali Farka Touré, and Baaba Maal had been its beneficiaries. But far from opening a floodgate, these fortunate few may only have jammed the openings in a very tight dam for some time to come. My attempts to explain this reality to lesser-known Malian musicians seemed to die in the air. Again I had an advantage—though one I wanted no part of—the illusion that I could be a star maker.

I found myself asking: When you put culture on one side of the scale, and hard goods, money, and opportunity on the other, how should the scale behave? Sometimes the way musicians protected and hoarded cultural knowledge rankled. "Why are you showing things to that white guy?" an observer had asked one of my teachers. "Don't you know he's going to go back to America and make money with our music?" On the other hand, I understood that sensitivity. For a little cash or an empty dream, too many African musicians had traded away their greatest assets.

During the blazing days of April and May, the sun directed life at the Tounkara compound. In the morning it fired the horizon, and the east wall of the courtyard cast a long shadow. Everyone congregated against that wall, the women with their work, the men with their chairs and conversation, and the children with their short wooden stools. As the sun burned its way upwards, that band of shade shrank minute by minute so that before noon, most people had moved outside, under the *nime* tree where the *mouton* had been tied up and dressed on the first day of Tabaski. The tree's dry, green, sickle-shaped leaves withered against the sky. Its branches seemed to shrivel under the sun's assault. But it cast a wide shadow on the street, and without it the sun would have driven everyone into the compound's baking verandahs and interior rooms.

One day, men came around with a ladder and clippers to trim trees throughout the neighborhood. They were collecting clippings to feed to their animals. Luckily, one of the children dashed in to warn Djelimady and he drove them off, shouting, "Don't you touch one leaf on that tree!"

I joined the family for lunch under the tree on the third and final day of Tabaski, a day when griots came to call. Djelimady was out inspecting potential houses with Douga. I found myself dozing after lunch but waited anyway, hoping that Djelimady might return and want to play music. I scanned the street groggily. An old man in a gray suit and a wicker pith hat motored past, hunched over his handlebars, teetering while keeping a fifty-pound sack of rice balanced on the back of his motor bike. A boy in white shorts ran down the street in the scalding white light of midday, chasing a deflated soccer ball.

The compound was exploding with flies, their tiny feet tickling our sweat-moistened skin. The clothesline that bisected the courtyard was black and fuzzy with them. As I ate beneath the tree, a young girl waved a fan to keep them off my food.

Adama Tounkara sat distractedly plucking at his *ngoni*. *"Mon ami,"* he said to me, "have you got 500 CFA for cigarettes?"

"What happened to all your millions from Babani?" I protested.

"But haven't you heard?" he asked. "It was all stolen from my room. It was locked in a metal box. They took the whole thing." In a few short weeks, Adama had rejoined the impoverished. *"Mon ami,"* he pressed, "I haven't had a cigarette all day." I gave him the money and he strode off with his *ngoni*.

Soon Djelimady pulled up in a taxi. He went into the courtyard muttering about houses. Djelimady had made his plans to move the family to the house where I was living, and weighing other options seemed to confound him. He emerged from the courtyard wearing only his navy blue shorts, and as he joined us under the tree for lunch another taxi pulled up and Ina Tounkara stepped out. Ina had never left Bamako since her arrival from Kita early in my visit, though she had now moved out to the fashionable Djelibougou neighborhood. She had come a long way from the talented but uncertain girl I first noticed sitting in a clothes hamper and taking musical cues from Adama Tounkara. Now she wore a frilly pink and white gown and a fine holiday hairstyle. She radiated confidence. With her first long, loping step away from the waiting taxi, Ina burst into song, showering praise on the family with her horn-like voice. As she moved among the Tounkaras sitting under the tree, Ina shifted grandly from one side to the other, the graceful sweep of her steps almost concealing her limp.

Ina sang strong and hard for some minutes before stopping to dry tears from her eyes. Djelimady handed her 5,000 CFA and others followed, clearly moved. Even I surrendered a small bill. Still tamping at tears with a tissue, Ina thanked us and got back into the waiting taxi to make her way to the next destination. That was the only time I ever saw a *jeli* cry.

Next came Badian, the young guitarist. About a week earlier, Badian had provided me with one of my greatest treasures. He had let me film him playing his versions of the Manding classics on guitar. This was no small matter, for Badian, you might say, played Stevie Ray Vaughn to Djelimady's B. B. King. Djelimady understood the histories of the *jeli* songs and their regional variations better than anybody, but Badian had extended the art of *bajourou*. He veered and jagged, throwing in clever rhythms and fingerings that seemed to define a new generation's approach to the music. Of course, like any good guitarist, Badian had been sensitive about being videotaped. A tape could be slowed down, paused. Fingerings could be precisely analyzed. Secrets could be revealed beyond the blur of notes on an audio recording. Djelimady had flatly refused to let me make such a video of his technique. A New York producer had actually proposed that I film an instructional video of Djelimady, but my teacher had sniffed at the terms. "You can't afford it," he'd told me when I described the project, and I had dropped the idea. Badian had agreed to let me film him as part of an exchange for my small electric guitar, which I was to give him on the eve of my departure. Badian's visit to the Tounkara compound that day was in keeping with Tabaski custom. It also provided him with an opportunity to remind me of my obligation to him.

Badian arrived on foot, looking suave in his silvery *boubou*. He began a round of greetings. No money changed hands, but apparently Djelimady's wife expected something from her husband's protégé. "I've got a problem with him," Adama Kouyaté said to me, gesturing with the ladle she was using to fill plastic bottles with *gimbré*. These yellow bottles had once contained automobile brake fluid; after a good scrubbing, they became the standard vessel for a serving of the sweet ginger drink.

"Oh?" I said. "What's it about?"

"It's about money," she replied with hushed resolution. Noticing none of this, Badian came to her and requested a bottle of *gimbré*. I could almost hear her steaming as she handed him one of the yellow bottles. Moments later, when Badian made his move to leave, Adama Kouyaté struck like a cobra. Leaping from her vat and bottles, she seized Badian by the embroidered collars of his *boubou* and began singing vengefully into his face. "*Soooolio kili!*"

Adama was calling the horses for Badian, who was now duty bound to pay her. Standing about where Douga had been flashing bricks of $100 bills a few nights earlier, Badian held out a single 10,000 CFA note and meekly protested that it was all the money he had in the world. Without releasing her hold on his collar, Adama led Badian like a doomed sheep around the corner to the boutique so he could make change. When they returned, she dragged him back into the shade of the tree and began again with the horses. *"Soooolio kili...!"* Adama boomed at her flinching captive. When she finished, Badian reached into his *boubou* and fetched a 500 CFA note. Adama seized the bill and released the young griot.

These events produced a party-like atmosphere under the tree. There was no beer, no music, only infernal heat and vaporous *gimbré*. Still, Djelimady, Madou Djan, and I fell into conversation. It was one of those rambling political dialogues they both loved so much. It proceeded illogically and led to unexpected places.

Madou asked me who I thought had really killed JFK. I told him I honestly didn't know.

"It was Castro," declared Djelimady, still in a mood to vilify the Cubans after his failed engagement in Havana. "No doubt about it."

Madou shook his head. "I think it was the Mafia," he said. "The assassination was too well organized for Castro." I floated the CIA theory, but both brothers rejected it, as though that organization were too abstract, too faceless an entity to take credit for such a notorious crime. Lee Harvey Oswald got no votes under the *nime* tree that day.

"And Malcolm X," said Djelimady, "I'll bet you don't know who killed him."

"That's easy," I said. "The Nation of Islam."

"Nooooo," he intoned, as if I had stepped right into his trap. I assumed that Djelimady would now defend the black Muslims of America. I knew the terms of that debate, and I felt comfortable enough with my host to let him know I didn't buy the Nation of Islam defense. For me, JFK was a mystery. This was not. But Djelimady had another agenda altogether.

Since our earliest conversations, Djelimady had been telling me that a Malian had actually discovered America. This startling notion could not have come to him entirely through griot history, since it relied on some rather speculative modern scholarship. Part griot lore, part Afrocentrism, and part conspiracy theory, Djelimady's explanation was, in its own peculiar way, unassailable.

The story begins with established historical fact. In 1310, at the height of the Empire of Mali, one of Sunjata's successors, Abu Bakr II, sent two hundred canoes down the Senegal river toward the Atlantic ocean on an exploratory mission. All but one of the vessels were destroyed in a storm. Abu Bakr persisted. He ordered another two thousand boats constructed, larger and sturdier than those in the first expedition. He then abdicated his reign to a new king—the much more famous Kankan Musa—and left Mali in order to lead this second expedition. The fourteenth-century Arab historian who reports these facts says simply that Abu Bakr and the two thousand canoes never returned. More recent scholars have picked up the thread, arguing that distinctively Manding cultural artifacts in Central America show an African influence that can only be traced to Abu Bakr's lost expedition, more than a century before Columbus. In other words, as Djelimady had always said, a Malian discovered America.

Djelimady further claimed that some members of Abu Bakr's expedition actually did make it back to Mali, and that there was some record of their American findings written down in Timbuktu. "*That's* why they killed Malcolm X," my guitar teacher now declared.

"I don't understand," I said.

"When Malcolm X went to Mecca, he was given documentation about Abu Bakr," Djelimady declared. "Everything was there. Malcolm X took it all back to America with him, but the Americans didn't want this to get out. So they killed him."

"Who, exactly?" I asked.

"I don't know," said Djelimady. "FBI, CIA. One of them."

Killing Kennedy had been too grand for the CIA. But this abomination, with its overtones of secret knowledge and racism, seemed to Djelimady a plausible U.S. intelligence operation. "Europeans and Americans are very advanced in technology," said Djelimady, "but they're a bit misinformed about history."

Just then, a blue Nissan pulled up alongside the tree and three stout African men got out. They wore splendid *boubous*: jade green, sky blue, and steel gray. With the tallest of the three—the blue one—taking the lead, they began an emphatic, orchestrated oratory, almost shouting praise upon the Tounkaras. "*Naamu,*" came the automatic response from Djelimady, to whom these incantations were directed. Each time the griots paused, Djelimady would again mutter, "*Naamu,*" the standard Bambara affirmation of *jeliya*. After no more than five minutes of this, Djelimady reached into his *boubou* and found a 10,000 CFA note. Without the slightest hesitation, he gave it to the tall blue griot, and the three visitors stopped their oratory and sat down. Djelimady made a show of searching his pockets for more money and came up with a couple of 1,000 CFA notes, which he also surrendered. His body language seemed to say that no amount of money would be enough to express his appreciation for their words.

I had never seen Djelimady part with money so willingly. Madou also gave, and before ten minutes had passed, the three talking griots had left with over 15,000 CFA, more than most Malian workers make in a week of hard labor. Djelimady offered scant explanation for this display of generosity, if that is what it was. "The one who spoke is a *gawlo*," he said blandly. "I can't remember his name." A *gawlo* is a Fulani praise orator. He falls below both the *jeli* and the *funé* in the hierarchy of griots. Therefore *jeli*s and *funé*s must give him money when approached. "They come to the Buffet sometimes," said Djelimady. "When they come, you have to give."

"But why?" I asked, returning to a familiar line of inquiry—why people give to griots. Djelimady just shrugged as though I were asking why the sun rose in the morning.

Sayan Sissoko, the *ngoni* player, had a better answer. "I know them," he told me later when I described these visitors. "They go everywhere during Tabaski. The tall one is a very big *gawlo*. The other two are *funé*s. These are griots for griots. When they come, you have to give to them."

Sayan implied that Djelimady gave money because he was afraid of what the *gawlo* would do if he did not give. Apparently, if they are not paid well, *gawlo*s can get ugly, hurling insults, verbally abusing the most vulnerable family members. Sayan said that an unappeased *gawlo* had been known to open a young woman's dress in front of the men, or even to lift his *boubou* and defecate in the middle of a family compound.

Tight as he was with money, Djelimady had actually seemed pleased to give to the *gawlo*, and I had sensed a certain satisfaction lurking behind the stalwart faces of givers at weddings and baptisms. The game seemed to be to present an impassive facade. But clearly the griots' words scratched an itch deep in people's psyches, an itch I could not feel and so could not imagine what it felt like to have assuaged. Perhaps this showed that Malians valued something that was both more enduring and more attainable than material wealth. On the other hand, I could never quite rid myself of the impression that it was all a scam. The question remained. Were the griots cultural saviors, or were they hustlers forever fixing society's gaze on a lost past?

Barou laughed at my attempts to comprehend the economics of griotism. "Forget about the money," he said. "You can't understand it that way."

"But Barou," I said, "you told me that those guys who hang off the backs of the *bashée*s all day make only 500 CFA a day."

"Yes," he said.

"And they work ten or twelve hours," I continued. "Out in the sun, running after customers, carrying people's loads, putting things on the roof, taking them off, forcing people to sit all crammed together, getting shouted at—all for 500 CFA."

"Yes," Barou agreed wearily.

"And then these *gawlo*s waltz in with a few fancy words and walk away with 15,000." Barou laughed. "From *Djelimady*, the same guy who could only give 5,000 to save you from losing your electricity. And you were his friend."

"Griots count more than friends," said Barou.

"Evidently."

"Look," said Barou. "We can ask the same kind of questions about you. We look at all the money that American movie stars and sports heroes make and we think, 'How can America let so many of its people live in poverty and then give millions to Arnold Schwarzenegger?'"

A friend of Barou's was listening to this exchange with interest. He was the official who had sped my airport arrival on my first night in Bamako, and now he came to my rescue once again. "You are right," he said, "we waste a lot of money on griots. And no one is worse than Sissoko." Babani Sissoko was clearly no national hero in this man's eyes. "Sissoko doesn't think about how he spends money," said the official. "How could he send a planeload of West Africans to Mecca? Doesn't he know there's a meningitis outbreak in these countries?" He was right. From Nigeria to Gambia, the airborne virus had been claiming lives mercilessly that spring. "If one of those passengers had the disease, how many might die in Mecca? Sissoko didn't think about that, did he? Just his own publicity. He is a fool. Worse. He's evil. Look at this country. Eight million people, and more than half of us are illiterate. What does this man do with all his money? He gives it to rich griots. What a waste!"

Griots, it seemed, held a mirror up to society. How you valued them depended upon your vantage point, and perhaps it has ever been so. Two hundred years before I lived in Bamako, the Scottish explorer Mungo Park lived among the Manding and observed their lives with acute perceptiveness. He was among the first Europeans to write about the *jeli*s, and he said this about them:

> They sing extempore songs, in honour of their chief man, or any other persons who are willing to give "solid pudding for empty praise." But a nobler part of their office is to recite the historical events of their country; hence, in war, they accompany the soldiers to the field; in order, by reciting the great actions of their ancestors, to awaken in them a spirit of glorious emulation.

One man's empty praise is another's best hope in battle. So it remains, two ideas side by side, as persistent as they are irreconcilable.

After Tabaski, Babani Sissoko flew to the Gambia. "To buy hotels," Djelimady told me. It seemed a routine enough excursion for the multimillionaire, and I fully expected Djelimady to vanish after him any day. If that happened, it would surely be the last I would see of my teacher.

"It's Djelimady who has not been correct with you," the Colonel declared over breakfast one Sunday. "You have come all this way to study with him, and he's off doing this, off doing that." I had made the mistake of telling the Colonel that in all these months, I had never actually been able to interview Djelimady. Having been my teacher, my host, my bandleader, and my friend, Djelimady now showed a decided reluctance to re-enter the journalist-subject relationship, even for a moment. Was he afraid of what I might now ask? Did he just dislike interviews? Most of all, I think he just felt he'd given enough. The Colonel didn't see it that way. He had never forgiven Djelimady for failing to entice Babani to visit us, and he was inclined to dwell upon any fresh news of the guitarist's shortcomings.

The longer I spent in Bamako, the more I found people trying to convince me that big and powerful people—Djelimady, the griots, Babani, even President Konaré—were in fact bad. In part, these criticisms grew from an unfortunate instinct in a poor society, the urge to bring down the successful. One African musician once put it to me in an aphorism: "A tall tree is hated by the wind." I tended to reject these denunciations, for it seemed that each time I verged on concluding that the griots were parasites, or that Djelimady was disregarding me, something would come along to renew my sense of wonder and appreciation.

An old man with piercing, faded eyes and missing teeth appeared among the Tounkaras during those final weeks. He slept in an empty room at the new house just the other side of the Colonel's room. He spent the day and evening sitting with the family at the Tounkara compound. The man was Sangana Coulibaly, the foremost hunter's musician of Kita, and he had come to stay as a distinguished guest of the Tounkaras. Sangana played the *simbi*, a seven-stringed antecedent of the *kora*. He knew by heart all the lineages and histories of Kita, especially the stories of the area's great hunters.

Djelimady had explained to me that in ancient times, long before Sunjata, a special caste of hunters held the responsibility of knowing societal history and family lineages and expressing them publicly in song. Hunters were the most exalted and treasured people in Africa. In addition to their rare knowledge of distant lands and peoples, they had magical powers and could commune with the spirits of their prey. They hunted among the herds and predators that roamed the forests and grasslands. Hunters provided many essentials: meat to sustain people; horns, claws and fur to decorate ceremonial finery; and the skins that gave voice to drums, lutes, and harps.

Over the centuries, as the Sahara has crept southward, the hunters' once fertile lands have gradually become parched into savanna where few animals can live, and eventually into barren desert. With those changes, people have come to rely on domesticated herds of livestock, and hunters are now figures of powerful nostalgia rather than daily providers. Djelimady had told me that there came a time when the musical and historical responsibilities of the old hunter bards with their *simbi*s passed on to the griots with their *balafon*s and *ngoni*s, and later, *kora*s and guitars. The hunter historians went on, but their sphere of influence narrowed to increasingly secret and cultish circles in places like Kita and, of course, Wasulu. Sangana was a marvelous holdover from the past.

The first time I met Sangana by the compound stoop, he picked up the *simbi* and played a little. The instrument's metal strings produced a thinner, less interesting sound than the *kora* or the *ngoni* has. After plucking quiet melodies, intangible airs with notes disconnected because they died out so quickly, Sangana began to sing. At first his song was little more than a distracted mumble, a bit like the whispery vocal improvisations of a Shona *mbira* player in southern Africa. Then, suddenly, Sangana unleashed a keening blast, loud and rough, not the elegant belt of a *jeli* but something darker, stranger, more ritualistic. Having gained everyone's attention, Sangana stopped abruptly and called for one of the children to take his *simbi* back into the courtyard. He was giving a clue, sowing seeds of interest, and then leaving us in a state of exhilarated curiosity.

Even without such displays, Sangana would have caught my eye. He was old and craggy-faced and always dressed in a dark brown *bogolon* robe and a hat with fur patches and a small tuft of black feathers rising above it. He did not speak much French, so we never conversed, but whenever I saw him, he shook my hand and smiled broadly, revealing his missing front teeth.

That Sunday, I played an afternoon wedding with Djelimady. Stormy clouds lingered, offering more empty promises of rain. Wind and passing trucks picked up the dust and made the air thick in the warm afternoon light. Occasionally, a large V-formation of egrets flew overhead. The wedding ended promptly at sunset, and back at the compound that night, Sangana played for the family.

Somehow people knew about this event. Basekou Kouyaté arrived with one of his brothers. Douga Sissoko and his cousin Tiekoro showed up in the Opel, followed by friends from the neighborhood who came on foot. Everyone assembled in the courtyard. One of the twins brought Sangana his *simbi*, and Djelimady and Solo took up their acoustic guitars. They began to play the song "Kulanjan," a proud and lyrical *simbi* piece that has become a mainstay of the Manding repertoire. Sangana took to his feet and fairly awed the audience with oratory for nearly an hour. At one point, Djelimady passed me his guitar so I could accompany. He watched me until I found my place in the music. Then he sat back and seemed to lose himself in Sangana's words.

Money began to flow. Adama Kouyaté gave 5,000 CFA. Djelimady gave more. Douga produced a small bundle of bills. Basekou gave too. By the end, Sangana's pockets bulged. Djelimady chuckled. "He has all the money he will need for the next year," he said, adding that Sangana had come to Bamako for exactly that reason.

Sangana wore a smile from ear to ear. But this event had touched the Tounkaras as well. If the *gawlo* who had regaled Djelimady under the *nime* tree knew how to scratch the Tounkaras' itch, Sangana had delivered a full psychic massage. The old hunter bard was from their place. Perhaps he had even attended the baptisms of Djelimady and his brothers. In any case, he knew the ways to unleash this family's collective ancestral power, their prized *nyama*, as well as anyone. His mere presence had filled the Tounkaras with anticipation, and now that he had delivered, the mood of satisfaction was palpable.

When the guests left, Djelimady became absorbed in a political program on television, one of those presentations I could never follow due to the rapid, expressionless French, political jargon, and inside references. It amazed me that even after half a year in Mali, I still found these political speeches and discussions so impenetrable. Ibrahim Keita, the prime minister and one of Djelimady's favorite politicians, was speaking. Djelimady smiled, still caught in Sangana's joyous spell. There were foam mattresses in the courtyard that evening, for just as the heat had moved daylight life out to the shaded street, it had moved sleeping into the courtyard. Djelimady and his wife lay side by side on a mattress, their heads propped up on pillows, their eyes gazing across the courtyard toward the droning television. They looked as happy together as I had ever seen them.

By the time I left Bamako, many of the residents of the Tounkara compound had themselves gone off to attend or play music at various weddings and ceremonies out of town. These departures simplified my leave taking. "You're lucky," Barou observed. "Everyone would have wanted to come to the airport, and they would all have expected gifts." Nothing so clarified my relationships with people as the act of saying goodbye. It presented the final opportunity to even up the score in the ineffable games of give-and-take we had all been playing. My friends were not bashful in staking their claims.

The last time I saw Adama Kouyaté, she lay on a blanket under the *nime* tree in the late afternoon light. She was having her hands and feet decorated for a wedding in Kita. The process involved cutting tiny strips of white medical tape with a razor and placing them precisely so that the spaces between the strips exposed a detailed pattern of bare skin across the palms and fingers of her hands and the soles and toes of her feet. After hours of this preparation, one of her daughters would smear henna over the taped areas and tie plastic bags around Adama's hands and feet. Later she would wash away the henna and remove the tape, and an intricate design would remain, black on Adama's brown skin, a sign of respect for the marrying couple.

"Banning," she demanded from where she lay being taped by her daughter Bintou, "when you leave, you mustn't be giving all your things to just anybody. Anything you don't take with you, you must leave for me." We went over her list: mattress, sheets, pillow, bedside light, desk, one fan, toiletries, two towels, leftover medicine. The small cassette/radio boom box would go to Madou Djan, and the power transformer to Solo and Yayi for their American electronic gear.

"What about the second fan?" asked Adama. "Djelimady said you have two." I told her I had promised the second fan to the Colonel. I laid on a little praise for him, listing the good things he had done for me to emphasize that the fan was not negotiable. Djelimady chortled at his wife's diligence in pinning me down on each item she was to receive. I had to demonstrate that I had understood and promise to comply.

My remaining days included other such inquisitions. I had begun the complex mental process of dividing up all my nonessential possessions to be apportioned among my friends. These gifts amounted to little of substance, but they contained messages. They were part of the expected ritual of departure.

One morning I woke up in a clammy bed of sweat. It was barely 6:00 A.M., but the electricity had gone out, stopping my fans. The earth's massive store of heat flowed unhindered into my worn, sweaty body. The little neighbor girls began their morning screams, and soon a rap on the door announced the arrival of Badian. Still looking smart in his Tabaski *boubou*, he had come to check on his guitar. He too wanted a precise list of what I would be turning over, how many sets of strings, how many picks, and so on.

"Capo?" he asked.

"No," I told him. "None left."

"Cassettes?" It went on like this, Badian's nervous eyes darting about my room looking for other things he might claim.

Hot, tired, achy, and irritable, I arrived for breakfast at the Tounkara compound, where new irritations awaited. First, Solo informed me in somber tones about his latest problem with the electronic gear he had brought from the United States. Rather than play weddings in the heat, Solo had taken to renting out his equipment. The most recent renter had not understood the need for the voltage transformer, a heavy block of metal that converted 220v to 110v current. The renter had bypassed this weighty obstacle and plugged Solo's PA amplifier directly into 220v current, grilling something inside.

"I know you have found someone who repairs these things," said Solo. It was true. Samakou had led me to a man in Lafiabougou who had successfully fixed Djelimady's amplifier, as well as one of my tape recorders. "Do you think you could take care of this?" asked Solo. I couldn't refuse him. "Do you think you could do it today?"

"All right," I said, suppressing annoyance.

Young Sambry Kouyaté was there, slouched in a lawn chair, watching this in a state of consternation. I knew what was bothering him. Sambry had asked me to accompany him to his home village to play at a wedding there. The village was Tokoto, just beyond Kita. Sambry had wanted us to go there together, leaving by train the following morning. He had said the trip would give him his first chance to play guitar at a wedding, but only if I came along with my two guitars. Sambry had tried to entice me by speaking of the wondrous things we would see there: artisans who made horses out of dyed cow skin, a spring of magical water, and, the big attraction, his mother. For Sambry, Tokoto was a place of enchantment, and I had regretted having to disappoint him. But time was simply too short.

Djelimady drove me into town, pausing briefly so we could drop Solo's amplifier with my repairman. The technician stood among dusty television sets and radios and wore his usual long face. He liked to worry me, but in the end he did good work and charged little for it. He said he would try to have the unit repaired by evening.

That evening, as I was walking to catch a *bashée* to the Tounkaras, a mobilette pulled up beside me. Riding it was a young *kora* player named Boubacar, who often palled around with Sambry, Adama, and the other young *jelis* who frequented the Tounkara compound. Boubacar was driving Yayi Kanouté's mobilette and he had a story to tell.

"Hop on," he said. "I'll give you a ride to the terminus." I laid my guitar across my knees and perched myself on the plush passenger cushion of Yayi's new motor bike. "I can't take you all the way," Boubacar shouted through the breeze. "I don't want Solo to see me."

"Why not?" I shouted back.

"If he sees me on Yayi's mobilette, he'll think more of his crazy thoughts." When I said nothing back, Boubacar realized that I was not up on the latest events among the Tounkaras. "Didn't you know that Yayi has left the compound?" he asked.

Boubacar explained to me that a few days earlier, Solo had angrily accused Sambry and him of fooling around with Yayi. Boubacar did not explain the exact nature of the charges, nor did he deny them. He only said that Solo had behaved so outrageously that Yayi had left the compound in a rage and gone to stay at her family home. As he dropped me off by the crumbling mosque at the Lafiabougou terminus, Boubacar said, "Yayi is going to Tokoto to sing at a wedding tomorrow. But don't worry. By the time she comes back, Solo should have calmed himself down."

As I walked the rest of the way to the compound, I considered the fact that I had spoken with Solo, Sambry, and Djelimady that morning, and none of them had given the slightest hint of these troubles. I began to piece things together. Solo had asked me to fix the amplifier, knowing that it would be going to Tokoto, though he would not. Sambry had requested that I come along with my guitar because he hoped to take Solo's place playing guitar for Yayi at the wedding. Djelimady, for his part, had pretended to be oblivious to all of this. "People in the family think Djelimady is slow," Barou had once told me, "but he isn't. He just likes to stay out of things, so he pretends not to notice."

Sambry was waiting outside at the stoop when I approached the compound. He wanted to know whether I had reconsidered coming to Tokoto. I had not. "Noooo, Banning," he moaned. "Truly I am not happy." Two of Sambry's friends were seated on stools, and they began to make fun of him. It was hard not to smile at Sambry's clownish mask of chagrin.

Djelimady was not there with the car, and it was approaching 9:00, our last chance to retrieve the amplifier. I made Sambry a proposal. We would get a taxi and retrieve the amplifier. When Djelimady got home, we would ask if Sambry could use Djelimady's second guitar, the one Solo had brought him from New York. Sambry rejected my idea out of hand, saying that he did not want to talk to Djelimady about the trip to Tokoto; it would be too awkward. Understanding more than he knew, I held my ground, arguing that Djelimady would want to help. "You can blame me, Sambry," I told him. "Say that I was going to give you my guitar, but that now I need it. What have you got to lose? The worst he can do is say no."

When we returned with the amplifier, I brought it to Solo, reporting that it had cost 5,500 CFA for the repair, plus 1,000 for the taxi. He thanked me profusely, ignoring my hint that he reimburse me. Soon Djelimady arrived and Sambry followed him into his bedroom for the confrontation. Sambry emerged moments later, grinning. Djelimady had consented. It pleased me to have helped engineer this resolution even though none of the Tounkaras had explained me what was really going on. I felt I had learned more than Manding guitar songs in my time with them.

The tallying of scores continued. Sali Sidibé managed to revive her cassette project, and I was called in to record my parts. The engineer set up his gear on a table under Sali's concrete entrance way. The producer, facing problems with another artist, could not allow the equipment to be in the studio for fear it might be seized. I pulled up a metal chair and plugged my guitar into the board, and we recorded among women filling their wash pails, lethargic children and nervous chickens, and Booboo, the compound's pet monkey, who continued his ritualistic bouncing without regard for the soaring heat.

When we finished, Sali called me over to express her pleasure. Her husband translated. "She says the next time you play these songs will be on a stage in America."

"*Insha 'Allah*," I replied, resorting to West Africa's favorite evasion. Sali smiled. The spark in her eye beamed confidence, as if she knew something I did not.

No such mystery attended my farewell to Adama Tounkara. Like his friend Badian, he had staked claims to key possessions of mine. One evening, he pulled up in front of the compound in his mobilette. *"Mon ami,"* he said, "I am leaving for Gao in the morning. I have a concert. What about the things you promised me?"

I rode with Adama to my house and he accepted the gifts without ceremony. I wished him well with the twins. I wanted to draw him out, to ask him when he might marry Miriam Diallo, and what his plans were for the future. I still felt affection for Adama going back to my earliest days in Bamako when he had rehearsed me so mercilessly, and I had stood by him through the naming of his sons. Adama stared ahead with dull eyes, as if I were already gone, as if he were looking at a ghost and the sight depressed him.

"You'd think I was *dying*," I complained to Barou. "All this melodrama."

"America is far," he replied. "People don't know whether they'll see you again." To his credit, Barou never asked me for anything. He had helped me every day from start to finish. He knew I would not forget him.

Strange weather moved over the city. Approaching the new bridge, I could see it across the river, a red cloud of dust that was enveloping Badalabougou and Kalaban Koro, where Djelimady and Madou Djan had gone to bury an aunt who had died that morning. The dust cloud roiled high over the land and blocked out the sky. It was moving fast. Before my taxi reached the other side of the bridge, swirling eddies of dust the color of dried blood whipped against the windows of the car. Feather-light shrubs and bushes flew around like tumbleweeds scratching at the windows. I could smell the promise of rain, a promise that had been building for weeks, like an unpaid debt between friends. Still, no rain came. The storm passed, having only thickened the city's coat of red silt.

We ate a feast that night—fish, rice, chicken and fries, even *tow*. With so many Tounkaras away, there was bounty. "You must eat," Madou Djan kept saying, sliding another large metal bowl of food my way. Just as I thought I was through, one of Djelimady's daughters came with fish: thick steaks of hearty Niger River *capitaine*, shot through with veins of garlic and green spices.

Djelimady and I lingered over dinner. He took the opportunity to reflect on stories from the past. He wanted me to know certain things. About the Cuba fiasco. About the misunderstandings that had surrounded the recording of the Bajourou record in 1992; he knew I had heard stories from Lucy Durán. Even about Sali Sidibé's troubles with the American rock singer Toni Childs in London. Characteristically, Djelimady focused on affixing blame for all that had gone wrong, and for the most part, the culprits in his eyes were the British handlers and producers. I took these as cautionary tales. To come to Mali and study, as I had done, was one thing. But if a foreigner planned to profit from Malian music, he had better not forget to reward the musicians equally. It was a masterful summing up on Djelimady's part, a mixture of reverie, philosophy, personal absolution, and warning.

After dinner, Djelimady, Madou, and I walked over to the nearby Hotel Logo, just at the edge of the big clearing where the *mouton* market had stood only a week before. All that remained now were the skeletons of the makeshift barns. Someone had told Djelimady that the great Guinean griot singer Sekouba "Bambino" Diabaté was staying at the Logo. It seemed unlikely, but sure enough, we found Bambino and his guitarist, Petit Kondé, loafing in a third-floor hotel room. "Eeh!" crowed Djelimady, and the smiles and backslapping began. "Come and see us," Djelimady encouraged them. "We're just going to sit out and play music."

Half an hour later, the Guineans ambled up and joined us on the stoop outside the Tounkara compound. I talked to Bambino for a while about Guinea. I asked after friends in Conakry and learned that one had recently died, a journalist known as Abede. Abede was a friend to musicians, and the following year, Salif Keita would honor him with a song featuring Toumani on *kora*. "Abede worked too hard," said Bambino, "right until the end." Bambino told me he was flying to New York in a week to record with the African-Latin group Africando. "Will I see you?" he asked.

The world felt small and connected at that moment, as though the Tounkara compound, for all its humble trappings, was an important place. I thought of all the musicians, scholars, businessmen, politicians, and friends who had visited there over the months I had been in Bamako. It seemed almost as though you could just wait there by the stoop, and everyone in the world you needed to see would come along sooner or later.

We got out our guitars. Djelimady, Kondé, and I passed two guitars among the three of us while Bambino sang *jeliya*, cool and sweet under a rising moon. The air was unusually fresh following the afternoon dust

storm. The street felt calm and familiar. The music sounded as beautiful as any I had heard.

On my last day in Bamako, I played with Djelimady at an enormous
wedding in Djelibougou. When we arrived at the celebrating compound
at eleven in the morning, the temperature was already approaching 120
degrees Fahrenheit. "Oh, it's hot," Djelimady complained. "This is the
hottest dry season I can remember."

A tent had been set up, covering one section of the large courtyard.
Women gathered there as drummers began to play. The family matriarch
sang with the drums. Meanwhile, the men congregated around the corner in the shadow of the building, near the cook fires. Djelimady regaled
them with talk of Babani Sissoko. We began to play music sometime after
noon. Sweat poured from the faces and hands of the musicians. Our
clothes became drenched and stuck to us. Thirst seemed unquenchable,
and when a bucket of plastic water bags came around, I bit into one and
sucked it dry in a single, long gulp. Weeks later, back in New York, I
would spend days in bed at the mercy of some waterborne intestinal virus,
just the sort of illness I had carefully avoided through seven months of
drinking bottled water. I doubt if even foreknowledge of that coming illness would have stopped me from drinking then. The moment I tossed
the empty bag in the dust, a mad thirst assailed me again, and I reached
for another.

That night, before going to the airport, I visited the Tounkara compound one last time. I brought Djelimady a few gifts, including 20,000
CFA, which I had carefully saved for him. He riffled through the items—
magazines, tapes, music for jazz tunes, guitar paraphernalia—and he
thanked me. He took me into his room and said, "Banning, I want you
to know that I am pleased with you. You have never been at fault during your stay. You have always been correct with me. If anyone has been
at fault, it was me." These were big words coming from Djelimady. For
all the risks inherent in our apprenticeship, we were parting as friends.

Once again, a strange turbulence worked the air that night. A restless
wind was picking up, filling the air with dust and detritus. I had invited
guests to visit the compound and say goodbye, but few came. Sali Sidibé
stopped by with her husband and Harouna, *kamalé ngoni* in hand. I
insisted that Harouna and Djelimady play one last song for me, and they
obliged, speaking each other's musical languages with uncanny sensitivity. Their Wassoulou-flavored version of the griot song "Lamban" played

like a recapitulation of all I had experienced with the musicians of Bamako. Had I been a record producer after all, this is what I would have wanted to record. It broke traditions. It fit no known format. It was brilliantly spontaneous music, the best-kept secret in Mali.

Joyce and Barou took me to the airport, Barou documenting everything using a small tape recorder I had given him as a parting gift. As we drove away from the Tounkara compound, we could see in the headlights billowing clouds of dust, dry shrubbery, and diaphanous plastic bags whipped up by the wind and charging across the open plain that stretched to the abandoned *mouton* market. By the time we reached my house to collect my things, the rains had begun, this time with a fury that left no doubt—the dry season had ended. Rain pounded the city. It roared against corrugated iron roofs. It made streets flow with mud and left whole neighborhoods without power. Brown rivers carried off the parched refuse of seven rainless months, and the songs of centuries played within me.

Afterword

Bee n'i dakan: Everybody follows the path of their destiny.

(Bambara proverb)

A lot has happened since I left Bamako in May of 1996. Djelimady Tounkara has moved his family to the house where Dirck and I lived in Lafiabougou. He has also taken a second wife, the daughter of the *chef des griots* in the Gambia. Djelimady wrote to me in 1997 to say he had accepted the chief's daughter a little reluctantly, but at the insistence of his friend Babani Sissoko, who arranged the marriage. Visitors tell me that the new wife's presence has changed the tenor of life among the Tounkaras, now for the first time a polygamous household. Djelimady's nephew, Adama Tounkara, has married Miriam Diallo, at last legitimizing their twin sons.

Some of the musicians I knew in Bamako have died. Fodé Kouyaté, the griot singer who invited me to play before twenty thousand people at Tabalé '95, succumbed to meningitis almost exactly a year after those concerts. He drove himself to the hospital complaining of headaches and was dead within hours. At around the same time, Sidiki Diabaté, Toumani's father and the man who pioneered the Malian kora tradition during the 1950s and '60s, died at the age of seventy-three during a visit to the Gambian village of Bansang, where he was born. Sidiki's body was returned to Mali for a state funeral. Dounanke Koita, the Bobo singer, has also died of an unknown illness. Mamadou Jatigui Diarra, the hunters' chief, has also died.

As for Babani Sissoko, things didn't go quite as Djelimady predicted, but I did meet the millionaire again, in Miami in 1997, at a time when he was facing charges from the U.S. government over a shipment of helicopters to the Gambia. My friend Kassim Kone, the anthropologist and linguist, had been employed by Babani's defense team, and he escorted me to Babani's Brickell Key penthouse. This time I approached Babani more clearly, aiming to write a magazine article that would examine his plight. As in Bamako, we waited a very long time to see him. At the start of our brief encounter, I described the book I was writing about musicians in Bamako, and Babani immediately ordered a $30,000 check to support my work. I could have refused it, for I knew that accepting his gift would undermine my journalistic ambitions. But Babani was not offering another interview, only the check, and in the end I felt it was more important for me to write about the music and let others investigate the man. I took Babani's check, and I never saw him again.

In the fall of 1998, a reporter for the *Miami New Times* revealed a major source of Babani's wealth during the years I knew him. An officer at the Dubai Islamic Bank in Abu Dhabi had confessed to falling under the "spell" of an African business man called "Baba" and had been quietly transferring money to him abroad. Inexplicably, no one at the bank had intervened to question these transactions. The total amount, withdrawn over a period of thirty months, reportedly came to 242 million dollars. In the wake of this revelation, some of Babani's associates were detained by Interpol. Air Dabia has folded. But Babani Sissoko continues to live in Mali, keeping a low profile but a free man.

The Super Rail Band of Bamako did not die after all. It is back in business with a new, young horn section, and sounding better than ever. They play once again at the Buffet Hotel de la Gare and also other venues around town. I have continued to practice and play the wealth of music that Djelimady gave me, and to find new applications for it. In 1998, I recorded a song with Thomas Mapfumo and the Blacks Unlimited, Zimbabwe's leading roots pop orchestra. Based on a riff that Djelimady taught me but transformed by the magic of the Blacks Unlimited, the song became a hit in Zimbabwe.

Oumar Diallo, a.k.a. Barou, came into some money after playing on a record by singer Rokia Traoré that did well internationally. Barou invested in recording equipment and now operates a small studio out of his home in Lafiabougou and plays bass for Ali Farka Touré.

Ali Farka Touré has remained on his farm in Niafunké. Nick Gold had to drive his equipment across the desert to the remote village to record a follow-up to Farka's Grammy-winning session with Ry Cooder. Salif Keita made a record with American rocker Vernon Reid. Habib Koita has toured the United States for the first time and was a sensation. Oumou Sangaré sang in the soundtrack for Oprah Winfrey's film adaptation of the Toni Morrison novel *Beloved*. Toumani Diabaté, along with Basekou Kouyaté and five other Malian musicians, made a fabulous record of acoustic African and American roots music with American bluesman Taj Mahal. The group Kulanjan toured the United States with Africa Fête in 1999. Mali now has more artists signed to major U.S. labels than any other country in Africa.

Glossary of Names

These names are listed alphabetically, by first name, as they generally appear in the text.

Abdoulaye Diabaté Singer/bandleader from Koutiala. Prominent Bambara pop star.

Adama Kouyaté Djelimady Tounkara's wife.

Adama Tounkara Djelimady Tounkara's *ngoni*-playing cousin.

Ali Dembélé Rail Band rhythm guitarist.

Ali Farka Touré Songhai musician from the northern town of Niafunké. Mali's most famous guitarist.

Alpha Oumar Konaré First democratically elected president of the Republic of Mali. Elected in 1992 and reelected in 1997.

Ami Koita Top ranking *jelimuso*, noted for her international pop adaptations.

Baaba Maal One of Senegal's top singer/bandleaders.

Babani Foutanga Sissoko Intermittently wealthy Malian and the country's most generous patron of the arts.

Badian (Boubacar Diabaté) Young *jeli* guitarist; a protégé of Djelimady Tounkara.

Banzumana Sissoko The most famous griot of Mali's colonial era. Died in 1987.

Basekou Kouyaté Innovative young *ngoni* player. A member of Toumani Diabaté's Manding instrumental super-trio.

Barou (Oumar Diallo) Freelance musician and producer, and my best councilor in Bamako.

241

Bouba Sacko Respected griot guitarist. Member of the Bajourou trio.

Colonel (Boubacar Keita) Tenant of Djelimady Tounkara's. In charge of security at the house where I lived.

Djelimady Tounkara Top Malian griot guitarist. My teacher and host in Bamako.

Djeneba Diakité Wassoulou singer. Married to guitarist Madou Bah Traoré.

Djiby Camara Bass player in Toumani Diabaté's Symmetric Orchestra.

Douga Sissoko Bamako businessman. Brother of multimillionaire Babani Sissoko.

Dounanke Koita Singer/guitarist/bandleader. Famed for creating pop music based on the music of the Bobo ethnic group. Died in 1997.

Fodé Kouyaté Popular griot vocalist. Died in 1996.

Habib Koite Singer/guitarist/bandleader. A rising star.

Harouna Kouyaté Nephew of Djelimady Tounkara, brother of Sambry Kouyaté.

Harouna Samaké Innovative *kamalé ngoni* player for Sali Sidibé.

Ina Tounkara Young relative of Djelimady Tounkara. Launched her career as a Bamako *jelimuso* during my stay.

Kalwani The most notorious cassette pirate in West Africa.

Kaneba Oulen Diabaté *Jelimuso* best known for her 1995 song critiquing Malian democracy.

Kankan Musa Fourteenth century king of the Malian Empire. Made lavish pilgrimage to Mecca, spreading Mali's gold and its reputation.

Kandia Kouyaté Top Malian *jelimuso*.

Keletigui Diabaté Mali's grand old man of the *balafon*. One-time lead guitarist in Mali's National Orchestra. Recently left Toumani Diabaté's instrumental trio to join Habib Koite's band.

Lobi Traoré Guitarist/singer. The Bambara bluesman.

Madou Bah Traoré Wassoulou guitarist, arranger and manager.

Madou Djan Tounkara Djelimady Tounkara's older brother.

Modibo Diabaté Husband of Wassoulou singer Sali Sidibé.

Modibo Keita First president of the Republic of Mali. Overthrown and killed by Moussa Traoré in 1968.

Mory Kanté World-renowned Guinean singer/bandleader. Started out playing *balafon* and then singing in the Rail Band.

Moussa Kouyaté The Tounkara family's griot.

Moussa Traoré Dictatorial president of Mali from 1968 until 1991, when he was overthrown in a popular uprising. Currently in prison.

Nainy Diabaté Popular *jelimuso* known for her energetic, electric pop.

Ouedraogo Mamadou Alto saxophonist for the Rail Band. Died in 1996.

Oumou Sangaré Mali's most popular Wassoulou singer/bandleader.

Ousmane Cherif-Haidara Oumou Sangaré's husband and manager.

Ousmane Kouyaté Guitarist for Salif Keita. Friend and protégé of Djelimady Tounkara.

Philippe Berthier French music producer, in Mali since 1980. Proprietor of Studio Oubien and Mali K7.

Sadio Kouyaté Popular *jelimuso* from Segu. Resides in New York as of this writing.

Sali Sidibé Veteran Wassoulou singer/bandleader.

Salif Keita Mali's most successful pop singer internationally. Became a singer despite his noble heritage. Got his start in the Rail Band.

Samakou Tounkara Djelimady Tounkara's eldest son.

Sambry Kouyaté Djelimady Tounkara's nephew.

Samory Touré Warlord who fought the French for eight years before his capture in 1898.

Sayan Sissoko Respected *ngoni* player in Bamako.

Sidiki Diabaté Pioneer of Malian *kora* music, along with Batourou Sekou Kouyaté and Djelimady Sissoko. Father of Toumani Diabaté. Died in 1996.

Solo Tounkara Djelimady Tounkara's younger brother. Married to Yayi Kanouté.

Sunjata Keita First ruler of the Malian Empire and subject of the seminal epic in the Manding griot canon. Ruled from 1230–1255.

Toumani Diabaté Mali's top young *kora* player and the prodigal son of the late Sidiki Diabaté, father of the Malian *kora* tradition.

Yayi Kanouté Bamako *jelimuso* and, as Djelimady Tounkara's sister-in-law, the diva of the Tounkara compound. Also daughter of legendary *jelimuso* Fanta Sacko.

Discography

There are more and more recordings of Malian music available each year, including a companion CD to this book, *In Griot Time, String Music from Mali* (Stern's Africa). The following is a selective discography of some of my favorite Malian releases.

Malian Artists on CD

Super Rail Band, *Mansa* (Indigo)

Super Rail Band, *New Dimensions in Rail Culture* (GlobeStyle)

Rail Band, *Salif Keita and Mory Kante* (Syllart/Stern's). The old days!

Bajourou, *Big String Theory* (Xenophile)

Ami Koita, *Songs of Praise* (Stern's Africa). Jeli pop.

Kandia Kouyaté, *Kita Kan* (Stern's Africa). Progressive jeli pop.

Kasse Mady, *Koulandjan Kela* (Syllart/Stern's). Mostly acoustic jeliya.

Toumani Diabate, *Kaira* (Hannibal). Solo kora.

Toumani Diabate with Ballake Sissoko, *New Ancient Strings* (Hannibal)

Mamadou Diabate, *Tunga* (Alula). Great kora debut from Toumani's US-based cousin.

Salif Keita & Les Ambassadeurs, *Seydou Bathily* (Sonodisc/Stern's)

Salif Keita, *The Mansa of Mali. . . . A Retrospective* (Mango)

Salif Keita, *Folon, The Past* (Mango)

Habib Koite, *Muso Ko* (Alula)

Habib Koite, *Ma Ya* (Putumayo)

Lobi Traoré, *Ségou* (Cobalt/Stern's)

Lobi Traoré, *Duga* (Cobalt/Stern's)

Amadou et Mariam, *Sou ni tilé* (Tinder). Bambara pop.

Abdoulaye Diabaté, *Bende* (Cobalt/Stern's). Bambara pop, très roots!

Zani Diabaté, *The Super Djata Band* (Mango). The quintessential pentatonic guitar rock recording.

Sali Sidibe, *Wassoulou Foli* (Stern's Africa)

Sali Sidibe, *From Timbuktu to Gao* (Shanachie)

Oumou Sangare, *Moussoulou* (World Circuit/Nonesuch)

Oumou Sangare, *Ko Sira* (World Circuit/Nonesuch)

Oumou Sangare, *Worotan* (World Circuit/Nonesuch)

Nahawa Doumbia, *Yankaw* (Cobalt/Stern's). Wassoulou music.

Ramata Diakite, *Na* (Cobalt/Stern's). Wassoulou music.

Néba Solo, *Kenedougou Foly* (Cobalt/Stern's). Rocking pentatonic balafon.

Boubacar Traoré, *Sa Golo* (Indigo). One-of-a-kind acoustic guitar and vocal.

Ali Farka Toure, *The River* (Mango)

Ali Farka Toure, *Radio Mali* (World Circuit/Nonesuch). Classic '70s recordings.

Ali Farka Toure with Ry Cooder, *Talking Timbuktu* (World Circuit/Ryko)

Ali Farka Toure, *Niafunké* (World Circuit/Ryko). Live from paradise on the Niger!

Taj Mahal & Toumani Diabate, *Kulanjan* (Hannibal)

Hank Jones Meets Cheick-Tidiane Seck and the Mandinkas, *Sarala* (Verve). Jazz encounters Mali

Compilations

Musiques du Mali, Volumes 1 & 2 (Melodie). Altogether, 4 CDs of vintage recordings of Malian music.

The Divas from Mali (World Network). Great collection of natural, acoustic recordings.

Divas of Mali (Shanachie). Features more electric pop.

The Wassoulou Sound, Women of Mali (Stern's Africa). The essential Wassoulou compilation.

Mali to Memphis (Putumayo)

Electric & Acoustic Mali (Hemisphere). Includes the only Dounanke Koita track ever released internationally.

Royaume du Mande (Sono Africa/Rendez Vous/Sterns). West African musicians praise the Malian Empire.

References

I consulted a number of texts in writing this book. I've listed the key ones below. There are many others to explore, but these should give the curious reader a start. I begin with a discussion of specific texts consulted in writing individual chapters.

My telling of the Sunjata story in Chapter 1 comes from D. T. Niane's version, as told by Mamadou Kouyaté of Guinea. As I sought to pin down the historical Samory Touré, I first read the account in Sanche de Gramont's *Strong Brown God*. Later I consulted Pakenham's *The Scramble for Africa*. The phrase "Manding swing" comes from Graeme Ewens's *Africa O-Ye!*

My summary of the history of the griots in Chapter 3 owes a lot to Roderic Knight's 1973 dissertation "Mandinka *Jaliya*" and to three essays from *Status and Identity in West Africa*, specifically "*Nyamakalaya*, Contradiction and Ambiguity in Mande Society," by David C. Conrad and Barbara E. Frank; "Power, Structure, and Mande *jeliw*," by Barbara G. Hoffman; and "*Jaliya* in the Modern World: A Tribute to Banzumana Sissoko and Massa Makan Diabaté," by Cheick Mahamadou Chérif Keita.

Robert Palmer's *Deep Blues* and Dena Epstein's *Sinful Tunes and Spirituals*, which the late Palmer recommended to me, were my main sources on surviving African-isms in American folk music. The detail about banjo players turning factory banjos into "fretless" instruments comes from Richard Nevins's notes for Yazoo's 3-CD series, *Before the Blues*. Kassim Kone was my source on the different types of slaves. My explanation of the origins of *sanakhou*—"bantering brotherhood"— comes from a note by G. D. Pickett in Niane's version of the Sunjata epic.

Some details on Salif Keita's story in Chapter 6 come from a film called *Destiny of a Noble Outcast*, released on video by Island. Many of the details about African Islam in Chapter 8 come from the two Trimingham books and from the Sudan essays in the three UNESCO *General History of Africa* volumes, 4–6. The UNESCO books also helped with the Wasulu history touched on in Chapter 11, although Lucy Durán's essay, "Birds of Wassoulou," was my major source for this chapter.

In Chapter 12, I borrowed J. Spencer Trimingham's image of the "wound cord" of African Islam. The background on Songhai comes from Trimingham's history and from the UNESCO volumes. The factual aspects of Abu Bakr's story, as told in Chapter 13, come from volume 4, *Africa from the Twelfth to the Sixteenth Century.*

Recommended Reading

Ajayi, J. F. Ade, ed. *General History of Africa.* Vol. 6, *Africa in the Nineteenth Century until the 1880s.* Paris: UNESCO International Scientific Committee for the Drafting of a General History of Africa, 1989.

Barlow, Sean, and Eyre, Banning. *Afropop!—An Illustrated Guide to Contemporary African Music.* Edison, N.J.: Chartwell Books, Inc., 1995.

Bird, Charles S., and Martha B. Kendall. "The Mande Hero, Text and Context." In *Explorations in African Systems of Thought,* ed. Ivan Karp and Charles S. Bird, pp. 13–26. Washington, D.C.: Smithsonian Institution Press, 1980, 1987.

Charry, Eric. "The Grand Mande Guitar Tradition of the Western Sahel and Savannah." *Journal of the International Institute for Traditional Music* 36, no. 2 *(The Guitar in Africa: The 1950s–1990s)* (1994): 21–61.

———. "Plucked Lutes in West Africa: An Historical Overview." *Gilpin Society Journal* 49 (March 1996): 3–37.

Chérif Keita, Cheick Mahamadou. "*Jaliya* in the Modern World: A Tribute to Banzumana Sissoko and Massa Makan Diabaté." In *Status and Identity in West Africa, Nyamakalaw of Mande,* ed. David C. Conrad and Barbara E. Frank, pp. 182–96. Bloomington: Indiana University Press, 1995.

Chernoff, John Miller. *African Rhythm and African Sensibility, Aesthetics and Social Action in African Musical Idioms.* Chicago: University of Chicago Press, 1979.

Condé, Maryse. *Segu.* New York: Ballantine Books, 1987.

Conrad, David C., and Barbara E. Frank. "*Nyamakalaya,* Contradiction and Ambiguity in Mande Society." In *Status and Identity in West Africa, Nyamakalaw of Mande,* ed. David C. Conrad and Barbara E. Frank, pp. 1–26. Bloomington: Indiana University Press, 1995.

Courtlander, Harold, with Ousmane Sako. *The Heart of the Ngoni, Heroes of the African Kingdom of Segu.* New York: Crown Publishers, 1982.

Davidson, Basil. *The African Slave Trade.* Rev. and enl. ed. Boston: Little, Brown & Co., 1980.

De Gramont, Sanche. *Strong Brown God: The Story of the Niger River.* Boston: Houghton Mifflin, 1975.

Diawara, Manthia. *In Search of Africa.* Cambridge: Harvard University Press, 1998.

Durán, Lucy. "*Jelimusow:* The Superwomen of Malian Music." In *Power, Marginality and African Oral Literature,* ed. Liz Gunner and Graham Furniss, pp. 197–207. Cambridge: Cambridge University Press, 1995.

———. "Birds of Wasulu: Freedom of Expression and the Expressions of Freedom in the Popular Music of Southern Mali." *British Journal of Ethnomusicology* 4 (1995): 101–33.

———. "Music Created by God: The Manding Jelis of Mali, Guinea and Senegambia." In *The Rough Guide to World Music*, ed. Simon Broughton et al., pp. 243–60. London: The Rough Guides, 1995.

———. "Djely Mousso." *Folk Roots* 11, no. 3 (September 1989): 33–40.

———. "Ali Farka Touré." *Folk Roots* 14, no. 5 (November 1992): 38–41.

———. "World Shaker." *Folk Roots* 15, nos. 7–8 (January/February 1994): 42–44.

Epstein, Dena J. *Sinful Tunes and Spirituals: Black Folk Music to the Civil War.* Urbana: University of Illinois Press, 1977.

Ewens, Graeme. *Africa O-Ye! A Celebration of African Music.* New York: Da Capo Press, 1991.

Hale, Thomas A. *Griots and Griottes.* Bloomington: Indiana University Press, 1998.

Hamdun, Said, and Noel King. *Ibn Battuta in Black Africa.* Princeton: Markus Wiener Publishers, 1994.

Hoffman, Barbara G. "Power, Structure, and Mande *jeliw.*" In *Status and Identity in West Africa, Nyamakalaw of Mande*, ed. David C. Conrad and Barbara E. Frank, pp. 36–45. Bloomington: Indiana University Press, 1995.

Jansen, Jan, and Clemens Zobel, eds. *The Younger Brother in Mande, Kinship and Politics in West Africa.* Leiden, The Netherlands: Research School CNWS, 1996.

Joris, Lieve. *Mali Blues, Traveling to an African Beat.* Melbourne: Lonely Planet Publications, 1998.

Knight, Roderic Copley. "Mandinka *Jaliya:* Professional Music of the Gambia." Ph.D. diss., University of California, Los Angeles, 1973.

Kone, Kassim. *Mande Zana ni Ntalen.* West Newbury, Mass.: Mother Tongue, 1995.

Maren, Michael. *The Road to Hell: The Ravaging Effects of Foreign Aid and International Charity.* New York: Free Press, 1997.

Niane, D. T. *Sundiata, an Epic of Old Mali.* London: Longman Group Ltd., 1965.

———, ed. *General History of Africa.* Vol. 4, *Africa from the Twelfth to the Sixteenth Century.* Paris: UNESCO International Scientific Committee for the Drafting of a General History of Africa, 1984.

Ogot, B. A., ed. *General History of Africa.* Vol. 5, *Africa from the Sixteenth to the Eighteenth Century.* Paris: UNESCO International Scientific Committee for the Drafting of a General History of Africa, 1992.

Pakenham, Thomas. *The Scramble for Africa: The White Man's Conquest of the Dark Continent from 1876 to 1912.* New York: Random House, 1991.

Palmer, Robert. *Deep Blues, A Musical and Cultural History of the Mississippi Delta.* New York: Penguin Books, 1981.

Park, Mungo. *Mungo Park's Travels in Africa.* Ed. Ronald Miller. New York: Dutton, 1969.

Roberts, John Storm. *Black Music of Two Worlds.* Tivoli, N.Y.: Original Music, 1972.

Trimingham, J. Spencer. *Islam in West Africa.* New York: Oxford University Press, 1959.

———. *A History of Islam in West Africa.* New York: Oxford University Press, 1962.

Index